Letters from
Georgian Ireland

Garden at Delville by Mary Delany, 30 December 1745.

Letters from Georgian Ireland

The correspondence of
Mary Delany,
1731–68

Edited by Angélique Day
Foreword by Sybil Connolly

The Friar's Bush Press

For Fergus

Published 1991
Friar's Bush Press
24 College Park Avenue
Belfast BT7 1LR
ISBN 0 946872 35 X
© Foreword Sybil Connolly
© Editorial selection and linking texts Angélique Day

Cover design Rodney Millar Associates, Belfast
Printed by W. & G. Baird, Antrim

CONTENTS

LIST OF COLOUR PLATES

Anemone, drawn by Mary Delany

FOREWORD

Mrs Delany, in our time

I first became aware of Mrs Delany through the Irish Georgian Society's quarterly journals.

She appealed to me because of the almost astonishing impact she made in so many different areas. Astonishing because, the eighteenth century was not a time when women were given much opportunity to be distinctive. Yet Mrs Delany, with her pleasant but homely appearance, her comfortable but by no means luxurious way of living, was held in high esteem by some of the brightest and most distinguished people of that era.

King George III and Queen Charlotte met her during one of their visits to the Duchess of Portland – herself a remarkable woman. Mrs Delany's obvious integrity appealed to them and in no time at all the Royal Couple were seeking her counsel on questions of morality, and many other aspects of life. In her later years she lived at Windsor in a Grace and Favour residence, given to her by the King.

In 1980, Ruth Hayden, a descendant of Mary Delany's, wrote a book entitled *Mrs Delany and her flowers*, which I immediately bought and read with enthusiasm. Three years later, in 1983, Professor Charles Ryscamp, who was then Director of the Pierpont Morgan Library, in New York, visited me in Dublin. As is my usual practice when I have guests, I put in his room a selection of books which I thought might interest him, amongst them was the book on Mrs Delany. On the evening of the first day, during dinner, Charles Ryscamp commented on the Delany book and told me that, as a young student of English, at Harvard University, he had been given the task of editing the eighteenth-century Walpole papers; in the course of which he had become, like me, totally fascinated with Mrs Delany; her friendships with Handel, Joseph Banks, Walpole, to name just a few, her wide range of talents including her embroideries and flower collages, the latter which had been given to the British Museum by Lady Llanover to whom Mrs Delaney had bequeathed them upon her death.

Under Charles Ryscamp's directorship, the Pierpont Morgan Library has, over the years, mounted superb exhibitions covering a wide range of subjects, from the paintings of Beatrix Potter to the Holbein drawings from Windsor Castle. That evening, Charles confided to me that it would be the realization of a long held ambition, if he could present, at the Library, an exhibition of the Flower Collages of Mrs Delany. A mutual friend who was dining with us, offered to underwrite the venture. And so began a journey which would take approximately three years from that evening and result in one hundred and twenty of Mrs Delany's Flower Collages, and some of her embroideries being displayed at the Pierpont Morgan Library in New York, in the autumn of 1986.

It was a journey that was not without its painful moments. Inevitably such exhibitions are costly to mount. In the case of Mary Delany's collages certain long and expensive preservation work had to be carried out before they could travel on the

6,000 mile journey to New York, and at the close of the exhibition, back again to London. Three curators travelled (first class) with the collages so that they could be transported personally, and stayed in New York for five days to supervise the hanging of their precious cargo; and then, at the close of the exhibition, they had to return to New York in order to transport the collages back, to the British Museum.

The success or otherwise of an exhibition is gauged by the number of people in attendance. Compared to Holbein and Raphael, even Beatrix Potter, Mrs Delany was unknown in the United States. Indeed, except for a select few, she was comparatively unknown in England and Ireland.

Early in 1985 I was in New York at a particularly 'low' moment; more money was being requested by the British Museum for extra preservation work. The costs involved seemed to be daily on the increase. Charles and I were asking ourselves if perhaps the whole idea of the exhibition was an exercise in self-indulgence. One morning, I woke up and one of the solutions to our problems seemed to be that we must, somehow, get Mrs Delany better known in New York.

One of the many fine qualities of the American people is that they will, generally speaking, listen with an open mind if they are approached with an idea; and if the idea appeals to them, they are not adverse to 'having a go'. A few months earlier I had been asked by John Loring, the design director of Tiffanys to design china for the store. Now, I approached him with the idea that I would design dessert plates and coffee cups which would echo the flowers on Mrs Delany's Collages, and that Tiffanys would advertise them in the *New York Times*, mentioning what they were and the dates and venue of the exhibition. John Loring liked the idea, and agreed my proposition. The same willingness to co-operate existed with Brunswhig & Fils when I suggested to them that I design two fabrics for them, one would echo Mary Delany's collages, the other the embroidery on her court dress. The next stop was the magazines. *Connoisseur, House and Garden, House Beautiful* were all receptive to the story of Mrs Delany, and in September 1986, when the exhibition finally opened at the Pierpoint Morgan Library, all three magazines carried four and five page stories in praise of the exhibition and its creator.

The attendance figures exceeded our wildest expectations. In 1986 Mrs Delany had been dead for two hundred years; nevertheless she took New York by storm.

Her influence lingers on. The plates and coffee cups which I designed for Tiffanys became, and remain, a best seller. The fabric for Brunswhig echoing the flower collages is still attracting attention, and the chintz design taken from the embroidery on her court dress covers the chairs in my own drawingroom.

Because of the success of these items I find myself with a second career and consequently I am busier than ever. Diligence was very important to Mrs Delany, and sometimes I smile to myself and think how happy she would be knowing that she is responsible for this state of affairs.

Sybil Connolly
1991

CHRONOLOGY

1700   Mary born at Coulston, Wiltshire, 14 May

1707   Anne her sister born

1711   Mary sent to live with her aunt,Lady Stanley, in London

1714   Mary spends time in Gloucestershire where she meets Sally Kirkham

1717   marries Alexander Pendarves, of Roscrow, Cornwall

1721   her father Bernard Granville dies; her sister and mother retire to Gloucester

1724   Pendarves dies

1731   first visits Ireland, meets Dr Delany in Dublin

1733   returns to London

1740   Anne, her sister, marries John Dewes of Wellesbourne, Warwickshire

1743   Mary marries Dr Delany in England, 9 June

1744   moves to Ireland after Dr Delany is appointed dean of Down (henceforth D.D.); moves to Delville outside Dublin; first visit to deanery of Down

1745   visits County Down

1746   her niece Mary Dewes born

1747   summer in County Down; autumn in England

1748   spring in England; summer travelling in Ireland

1749   visits her brother at Calwich in England, and tours around

1750   returns to Ireland in spring; visits County Down in the summer

1752   visits Wicklow in May and then County Down, August to October

1753   after vising County Down in summer, journey to England

1754   Delanys return to Ireland with Sally Chapone

1755   Delanys return to England, visitng Bath in the autumn

1756   Delanys in England on legal business

1757   D.D. unwell, they visit Bath, Letitia Bushe, her friend, also ill

1758   Tenison lawsuit finished; return to Ireland in the June, then go to County Down and tour round the north

1761-2 in England; Anne Dewes dies in Bristol 1761

1763   return to Ireland after her sister's death; visit County Down

1764   marriage of Dr Sandford and Sally Chapone

1767   last visit the dean makes to England, to Bath for his illness

1768   Dean Delany dies in Bath; Mary buys a house in St James Place, London

1771   Georgina Mary Port, her great neice, born

1773   begins her cutpaper work series of flowers or Flora

1776   meets George III and Queen Charlotte

1782   because her eyesight is fading, work on the Flora ceases

1783   meets Fanny Burney, later Madam D'Arblay

1785   death of her friend, duchess of Portland; goes to live in Windsor where she has a grace and favour house plus pension

1788   Mary Delany dies

NOTES AND EXPLANATION OF SOURCES

Mary Granville (1700–88), later Mrs Pendarves, finally Mrs Delany, is the writer of the letters extracted here. This selection focuses on her life in Ireland during her visit first in 1731–32 and during the 25 years of her marriage to Dr Patrick Delany, dean of Down between 1743 and 1768. We have chosen to extract the subjects encountered in the letters in order to highlight their value for social and artistic history. These letters have a well-deserved reputation for lively observation of society and life in eighteenth century England and Ireland. Most of them were written to her sister Anne Dewes, whose granddaughter, Georgina Mary Port, later Mrs Waddington, was their preserver. She first arranged them, and the onerous and entirely magnificent task of transcribing and editing them was carried on by her daughter, Augusta Hall, Lady Llanover. This woman was a worthy descendant of Mary Delany, and had similar energies. She was married to Benjamin Hall, M.P. for Abergavenny, (1802–67); besides considerable researches into Welsh history, including ancient Welsh cookery, she saw through to publication six volumes of Mary Delany's letters (1861–62) – a monumental task. The originals of many of Mary's letters are in nine bound volumes and cases in Newport Central Library, Gwent; all the papers relating to the publication of the six volume series are in Aberystweth, at the University Library of Wales and, outside the scope of this book, some later letters exist in the Lewis Walpole Library, America.

The original letters are written in a fine, cultivated hand, and although the Llanover edition does cut some of the more frank vocabulary to suit a Victorian audience, and edits out some of the domestic detail, particularly the tender familial greetings that prefaced and ended many of Mary's letters, we have chosen, in this selection, to remain with the admirable Llanover edition *Autobiography and correspondence of Mary Granville, Mrs Delany*, (London 1861–2). This relates to the fact that there is not a full run of the letters in Newport; and also to the nature of this selection which is intended to give a portrait of Mary Delany in her Irish context. We hope a further generation of scholars may work on a completely unexpurgated text of Mrs Delany. This may eventually supply the minute verbal detail which we will have to pass over: for instance, in a letter written during her first Irish visit, (11 March 1731/32) describing a rejected suitor, one of the Brownlows, the original reads 'Hang my Lord Tirconnel, I don't relent or repent one bit', while the published edition reads 'as for my Lord Tyrconnell, I don't relent . . .' We are convinced that the freshness and the force of the letters have been retained in the Llanover edition even if some of the original phrases are omitted. The choice of letters and the selection of extracts from them are planned to show the great range and quality of her observations on life and society in Ireland.

What is striking about the originals is the fluency and elegance of the author's hand – there are very few second thoughts! Most of the letters reproduced here, in selection, are written to Anne Dewes, the author's younger sister. Where the letters are not addressed to her, we have indicated the correspondent; these include her letters to Swift which are not among the originals in Newport. We have included two of Anne Dewes' menus made out on the back of envelopes found among the originals in Newport. Other original letters included which were not published in the Llanover edition are from Dr Delany.

Up to 1752, the Julian calendar was still in use in England and Ireland, with the new year beginning on 25 March. The Gregorian calendar, with the new year beginning on 1 January, was used from 1582 in continental countries like France and Spain. Therefore Mary Delany dates her letters written during the first three months of the year up till 1752 according to both calendars, thus 6 January 1745/ 6, the old style or Julian year being 1745, the new style or Gregorian year being 1746.

We have used the page references from the printed volumes of the Llanover edition and have used the volume numbers found in the index (volumes i, ii, iii, iv, v). We have amended the punctuation and capitalisation of the Llanover edition to conform more closely with modern usage. To convey the full force of her impressions, Mary Delany used capitalisation and underlining throughout her letters. We have reproduced the underlining with italics. Mary was not worried (as her editors may have been) by inconsistencies of spelling; most spellings have been modernised although a few idiosyncratic spellings, including personal names, remain to give the flavour of her style. The term Mrs was used by Mrs Delany to refer to unmarried as well as married friends and has been retained: it is an abbreviation of Mistress and as such implied respect rather than marital status.

Mary Delany

CHAPTER 1

BACKGROUND TO MRS DELANY'S LIFE IN IRELAND

Mary was the eldest daughter of Colonel Bernard Granville, brother to George, Lord Lansdowne, friend of Alexander Pope and Jonathan Swift, and members of the family were important in government circles of the time, including their cousin John, Lord Carteret, and Lord Granville. Her mother was born a Westcombe, the daughter of a former consul of Cadiz. When Queen Anne came to the throne and the Whigs gained political supremacy, the Granvilles were in disfavour politically because of their high tory allegiance. Her father relied for money on his wealthier brother, and lived in Gloucestershire with his family. Her father's sister was married to one of the commissioners for customs, Sir John Stanley, and took Mary into her household in London, where she acquired an education and social graces. Then Mary rejoined her parents, her two brothers and younger sister, in their quiet country home in Buckland on the borders of Gloucestershire and Oxfordshire where they lived in a modest way. At that time she met her friend for life, Sally, daughter of Lionel Kirkham, who was rector of Stanton, a village near Buckland. Sally, nicknamed Sappho because of her learning, was the mother of Mary's godchild Sally Chapone.

At the age of seventeen, in 1717, her paternal uncle Lord Lansdowne, with whom she often stayed at Longleat in Wiltshire, his wife's home, persuaded her into marriage with Alexander Pendarves, someone as old as himself and part of a political connection with which he sought to secure his influence in the country. This unhappy experience of uncongenial marriage was not helped by their living in a remote part of the world, Roscrow Castle, near Falmouth in Cornwall, and, when they came to London, lodging in Soho, an unfashionable quarter. She fulfilled her duties as a wife faithfully and he died in 1724. However, despite her uncle's hopes, Mr Pendarves did not leave her sufficient income to live independently and she rejoined her Aunt Stanley's household, her husband's principal heir being his nephew, Francis Basset, who repaid her the income on her jointure.

Although she had joined her family again, she retained some independence and spent the next few years enjoying high society. She frequented the opera, where she and her brother Bernard were promoters of the new Italian style of opera and George Frederick Handel, the composer. She had many admirers, but rejected all suitors chosen by her family. The only man to turn her head was Charles Calvert, Lord Baltimore. However, his intentions did not seem to include marriage, and in 1730, he married the daughter of a rich merchant. It was to counter this disappointment that Mary accepted an invitation to visit Dublin from her great friend, Anne Donnellan who was known as Philomel or Phil. In the eighteen months she spent in Dublin and the country, visiting the friends and family of her hosts, she combined a dashing social life, with many visits to remoter parts and met with Patrick Delany, her future husband. At the time of her arrival in Dublin, he was on the brink of marriage to a wealthy widow. His close circle of friends included the famous dean of St Patrick's, Jonathan Swift and fellows from the University of Dublin, Trinity College, as well as some of the most witty and learned of women, like Constantia Grierson, wife of the famous Dublin printer, Letitia Pilkington, the playwright, and the beautiful Frances Kelly, much admired by Swift: he entertained these and others, in his lovely home, Delville, just outside Dublin.

When Mary left Ireland, she did not intend to return, and she resumed her stylish life with her uncle Stanley in London (her aunt died c.1730) and her great friend, Margaret Cavendish, the duchess of Portland with whom she often stayed at Bulstrode in Buckinghamshire. However, she maintained correspondence with her many friends from Ireland, including Dean Swift and the Delanys. Patrick Delany's wife died in 1741. In 1743 he wrote to Mary and asked her to be his wife. She agreed surprisingly quickly, given the disapproval of her family, particularly her brother, to the match. Delany was not able to boast of great rank and fortune, but was able to offer her a comfortable income, an attractive house, and above all, his devotion. He was not young and handsome, but he was humane and learned. She was not wealthy, so Dr Delany was no fortune hunter; but she was vivacious and attractive, witty and accomplished. The prospect of such good companionship appealed to them both. They were married and in 1744, after she managed, through family influence, to secure the deanery of Down for her new husband, they set off for Ireland.

Despite a few shadows, such as the lawsuit with the Tenisons over his first wife's will, his health, and living so far from her beloved family and friends in England, the Delanys lived a full and generous life : entertaining; working at their studies, crafts, house and garden; and enjoying the amusements offered in Dublin, from theatre and music to philosophy lectures at Trinity. They paid visits to friends and travelled occasionally to different parts of Ireland. They spent some summers in County Down so that the dean could fulfill his pastoral obligations, and later, they spent more time in England, sometimes a year at a time. Her letters during these years form a kind of journal to her sister, Anne Dewes. She confided all sorts of news to them. They are sprinkled with puzzles and conundrums which they used to exchange for their own amusement, and they employed pet names, and sometimes classical names to disguise some of their subjects of gossip. Anne Dewes' family was a constant source of interest. The Delanys started married life with some of the Dean's relatives, the Greens, living with them. Later her goddaughter, Sally Chapone, lived with them, eventually marrying Dr Sandford, their librarian cum chaplain. Her sister's health deteriorated in 1760 and she died in 1761, while the Delanys were with her. Henceforth the letters are written to her niece Mary Dewes, and her nephews, Court, Bernard and John Dewes, her friends, the duchess of Portland and others in that circle.

Mary's life was very much influenced by her family; at first, by the power of her male relatives, and later by the ties of affection that drew her to her sister's family. Her elder brother Bernard became head of the family when he attained his majority. He never married, but lived at Calwich in Derbyshire, a batchelor of great culture. He eventually made his sister Anne Dewes' child, John, his heir. Bevil, her younger brother, the black sheep of the family, emigrated and features very little in her Irish letters. Her marriage to Dr Patrick Delany was the most independent step she made outside her family.

DOCTOR PATRICK DELANY, DEAN OF DOWN

Patrick Delany (1685/6–1768), the humorous and learned clergyman whom Mary married in 1743, was a delightful man, as well as a charitable and thoughtful pastor. He came of farming stock, went to school in Athy and on to Trinity College, Dublin where he took orders in the Church of Ireland, and became a senior fellow. There he held briefly the Archbishop King lectureship and a chair in oratory and history. He taught many pupils through whom he gained a steady income and a wide acquaintance all over Ireland.

From the 1720s, as well as his university offices, he was chancellor of St Patrick's, Dublin; vicar of Davidstown, County Kildare; and rector of Derryvullen in Fermanagh. He was elected prebendary of St John's in Dublin but was never instituted due to the intervention of Primate Hugh Boulter, who was anxious to iron out irregularities, particularly in the holding of plural benefices. However, in this case, Boulter's main aim was to preserve the succession of fellowships at Trinity College. Boulter did not want a senior fellow to become permanent by virtue of a comfortable income from a Dublin parish.

Dr Delany always maintained a connection with Trinity, although when he married he had to give up his fellowship. He made a reputation for himself as a considerable preacher and published both theological and literary works. As we have seen Patrick Delany was in the circle of Swift's friends that entertained Mary in her first visit to Ireland. In 1732 he married Margaret, widow of Richard Tenison of Thomastown, County Louth and moved out of Dublin to Delville, a villa near Glasnevin.

[This account of her introduction to Patrick Delany comes from an autobiographical note Mary wrote for her friend the duchess of Portland]

I was so well pleased with my visit abroad that, instead of staying six months (the time I at first proposed) I staid eighteen. Amongst many agreeable acquaintances I made there, was the person to whom I am now married. The character he bore in the world, and his particular attachment to the Baron and Baroness, my relations and particular friends, made me wish to be acquainted with him. He was then married, lived in a very agreeable manner, reserved one day in the week for his particular friends, amongst which number were those of the best learning and genius in the kingdom. I thought myself honoured by being admitted into such a set, and Silvia [Mrs Donnellan] and I never failed making use of a privilege so agreeable to both of us. She made a considerable figure in society so well suited to her.

By this means I grew intimate with Dessario [Dr Delany], and had an opportunity of observing many excellent qualities which cannot be known in barely being acquainted with those talents which must be allowed shining ones, and have distinguished him for many years. His wit and learning were to me his meanest praise; the excellence of his heart, his humanity, benevolence, charity and generosity, his tenderness, affection, and friendly zeal, gave me a higher opinion of him than of any other man I had ever conversed with, and made me take every opportunity of conversing and corresponding with one from whom I expected so much improve–ment.   i pp296–97

Here is one of her first references in her letters to the man whom she later referred to affectionately as her "own D.D."

Dublin, 1732/3

But Mr Delany will make a *more desirable friend*, for he has all the qualities requisite for friendship – zeal, tenderness, and application; I know you would like him, because he is worthy.   i p402

After Dr Delany's marriage she mentions him in her correspondence.

Killala, 7 May 1732

Mrs Percival [mother of Mrs Donnellan and Mrs Clayton] is at a lodging at Little Chelsea, and Dr Delany with her, who has just married a very rich widow: Gran [Anne Donnellan's maid] has writ me a very comical account of their way of living; she has an excellent talent at description. Mrs Mahone's being in the house with us has put a stop to our studies for some time. I writ you word that we had read Dr Delany's and were about Dr Berkeley's; I wish if Mrs Chapon could get them to read she would, and send me her judgment of them; and also let me know (if you have an opportunity of reading them) *your* opinion.   i p369–70

Mary corresponded with Dr Delany and his wife at intervals; their mutual friend Dean Swift was invariably mentioned and these extracts are contem-porary with the exchange of letters between Mary and the famous dean of St Patrick's. Patrick Delany's neice was being trained up by Mary as her maid.

Dr Delany to Mary, Dublin, 8 February 1735, extracts from unpublished manuscript: Newport Library, Gwent.

I will tell you sincerely: I have sometimes fallen in upon the Dean when he was writing to you. He has sometimes shown me his letters and that exacted a sight of yours. I needed no more to convince me how poor a figure I should make in a correspondence where he was at best but second, though I must own that till then, I thought him your best letter writer in the world. Be advised madam, abate a little of that ease and politeness, that delicate and fine turn of thought and phrase and come down some degrees nearer to the level of common politeness, or take my word for no man of common sense will long be your correspondent. You will too late find the truth of that part of Solomon's fine compliment to his mistress and be convinced that a fine lady can be in this respect "terrible as an army with banners!"

The complaint of my friend [Dean Swift] is indeed a kind one but they forget that I am a hermit and that hermits don't visit their friends but their friends them.

Thursday is still sacred to them and if they will not come to the sacrifice, the priest I hope, is not to be blamed.

I am very glad to find from your account of George that one of my nieces has found the way to my esteem. I beg to assure you madam and I beg you to assure her that her good behaviour to you will not only recommend but endear her to me. Your goodness to her is beyond all acknowledgment!

Here, Dr Delany puts his anxiety about the poor before his financial duty to his neice and expresses regret over his extravagence at Delville.

Dr Delany to Mary, Dublin, 26 January 1739, extracts from unpublished manuscript; Newport Library, Gwent.

Madam: I received the favour of your letter with equal pleasure and confusion, too well knowing how ill I am entitled to that honour but you are born to conquer in every character and I submit with pleasure.

The rigours of our seasons began and I am sorry to tell you, continue with yours. The poor of this city and country are in a miserable condition and though more than usual charity exerts itself in their favour, I am afraid many thousands will perish. The little scene about us seems less distressed than others because it is less and the charity of the neighbourhood can extend to it. I never wished so much for wealth as I do now, and never with less passion to be enriched by it. But these wishes come too late after a continued expense on building.

I mention this partly as an apology for not sending the fifty pound I promised her [his niece] which however I will not fail to remit with interest as soon as I am able and I beg you will assure her with my best wishes that your regard for her has greatly endeared her to me.

My wife and Miss Tennyson beg you to accept their best wishes and respects and hope when you next do me the honour of a letter it will not be when you are confined to company.

His wife died in 1741. In the spring of 1743 he travelled to England, and wrote his most important letter to Mary. Since they had continued their friendship by letter it is not so startling to read the following proposal.

Dr Delany to Mary, Dunstable, 23 April 1743

You, madam, are not a stranger to my present unhappy situation, and that it pleased God to desolate my dwelling; I flatter myself that I have still a heart turned to social delights, and not estranged either from the tenderness of true affection or the refinement of friendship. I feel a sad void in my breast, and am reduced to the necessity of wishing to fill it. I have lost a friend that was as my own soul, and nothing is more natural than to desire to supply that loss by the person in the world that friend most esteemed and honoured; and as I have been long persuaded that perfect friendship is nowhere to be found but in marriage, I wish to perfect mine in that state. I know it is late in life to think of engaging anew in that state, in the beginning of my 59th year. I am old, and I appear older than I am; but thank God I am still in health, tho' not bettered by years, and however the vigour of life may be over, and with that the *vigour of vanity*, and the flutter of passion, I find myself not less fitted for all that is solid happiness in the wedded state – the tenderness of affection, and the faith of friendship.

I have a good clear income for my life; a trifle to settle, which I am only ashamed to offer; a good house (as houses go in our part of the world), moderately furnished, a good many books, a pleasant garden (better I believe than when you saw it) etc. Would to God I might have leave to lay them all at your feet.   ii p210–11

Mary Granville, mother of Mary Delany.

Mary took counsel with the immediate members of her family, her mother and sister, but did not give a definite answer. So Patrick took up his pen again.

Dr Delany to Mary, 3 May 1743

Permit me, madam, to beg to know my fate as far as it depends upon your friends in Gloucester: if it be favourable, be so good as to signify it to me, by *allowing* me the honour to call them *my friends*; I must be theirs, at all events; since I cannot cease to be with perfect affection and esteem, yours.

May every day of your life be as happy as I hope to find this and the next: and may the felicity of making mine such be only yours. Pardon the presumption of this well intended wish, in, madam, Your most obedient and not wholly unselfish servant, Pat Delany.   ii p212

At first, Mary had to withstand family disapproval and even at her age (she was in her forties) had to be encouraged to break her deference to their wishes.

Dr Delany to Mary, 6 May 1743

Madam, Though I can scarcely hold a pen in my hand, I cannot help attempting to inform you that I apprehend, from a moment's conversation with your brother this morning in the street (for he was gone out before I could reach his house), that his visit at Northend has made some change in his sentiments in relation to me. I beseech you, madam, leave me not to the caprice of any of your friends; and much less to the mercy of every humour of every friend. Where you *owe duty*, pay it; and let me rise or fall by the determination of *duty*; but let not the decision depend upon the fickle, the uncertain, and the selfish. God has blessed you with noble sentiments, a good understanding and a generous heart; are not these, under God, your best governors? I might venture to pronounce that even a parent has no right to control you, at this time of life, and under your circumstances, in opposition to these; and a *brother* has no shadow of right.   ii p213

Her sister Anne was an ally at this time

Anne Dewes to Dr Delany, Bradley, 3 June 1743

Sir, Though it is very natural to like those persons who are valued and distinguished by a favourite friend, yet I must assure you that my respect and admiration you have had, long before I could imagine there would be any other attachment than what is due to uncommon merit; but I now with great willingness and pleasure will add sisterly affection and esteem, which I dare say must increase upon acquaintance, and as you *make her happy* who is endeared to me by the strongest ties of love and obligation. If you find she has not entirely misplaced her friendship and will add yours to it, I shall be vastly glad, and if the most ardent prayers and wishes for your mutual happiness is any degree of merit, then I own I have a great deal, and fear I can claim no other.

*Anne Dewes, sister
of Mary Delany
and the main
recipient of her
correspondence.
From a drawing by
Mary Delany.*

The just sense you have of my sister's extreme worth gives me infinite delight, I never thought she could meet with anybody sensible enough of those delicacies in her disposition that complete the most amiable part of a woman's character, but now *I believe she has*; which will greatly alleviate what I shall suffer by her absence. Her absence is a subject, I will not mention, for as I now sincerely desire to promote your happiness, I trust in your generosity to deprive me of as little of mine as is in your power to avoid; and shall put Mrs Pendarves [Mary] in mind how much joy and satisfaction she retards by staying in London longer than is absolutely necessary. ii p216–17

They married on 9 June, 1743. It was probably a very private marriage because at the time, her brother and other influential relations were still set against the match. The description of Mary that follows was written for publication by Delany at a later date but when Mary vetoed this, was sent as a Christmas present for Anne Dewes, his sister-in-law.

Her stature was in a middle proportion . . . and every part and proportion perfect in their kind, fitted alike for activity and strength. Her walk was graceful, beyond anything that ever I saw in woman; and her dance would have been equally so, would her diffidence have permitted it. She was bashful to an extreme, and if I may use the expression, even blamably so. The case was the same with her playing [the harpsicord].

She could not bear the attention of others to her, and whenever she found she was attended to in a very extraordinary manner, she blushed and fluttered herslf into a confusion which quickly forced her to give over. With a person finely proportioned she had a most lovely face of great sweetness, set off with a head of fair hair, shining and naturally curled; with a complexion which nothing could outdo or equal.

Her eyes were bright . . . and she is almost the only woman I ever saw whose lips were scarlet, and her bloom beyond expression. The sweetness arising from united graces was guarded by a dgnity which kept all admirers in awe insomuch that she was the woman in the world to whom that fine description of Solomon could best be applied: *fair as the moon! clear as the sun ! but terrible as an army with banners!* iii pp388–89

The following description of herself is less flattering (and it dates from 5 years after they married) but it is surely a modest exaggeration.

Mary to Margaret, duchess of Portland
Delville, 14 February 1748/9

As to my dearest friend's wish about my phiz, it should be accomplished were it in my power; but it is given up by the whole college of painters to be an impossible face to draw *like*, as there is *no settled countenance* to copy! but *ill-conditioned* muscles, that grow crabbed and cross at the time when they ought to be in the best humour! Add to this a *muddled complexion, deep lines and furrows,* which time has bountifully and amply displayed, and for the size of the person belonging to that same face – *it is a porpuss grown.*   ii p504

After the wedding, Mary used her influence to obtain preferment for her husband and hoped that preaching before the king would provide an opportunity for his advancement. Patrick Delany had a reputation for considerable skills as a preacher.

Clarges Street, London, 30 November 1744

I believe I writ my mama word all the particulars of the settlements and so forth. D.D. preaches on Sunday next before his Majesty; it is unlucky for him that my Lord Carteret [a cousin] will not be able to attend in the closet, for he had determined to have said something in his favour. This was written in the morning. At eleven we went to Northend; at my return I made a visit to the Percivals [connections of the Donnellans], dressed and dined at Whitehall, made visits in the afternoon, drank tea with Lady Andover, who is come to town to lye in, and, poor thing! has had a fever. Cousin Fo[ley] came to town to-day, I sat an hour with her in my way home, and am now by my fireside with my own D.D., who bears all my flirtations and troubles with *unchangeable good humour* and only makes me regret every hour I spend from him.   ii p287–88

Soon he was appointed dean of Down, an office which carried with it an income of approximately £2000 a year, mostly derived from tithes or church dues from all the inhabitants of the parishes in the deanery.

Clarges Street, London, 8 May 1744

Well, my dear sister, I told you that I should not write to you this post, and I should have been as good as my word but that the *Dean of Down* desires me to make his compliments to you, and to present his humble duty to my mother. He has a most sincere regard for you, and only wishes and waits for an opportunity of telling you so in person; in the mean time hopes you will accept of his *devoirs* from *my hand*, and I believe there is nobody in England excepting myself (and D.D. is not jealous I assure you) for whom he has a greater value, and we have had several private conferences on that subject as well as many others. I am very glad to find, by your letter to my brother, that you did not apprehend D.D. to be as bad as he really was: but I suffered greatly, for nobody for the time could suffer more than he did, but I thank God he mends very fast. Yesterday he din'd in the parlour, and just as dinner came upon the table, Lord Carteret came to the door and came in.

He desired we would send the servants away, and when they were gone he told D.D. he was come from the Duke of Devonshire to offer him the Deanery of Down, and that the first small bishoprick that fell in he might have if he cared afterwards to quit Down; but the deanery is a much better thing than any small bishopric, and we are well pleased with the possession of it.

As soon as D.D. is well enough to go abroad he is to kiss hands, but that cannot possibly be till the beginning of the week, which will put off the happy hour of our meeting still longer.

Our dear Duchess raps at the door, and this cannot be finished 'till she is gone: she is pure well, – but has staid so long I can say but little more. I shall send to my brother your new gown to send because you may want to wear it, and two prints for you of the Giant's Causeway, which I desire your acceptance of, they are curiosities. Well, good night, I must sign and seal.   ii pp300–301

Mary continued to hope for higher office for the dean. Meanwhile her brother maintained his disapproval of Patrick Delany despite the change of attitude which the other members of the Granville family showed. Mary tried to repair the relationship.

Delville, 19 July 1744

You may have seen D.D. mentioned in the newspapers for the bishopric of Ferns, but I hope it will not be offered him, at least not these two months, for till then he will not be entitled to the rents of Down, and it will do us more harm than good, and the income is not better. I wrote to my brother last post a very long and kind letter, with an account of things here, and an invitation to be *a witness* and *sharer of my happiness* – (such a letter as you may imagine) but I should not have wrote *after what is past* without the consent of D.D., whose generosity and tenderness for me will not let him oppose anything that gives me satisfaction: it is the second letter I have wrote to my brother, but I have not yet received one line from him.   ii p313

In 1743 the bishop of Down, John Ryder, was an Englishman who had just been translated from the see of Killaloe. Many of the senior posts in the

eighteenth century Church of Ireland were held by Englishmen, to the disad-
vantage of Irish clerics, an issue Jonathan Swift raised in vain. Because these
churchmen wielded significant power in the temporal as well as ecclesiasti-
cal spheres, they often preferred to live near the centres of political activity,
either Dublin or London, rather than reside in their dioceses. The diocese of
Down had suffered from some neglect. The cathedral at Downpatrick was in
ruins, and many of the older churches needed refurbishment, if not complete
rebuilding. This state of decay in rural dioceses was not uncommon throughout
the British Isles but was worse in Ireland where the tumultuous events of the
seventeenth century, the 1641 revolt, and the Williamite wars left devastation
in their wake. In an area such as Ulster, where both Presbyterians and
Roman Catholics were in opposition to the payment of tithes, it required more
energy and commitment to attend to matters of church administration and
improvement than many churchmen were willing to show. The dean however
took his responsibilities seriously and immediately planned a visit to County
Down on his return to Ireland. Mary looked forward to the trip in a light
hearted vein.

Dr Delany was instituted as dean of Down in 1744.

Delville, 26 July 1744

D.D. had institution last Tuesday from the Bishop of Down, and has taken out his
patent, so now he is a Dean in all the forms; we propose setting out for Down on
Monday se'night, please God he is well. I hope we shall have a pleasant jaunt, but I
believe it is too late, and the days will be too much shortened, to think of going so far
northward as the Giants' Causeway, which is above fifty miles from Down. Miss
Forth (that lived with Mrs Clayton), is now with her sister Hamilton [Dorothea Forth
had married Francis Hamilton, rector of Dunleer, County Louth,in 1733]; they are in
our road to Down, and we design making them a visit in the way.   ii p318

Delville, 28 August 1744

I am at present in a great hurry, for at last we are obliged to go to Down. The Dean
thought his presence might have been dispensed with, but upon examination finds
there are forms that cannot be done by proxy, so to-morrow, please God, we set out
for Down. The roads are excellent, the weather very good for travelling, and I hope
the journey will be pleasant; the seeing of new places is entertaining, and we are
going into such a hospitable country, that we shall not lie at an inn all the
way.   ii p321

The Dean was very good to his family, providing for nieces and nephews.
Mary had already taken one niece as a personal maid after her first visit to
Ireland. When she returned as Mrs Delany another niece remained part of the
household even after she married Councillor Green, a lawyer.

Delville, 10 January 1744/5

Did I not write you word of an humble servant of Miss Delany's, a Councellor Green? he has been here and made his proposal, and is accepted; he is really a very handsome, agreeable man, modest, and has long had an affection for her, and I think she will make a very proper wife for him: without being at all handsome, she has something engaging in her looks and very proper in her behaviour: so now my thoughts are busy about her. Her uncle gives her her fortune and her wedding clothes; I hope we shall settle her happily, but she will be a great loss to me at home, for she is very useful and diverting, and gives us many a hearty laugh.   ii pp335–36

Delville, 19 January 1744/5

As also of the wedding in hand which goes on very well; and next Monday I go to Dublin to buy the clothes. D.D gives her five hundred pounds for her portion, and sixty pounds to buy clothes; I believe the knot will be tied about the middle of next month. I hope she will be happy; the prospect is fair, and she has engaged my good wishes by her very obliging behaviour.   ii pp338–39

Delville, 31 January 1744/5

Did I tell you of another wedding in hand here? a nephew of D.D's, who is a kind of steward to us, and a sober good sort of young man bred up to farming affairs. He is going to be married to a very clever girl, bred up in the same way – a niece of Mrs Barber's; the Dean *gives* them a very comfortable farm about twelve miles off, and they are to supply us with all farming affairs. When this is done the Dean has not a relation left that he has *not portioned or settled* in some comfortable way; and if I were to tell you all the particulars of his benevolence and his goodness towards them you would be astonished that his fortune had answered so well the beneficence of his heart.   ii p339

His household at Delville accommodated relations, friends and cats. The Greens seem to have been constantly at Delville, much to Mary's pleasure.

Delville, 2 March 1744/5

I give you a short account of our wedding day which passed off as well as such things generally do. They are still in the house with us, and will stay till the beginning of May that we go to the north. Mr Green is an agreeable man to have in the house as he is very well bred and easy, conversable, and reads to us while we work in the evenings, so that we spend our time very pleasantly. Miss Harman, a cousin-german and friend of Mrs Green, is now with us – a modest young thing, obliging and good-humoured; and you know I like to indulge friends as I love to be indulged myself; we have had a good deal of company on this occasion, and next week we return visits and have many dinner invitations on our hands. The Councellor Green has three brothers, the two eldest great sugar bakers, and one of them made a present to the bride of a bill of fifty pounds the day after she was married.

Have I told you of a pretty tortoiseshell puss I have? the sauciest and prettiest and most indulged little animal that ever was everybody's favourite. After this important sentence I have no more to add, but that I am with the utmost tenderness yours.   ii pp340,342

However, Mary, at this early stage, still hoped for a bishopric for her husband although the deanery of Down was said to be more valuable than some of the lesser bishoprics. The disposal of church benefices by patronage was taken for granted at the time. John Stearne, bishop of Clogher, benefactor of Trinity College, died in 1745 and raised her hopes.

Hollymount, Down, 21 June 1745

The death of the Bishop of Clogher *may* make an alteration in our affairs, and if it does, I fear it must in our schemes; for should D.D. be made a Bishop, he must attend the Parliament this winter, and our journey to England cannot be undertaken till the spring, as the bishopric must be taken if offered, or it may not again be offered; though a small one will not be accepted. I believe *he* will be condemned in general for this, but I own I think him *quite in the right*; I am better pleased to have him remain Dean of Down, than have him at the fag end of all the Bishops! If they give us Kildare I shall be at the height of my wishes as far as they regard *any worldly preferment*; though Clogher is more considerable by five hundred pounds a-year; but the Deanery of C[hrist] Church being annexed to the Bishopric of Kildare obliges a residence in or near Dublin, and so *Delville* might be our palace. The deferring the pleasure of seeing my dear friends in England this year, will be a vast disappointment to me, but if this happens, I shall have the joy of being with them a whole year instead of half a year, for if D.D. continues Dean of Down, he *must* be here next summer to finish the good works he is now laying the foundation of, and we shall hardly be able to leave this place till towards September.

D.D's constant attention to me, his indulgence on all occasions, his tenderness, and the regard he has for *all those I love*, testify his affection with more force than the muses can dictate; *they* indeed help to illustrate a growing passion, but when once it is arrived to the dignity of a settled friendship *their aid* is not wanted, though at all times their company is desirable and agreeable.   ii pp364–65

Hollymount, 28 June 1745

Lord G[ranville?] went to my Lord C[arteret] as soon as he was told of the Bishop of Clogher's death, and *demanded* that Bishopric for D.D. Lord C. said *it was engaged to a Bishop*; but explained no farther (I suppose the removes not being yet settled), and added he should "*not forget his friend.*" If the Bishopric is to given to a Bishop, it will of course occasion removes. I heard some time ago that Lord C. had declared that whenever he had a good Bishopric in his power he would give it to the Bishop of Cloyne (Berkeley); and *if he does* I shall honour him for distinguishing a man of so much merit, and may then have reason to hope D.D. will have a fair chance of being preferred as he deserves. Cloyne is a middling Bishopric, not to be refused, but I own Kildare *alone* is what I wish for.   ii pp366–67

Dr Patrick Delany, Dean of Down (1684/5–1768)

Ironically, it was their friend Robert Clayton who was appointed to the bishopric of Clogher from Cork and dashed Mrs Delany's hopes for her husband.

Delville, 24 August 1745

You have heard that the Bishoprics are settled; Cork to Clogher, the Bishop of Dromore to Cork, and Dr Marley *(a worthy and ingenious man)* to Dromore. ii p380

Delville, 8 February 1745/6

It is well for me that the Dean so well understands and feels the little cares and anxiety that belong to affection, otherwise I should sometimes try his patience; but he is so far from condemning me that he is *ready to join with me* in every mark and testimony of love to my friends.   ii p420

In this fond correspondence the Dean shows how much confidence he has in Mary to manage the Delville household during his absence on deanery duties. At this time he was engaged in a dispute with Judge Ward, the local landlord, over the payment of tithes. Ward supported the local weavers who objected to paying tithes on their weaving income when it was only a part-time occupation, and pleaded poverty: the dean refused to accept this, suggesting that a reduction of church tithes would merely increase the landlord's rental. In 1748 the dean published An Essay towards Evidencing the Divine Original of Tythes.

Dean Delany to Mary
Mount Panther, 15 August 1747
extracts from unpublished manuscript: Newport Central Library, Gwent.

My hand being weary with a long letter to Judge Ward which tho' dated yesterday was written today, Mr Sturgeon [his curate], who is very much your humble servant does me the favour to be my amanuensis to you. I am very much pleased with your account of your last jaunt; but much more, with the recovery of your health, your sleep and your spirits; for which I sincerely thank God, and earnestly beseech you to take more care of yourself for the future; to exercise more in your garden, and out of it; and to toil less at your painting: well knowing that the finest drawing and colouring of any angel upon the earth would make me but little amends for the slightest sinking of the least line in your countenance or change in your complexion.

My dearest life, you may be perfectly assured that I entirely approve of your oeconomy and conduct, in every respect and that I am truly thankful to God for your aggregate blessing of so many distinguished advantages and excellencies bestow'd upon me in one wife and friend. God in his goodness make me in some measure worthy of it.

As time passed, the Delanys became content with life as it was and gave up aspirations to the bishopric.

1751

The newspapers inform us positively of Lord Granville being President of the Council. I hope it will prove to his honour, and the good of the nation; *his abilities are sufficient*, and therefore the greater his reproach if he fails. As to any good that may accrue to us from his present situation, I think little of it, though I believe he would now *rather* prefer D.D. than any of his acquaintance; but great men are so hampered with their engagements to one another that they cannot always do what perhaps they wish to do. We are really neither of us anxious about it; indeed we have no reason, for if we can discharge the duty of our present station, I think we have nothing farther *in reason to wish for now* on our own account.

Last Saturday we had our music and company, and everybody seemed pleased, so much that I wished for my dearest sister over and over again. I am a prisoner till my horses are well, but what care I? I indeed wish to see my two agreeable Hamiltons; but I have good company at home, and a world of employments.   iii p40–41

Though her marriage was a particularly happy one, Mary missed her sister and the society she was used to in England. Mary and the dean compromised over her desire to visit England and her family and his pastoral responsibilities and went to England every third year. The troublesome Tenison lawsuit took up much time. While the dean was active in Down, he never moved there permanently and had to bear the criticism that he was an absentee. He had his difficulties there and was embroiled in a dispute about payment of tithes with the weavers and their spokesman and landlord, Judge Ward. Although the Dean insisted it was a matter of principle, it is tempting to speculate that he had to insist on their full payment in order to finance his building and improvements there. This tithe dispute probably set in motion another quarrel with the litigious Presbyterians in the deanery.

Delville, 3 January 1752

I have indeed often thought of late my lot *most singularly happy*, more so than is generally met with in this world of woe: a husband of *infinite merit*, and deservedly most dear to me; a sister whose delicate and uncommon friendship makes me the envy of all other sisters; a brother of worth and honour, and a friend in the Duchess of Portland not to be equalled, besides so many other friends, that altogether make up the sum of my happiness. But what a debt have I to pay! I am truly sensible of my own unworthiness, and that all these advantages are not to be enjoyed without a considerable allay, and as my most inmost thoughts have ever been laid open to the sister of my heart, I must now unburthen my mind.

D.D's love to me I think is as unquestionable as any mortal love can be, and the generosity of his sentiments as well known, but he is *most extremely harassed* with his law-suits, (that of the Tennisons, and that about his tythes in the deanery); and another is commenced against him by a mistake committed on his side of a form at law by the Presbyterians – those querulous people! I thank God his fortune is too good to suffer very considerably by these attacks, but suffer in some degree we must, and it is absolutely necessary we should act with caution and prudence till we are so happy as to get out of the jaws of the law – that beast of prey!

There is murmuring at his not living more at his deanery, and being absent so long from it when we go to England. This you may believe is vexatious to me, as it is *entirely* on my account he goes, and he is so generous as not to retract in the least from his *promise to me and to my friends* of my going to England *every third year*, though I am very sensible it is not quite convenient to him. What can I – what ought I to do in this case? were *only duty* concerned, ought I not to consider *his* interest, honour, and satisfaction? but with the additional affection I have for him, is it possible for me to avoid making him a sacrifice on such an occasion? and a *greater* than that of giving up for *one year more* my friends in England I cannot make!

I am unfortunately circumstanced in one respect, that *some* of my friends *cannot*, others *will not* take their turn of making me a visit. I have had the pleasure of spending three years with them, and not one month has yet been bestowed upon me! To you my most dear and most indulgent sister, I should not say this.   iii pp70–71

This was a worrying time when the Tenison lawsuit seemed to have succeeded against them, however, the Delanys pursued their cause through other courts and were eventually vindicated in 1758.

Mount Panther, 18 July 1752

This is by way of a little preparation to something that, I fear, will give you concern – the loss of our lawsuit, which has been carried against us. I hope God will graciously permit him to vindicate himself, *and make his innocence appear as clear as the noon day*, and those who are *really and truly* his friends and mine cannot value him the less for a calamity occasioned by his too great *disregard* of the things of this world and *too great security* in his own integrity.   iii pp138–39

Delville, 4 November 1752

I am perfectly well, and so is, I bless God, D.D., and one consolation we have, which no malice of our enemies can destroy – a conscience *perfectly clear of the charge*. iii p169

Delville, 8 March 1753

I am glad you are easy about our northern journey, for I believe it will do us both good, and I should be sorry when I am so happy as to enjoy my friends in England to give D.D. reason to feel I had been the occasion of his neglecting his duty; for indeed it is my *pride and happiness* that he does most conscientiously discharge it as far as lies in his power. With all my diligence I am afraid I shall not be able to finish the picture I have begun for the Duchess of Portland, as our time for going to the north is fixed for the 20th inst. D.D. must administer the sacrament the first Sunday in the month, and Easter day; and preach another – for he is not able to do both, and he has four churches to preach at besides, so that we cannot return before the middle of May, but time, my dearest sister, will fly, though it seems to do so less when we are impatient to see a beloved friend; but I know you wish the Dean should visit England with his mind free from any regret.   iii pp211–12

The unforeseen death of one of the first Mrs Tenison's beneficiaries consider-ably increased the dean's income and disconcerted his opponents.

Delville, 6 July 1754

This morning we had an account of Mrs Townley's death; she died last Wednesday was se'night [i.e.,a week ago last Wednesday] at the Bath, and by her death a rent-charge jointure of £600 a-year falls in to the Dean. The poor woman has been in a miserable way for many years, but I did not think in danger of dying, as her disorders were called hysterics. I believe the Townley's will mourn in good earnest for their cousin, as this will enable D.D. to withstand everything without suffering any very great inconvenience.   iii pp283–84

Sometimes Patrick Delany went to the north on his own. On this occasion, Mary was nursing her goddaughter Sally : notice his gallantry in the face of all circumstances.

Dr Delany to Mary
Mount Panther, 20 August 1759
extract from unpublished manuscript; Newport Central Library, Gwent.

You remember, my dearest life, Indiana says upon some occasion "all the rest of my life is but waiting until he comes". I can truly say so of your letters: I feast upon them for a post present and a post to come.

The judges dined with me yesterday; and were very easy and agreeable; but J.I. Canford [?Crawford, Dean Delany's agent] went away much sooner than I expected, and left me much vexed that I lost the opportunity of drinking his fair niece and doing her merits that justice which I fear he doth not. This was not my only misfortune: I forgot my spectacles and with great difficulty hammered out my sermon; and was (I hope sufficiently) mortified, but I thank God I find my self less and less fatigued every time I preach and I sometimes fancy I walk with more activity.

I am sorry you have lost your very agreeable companion and I my correspondent , but I thank God mine is a much less loss [may refer to Mrs F. Hamilton who was helping with Sally]. Your letters fully supply the place of all others. Their elasticity (like that of the air) expands and leaves no emptiness about them.

My dearest life you reckon wrong; you should only count by months, whilst there is any part of another month to come and then you may begin to count by weeks. The first week of the next month will I hope bring me to your care of my greatest happiness: but I desire I may not be expected to a day.

I am heartily glad to hear your, and my English friends are well. God long preserve you to them and to me, to the remnant of my span: till then and for ever after, be

The Quoile Estuary, Co. Down, by Mary Delany, 29 August 1763.

blessed up to your warmest wishes of my dearest life, your most affectionate and faithful P.D. my best wishes to all about you.

The dean, now in his eighties, became more frail and travel was difficult.

Mary to Viscountess Andover
Delville, 8 June 1765

The Dean has been so much out of order with his old complaint, and of consequence my spirits so much affected, that I have avoided writing to my dear Lady Andover till I was a more reasonable creature: I thank God he is rather better; he has given up his house in the Deanery, being unable to bear so long a journey without great inconvenience.   iv p48

Mary to Viscountess Andover
Delville, 18 November 1766

I have been sadly anxious for some time past for my dear D.D., he has been *very ill*, and reduced very low, which, to a man of his years, must give cruel apprehensions; however, I thank God his good constitution has at present got the better, and he is as well as he has been for some months past.   iv p88

The dean went with Mary to take a cure at Bath in 1767. When he died the following year at least Mary was near her own family circle.

CHAPTER 2

SOCIETY

DUBLIN: FIRST IMPRESSIONS

On her first visit to Ireland, through her family connections and her friends, the Claytons and Donnellans, Mary was introduced to several circles: the viceregal court; gentry; and clergy, including the university set of Trinity College Dublin. This world was very small and broadly defined by the religion of the established church, politics and loyalty to the English administration in Dublin. It was a charmed life for those in the right circumstances and conviviality was the order of the day. Her first visit to Ireland was a great success. She stayed in the Dublin home of the Claytons, relatives of her friend Anne Donnellan. Robert Clayton, who had become bishop of Killalla and Achonry in 1730, commissioned Richard Cassels to build a mansion in 1730 on the south side of Stephen's Green.

The lord lieutenant and viceroy of Ireland at the time of her first visit was Lionel Sackville, duke of Dorset. Until 1767, the lord lieutenants stayed in Ireland, at Dublin Castle, during the six months of the Irish parliamentary session, generally returning to England to re-establish their presence in the important social and political spheres there for the other half of the year. Ireland was considered by many of the viceroys to be banishment, although Dorset sought the post. His younger son, Lord George Sackville, made his presence felt in Dublin social circles. The Dorsets succeeded Mary's cousin John, second Baron Carteret, a friend of Swift.

Dublin, 26 September 1731

You are by this time, I hope, perfectly satisfied about every thing relating to my journey. I must now proceed and give you an account of men and manners. Last Tuesday I wrote you word of my having been at the Castle in the morning. We went again in the evening; the apartments consist of three rooms, not altogether so large as those at St James's, but of a very tolerable size. In the farthest room there is placed a basset table [a card game resembling faro], at which the Duchess of Dorset sits down after she has received and made her compliments to the company. It is very seldom any ladies sit down to basset, but quadrille parties [another card game played by four] are made in the other rooms, and such idle ones as I saunter up and down, or pick up some acquaintance to chat with, just the same as at St James's. There were several very pretty women; the top beauty is Lady Ross, a sweet agreeable creature.

Her first introductions in Dublin, apart from family, were to people who would become part of her intimate circle at Delville. Here she comments on the sociability she found in Dublin.

24

Great preparations are making against the birthday. There are to be no balls at Court, but on such public days; Lady Carteret used to have balls once a week, but they brought so great a crowd that the Duchess, who is of a quiet spirit, will avoid them.

Most of the Moncks [of Charleville, cousins through the Stanleys] are at present out of town, but I expect them thick and three-fold soon. Yesterday I spent an agreeable afternoon at Mr [Henry] Hamilton's, Mr Usher met us there. I never saw a couple better suited than Mr Hamilton and his wife [she later became Mary's particular friend]; they are both genteel and perfectly well-behaved, without any affectation; their house, like themselves, looks cheerful and neat. Whist was played till supper, but there were always three that looked on, who all took their turn of play, except your humble servant. We had a very pretty supper, neatly served, and parted between twelve and one. I don't believe I shall meet with people I like better during my stay here; they are both young, and have four children, whose behaviour shows the sense of their parents.

As for the generality of people that I meet with here, they are much the same as in England – a mixture of good and bad; all that I have met with behave themselves very decently, according to their rank, now and then an oddity breaks out, but none so extraordinary but that I can match them in England. There is a heartiness among them that is more *like Cornwall* than any I have known, and great sociableness. I apprehend from that way of living there must arise a good deal of tittle-tattle, but I have not heard much yet.

Wherever I go I meet with great civilities; I don't take it as paid me on my own account, but that of those I am with, who are here highly regarded, and indeed their friendliness and kindness to me increases every day.

They study to entertain me, and I have no uneasiness on their account but that they may think I am not so cheerful as they would have me; but as I grow older, though I feel as much warmth as ever, I have not so lively a way of shewing it. I attribute it a great deal to the fear I have always had of appearing too gay; a wrong notion I am now convinced, and it hurts the temper.   i pp289–92

Phoenix Park, one of the largest and finest urban parks of any European capital, covers 1,752 acres, part of lands seized by the crown from the priory of Kilmainham in the sixteenth century.

Dublin, 4 October 1731

The chief entertainment of this week I have forgot to mention, which was the review on Friday morning last. The park, justly called Phoenix Park, was the place of show. One regiment of horse and three of foot, who all performed their parts well. The Duchess of Dorset was there in great state, and all the beau monde of Dublin. The weather favoured us, and we were very pleased with the sight. But I must not pass over in silence the beauties of the park, which is a large extent of ground, very fine turf, agreeable prospects, and a delightful wood, in the midst of which is a ring where the beaux and belles resort in fair weather; indeed, I never saw a spot of ground more to my taste, it is far beyond St James or Hyde Park. Nobody's equipage outlooked ours except my Lord Lieutenant's, but in every respect I must say Mrs Clayton's

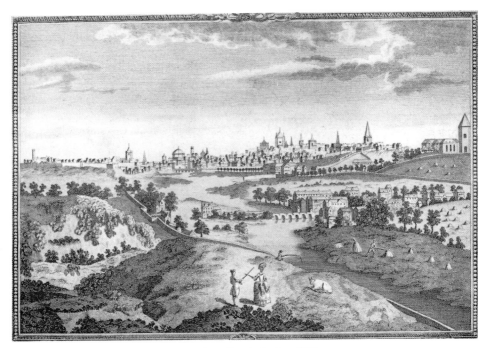

Dublin from Phoenix Park, c. 1753.

outshines her neighbours, not that that is easily done here, for people understand not only living well, but politely.

Yesterday we went to Christchurch, one of the cathedrals. I cannot say they have much reason to brag of the architecture of it, but they have good voices and a very sweet organ.   i pp294–95

When her cousin Carteret left Ireland he said, "When people asked me how I governed Ireland, I say that I pleased Dr Swift." Probably this friendship aided her introduction to Jonathan Swift, whose circle included Dr Delany.

Dublin, 9 October 1731

This morning we are to go out of town to a house of Dr Delany's called Delville: we carry a cold scrap with us, and propose spending the day very agreeably; it is about three miles off.

On Saturday morning we went in the coach and six to StillOrgan, a seat of my Lord Allen's, four miles from Dublin, very fine and charming prospect of the sea all the way, like the harbour of Falmouth. On a rising ground in the park there is erected an obelisk, very well built, from whence there is a very fine and extensive view. The house is like one made of card, the gardens laid out in the old fashioned taste, but capable of being made a fine thing; nothing can be prettier than the situation.

I must say the environs of Dublin are delightful. The town is bad, enough, narrow streets and dirty-looking houses, but some very good ones scattered about; and as for Stephen's Green, I think it may be preferred justly to any square in London, and it is a great deal larger than Lincoln's Inns Fields. A handsome broad gravel walk and another of grass, railed in round the square, planted with trees, that in the summer give a very good shade; and every morning Miss Donnellan and I walk there.

Yesterday being the anniversary of the King's coronation, we, like loyal subjects, went to the Castle; there was a ball very decently ordered, and French dancing in abundance. Your friend Index [Hon. John Percival, related to the Donnellans], who often speaks of you, played his part very well there, and had the prize. I danced three country dances with Mr Usher in a vast crowd; after that we were summoned to supper, where everything was prepared with great magnificence. Three large tables beside the Duke's, covered with all sorts of provision disposed very well. I never saw so much meat with so little confusion. After that they went to dancing again; it was so hot and crowded that our courage would hold out but for half a dance. Between twelve and one we came home, and were very well pleased to lay us down.

She met some of the liveliest intellects, including Constantia Grierson, wife to the printer and friend of Swift, and Letitia Pilkington (1712–59) the writer.

I have just began an acquaintance among the wits – Mrs Grierson, Mrs Sycon, and Mrs Pilkington; the latter is a bosom friend of Dean Swift's, and I hope among them I shall be able to pick up some entertainment for you.   i pp299–301

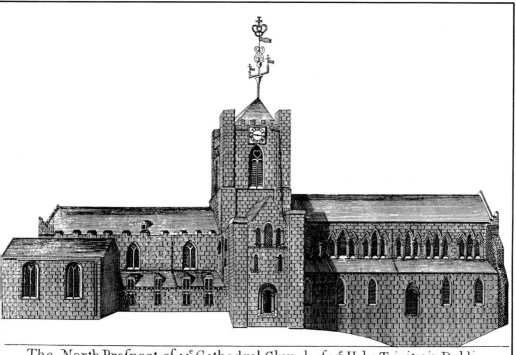

The North Prospect of yᵉ Cathedral Church of yᵉ Holy Trinity in Dublin

Christchurch Cathedral, Dublin, 1766.

Here she mentions Edward Lovett Pearce (1699–1733), architect of some of Ireland's most handsome buildings including the Irish houses of Parliament, now the Bank of Ireland.

Dublin, 4 November 1731

The birthday, as you may remember, happened on a Saturday. In the morning we all attended their Graces at the Castle in our best array, as I wrote you word after my return. Sunday we stayed at home; on Monday at eight o'clock went to the Castle. The room where the ball was to be was ordered by Capt. Pierce, finely adorned with paintings and obelisks, and made as light as a summer's day.

I never saw more company in one place; abundance of finery, and indeed many very pretty women. There were two rooms for dancing. The whole apartment of the Castle was open, which consists of several very good rooms; in one there was a supper ordered after the manner of that at the masquerade, where everybody went at what hour they liked best, and vast profusion of meat and drink, which you may be sure has gained the *hearts* of all guzzlers! The Duke and Duchess [of Dorset] broke through their reserved way and were very obliging; indeed it was very handsome the whole entertainment, but attended with great crowding and confusion.   i p309

The Wesleys were in the same circle as the Donnellans and Claytons.

Dublin, 16 November 1731

You guess very rightly, your favourite Miss Wesley [of Dangan] performs miracles at the Castle, and is by much the best dancer there. You may imagine such a little pretty creature does not want for praises: were I her mother, I should not expose her to so many, she is of an age to be spoiled by them, unless she has an uncommon share of sense. Mr and Mrs Wesley receive your compliments very kindly, and heartily return theirs. No, madam, I *do not dance* in *every crowd*, though I always have an agreeable partner at hand, and I did not dance on the birthnight.

At night Lord Mountjoy gives a ball to the Duke and Duchess of Dorset; he has invited my cousins, and told them he designed to ask me. The ball at Mrs Graham's [daughter of Lord Lansdowne, cousin of Mary's, living at Platten, Meath] will be next week I believe. Humphrey Matthews [of Thomastown] asked particularly after you; he is but just come to town. We are soon to have a *story-telling evening*: who shall I wish for to listen to him, I wonder?

Mr Barnard was here last night at our assembly (which was as much crowded as ever I saw my Lady Stafford's, and more agreeable, except in one respect, which you will not be at a loss to guess at); he is very conceited and silly, and said many things he intended to be taken for wit. He jeered me extremely upon liking Ireland, and had he been an Englishman I should have thought him very rude, for saying so many disobliging things of a place where I am so civilly treated. Phill gave him a rub or two about the lamps in Pall Mall that would not burn bright for him, and he had not much to say for himself.   i p312–15

Public performances of music were often the occasion for society gatherings.

Dublin, 25 November 1731

Monday being St Cecilia's day it was celebrated with great pomp at St Patrick's cathedral. We were there in the greatest crowd I ever saw; we went at 10 and staid till 4; there is a fine organ, which was accompanied by a great many instruments, Dubourg [leader of the viceroy's musicians] at the head of them; they began with the 1st concerto of Corelli; we had Purcell's Te Deum and Jubilate; then the 5th concerto of Corelli; after that an anthem of Dr Blow's, and they concluded with the 8th concerto of Corelli. Perhaps you think this was entertainment enough for one day; pardon me, we are not here so easily satisfied as to let one diversion serve for the whole day and we *double and treble* them.

Lord Montjoy [Thomas Windsor] made a fine ball for the Duke and Duchess of Dorset and their retinue, our house was among the invited people, and Monday was the day fixed on. After our music we returned home, eat our dinner as expeditiously as we could, and by seven (the hour named) we were all equipped for the ball; Mrs Graham, Miss Granville, and Miss Usher called on us, and we all went away together, nobody was admitted but by tickets. There was four-and-twenty couple, 12 danced at a time, and when they had danced 2 dances, the other 12 took their turn. No lookers on but the Duchess and Mrs Clayton, who thought it beneath the dignity of a Bishop's wife to dance.

The Duke danced with Lady Allen (the Duchess had the headache) Lord Mountjoy with Lady Caroline [Sackville], Mr Coot with Lady Lambert, Capt. Pierce with Mrs Donellan, and Mr Usher with me; the rest were people you don't know at all; Index [admirer of Anne Granville's] would not condescend to dance more than minuets.

Before the dancing began, the company were all served with tea and coffee; at 9, every lad took out his lass. At 11, those who were not dancing followed the Duke and Duchess up stairs to a room where was prepared all sorts of cold meats, fruits, sweetmeats, and wines, placed after the same manner as the masquerades. We eat and drank as much as we liked, and then descended to make way for the rest of the company. Mrs Clayton went away at 12, the Duchess soon after that, and Phil and I staid till 1, and then with much difficulty made our escapes, the rest staid till 4 in the morning. On the whole, the entertainment was more handsome than agreeable, there being too much company.

The next morning we rose at 9 o'clock, put on our genteel dishabille [dress], to the Parliament House, at 11, to hear an election determined: the parties were Brigadier Parker the sitting member, and Mr Ponsonby the petitioner, Mr Southwell's interest was the first, and the last was Sir Richard Mead's. I believe we were the most impartial hearers among all the ladies that were there, though rather inclined to Mr Southwell's side, but the cause was determined in favour of Sir R.M's. I was very well entertained there. Our cousins were also there.

About 3 o'clock Mrs Clayton went home to dinner with her Bishop; we were stout, and staid. Mr Hamilton, a gentleman I have mentioned to you, brought us up chickens, and ham, and tongue, and everything we could desire. At 4 o'clock the speaker adjourned the House 'till 5. We then were conveyed, by some gentleman of our acquaintance, into the Usher of the Black Rod's room, where he had a good fire, and meat, tea, and bread and butter. Were we not well taken care of? When the House was assembled, we re-assumed our seats and staid till 8; loth was I to go away then, but I thought that my kind companions were tired, and staid out of compliment to me, so home we came.   i p316–19

The gaiety continued although not all dancing partners were agreeable.

Dublin, 4 December 1731

I should have wrote to you last post, but I was to go to a ball at the Grahams, and I was afraid of making too much use of my eyes, lest I should dim their lustre, but I need not have been so careful, for there was not a man worth darting at. Our company was as follows: Lord Charles Hay, Mrs Graham, Mr Graham, and Mrs Hancock (Miss Vesey that was, I believe you saw her at the Bath). He was to have danced with me, but Mrs Hancock's husband is so jealous of her, that she must not dance with an unmarried man.

Sir Richard Mead danced with Miss Kelly, [Swift's admired] who keeps her beauty very well. The rest of the men are not worth naming, poor dull wretches, very ill chosen I am sure.

I wanted my good partner Mr Usher; in his stead I had Captain Folliat, a man six foot odd inches high, black, awkward, ramping, roaring, I though he would have shook my arms off, and crushed my toes to atoms, every moment he did some blundering thing, and as often asked "my ladyship's pardon." I was pitied by the whole company; at last I was resolved to *dispatch him* with dancing since he was not worth my conquest any other way; I called a council about it, having some scruples of conscience, and fearing he might appear and haunt me after his death staggered my resolutions, but when it was made plain to me that I should do the world a great piece of service by despatching him, it solved all my scruples, and I had no more qualms about it. In the midst of his furious dancing, when he was throwing his arms about him most outrageously (just like a card scaramouch on a stick), snap went something, that we all thought had been the main bone of his leg, but it proved only a bone of his toe. Notwithstanding which (like Widdington) he fought upon his stumps, and would not spare me one dance; we began pegging it at eight, and continued our sport till one, *without ceasing.*   i pp324–25

Dublin, 9 December 1731

On Tuesday Phill and I went to the Castle, got a very snug seat in the ball-room, and made ourselves very merry with some good figures that exposed themselves there. I am out of conceit with dancing at the Castle – it is so intolerably crowded. Yesterday was our day, we had a good deal of company, my table is flocked to, and is generally made up of beauties, excepting your humble servant. Lord Charles Hay has made acquaintance with me as a thing whose face he was used to in London; I am jeered about it, and so I am upon some other things of that kind.

To-morrow we go to a concert of music, on Saturday to the poppet-show, on Monday to the ridotto [a party with music and dancing]; Mr and Mrs Wesley are in the country for a few days; they are much at your service; after Xmas I go to Platten, Mr Graham's [married to her uncle Lansdowne's daughter] country-house, 20 miles from Dublin. We are to spend a fortnight there: they design inviting as much

A caricature: Sir Thomas Kennedy, Lord Charlemont, Mr Ward and Mr Phelps by Joshua Reynolds (1723-92).

company to go down with them as will make 6 couple for country dances, and we are to dance *every night*.   i pp328–29

Dublin, 14 December 1731

Yesterday Phill [Donnellan] and I went to the ridotto with a whole train of young things at our heels. I like it the least of any diversion I have seen here. There was a vast deal of company, two rooms of dancers; above 20 couple in each room. I danced with Mr Usher [cousin of the Donnellans] 2 dances, and had like to have been torn limb from limb; the Duke of Dorset was there, and Lady Caroline Sackville; the Duchess is very ill of a fever. We staid till 12 o'clock; Index [Hon. John Percival] came home with us by way of a guard.

   Pray how does your Pussey do?   i p332

Dublin, 17 January 1731/2

Would it were so, that I went ravaging and slaying all odious men, and that would go near to clear the world of that sort of animal; you know I never had a good opinion of them, and every day my *dislike strengthens*; some *few* I will except, but *very few*, they have so despicable an opinion of women, and treat them by their words and actions so ungenerously and inhumanly. By my manner of inveighing, anybody less acquainted with me than yourself would imagine I had *very lately* received some very ill usage. No! 'tis my general observation on conversing with them: the minutest indiscretion in a woman (though occasioned by themselves), never fails of being enlarged into a notorious crime; but men are to sin on without limitation or blame; a hard case! – not the restraint we are under, for *that I extremely approve of*, but the unreasonable license tolerated in the men. How amiable, how noble a creature is man when adorned with virtue! but how detestable when loaded with vice! Yesterday was our assembly, and a notable one we had.   i p333

Mary to her brother, Bernard Granville
Dublin, 7 March 1731/2

'Tis fit in return for the account you give me of your amusements, that I let you know what we do here. Why, on the first of March we went to Court in the morning, heard a song of Dubourg's [Matthew Dubourg, leader of the viceroy's musicians], (not so pretty as the last) after that compliment was over and we had refreshed ourselves by dinner, we went again at seven.

   The ball was in the old beef-eaters hall, a room that holds seven hundred people seated, it was well it did, for never did I behold a greater crowd. We were all placed in rows one above another, so much raised that the last row almost *touched the ceiling!* The gentlemen say we looked very handsome, and compared us to Cupid's paradise in the puppet-show. At eleven o'clock minuets were finished, and the Duchess went to the basset table.

   After an hour's playing the Duke, Duchess, and nobility marched into the supper-room, which was the council chamber. In the midst of the room was placed a holly tree, illuminated by an hundred wax tapers; round it was placed all sorts of meat, fruit, and sweetmeats; servants waited next, and were encompassed round by a table, to which the company came by turns to take what they wanted. When the doors were *first* opened, the hurly burly is not to be described; squawling, shrieking, all sorts of noises; some ladies lost their lappets, others were trod upon. Poor Lady Santry almost lost her breath in the scuffle, and fanned herself two hours before she could recover herself enough to know if she was dead or alive. I and my company were more discreet than to go with the torrent; we staid till people had satisfied their curiosity and hunger, and then took a quiet view of the *famous tree*, which occasion'd more rout than it was worth. I have enclosed you the newest piece of wit now stirring; the author they say is Mr Fitzmorris.   i pp337–38

Here Mary visits Castletown (Conolly) so called after Speaker William Conolly, who built it between 1719 and 1722. He was of obscure origins and became one of the richest Irishmen in that age, engaging the Florentine Alessandro Galilei to design this mansion although Edward Lovett Pearce (Captain Pierce, "our sleepy lover" in the correspondence, who gained a knighthood) made contributions.

Dublin, 11 March 1731/2

But I did not tell you what I did on Thursday last. Why Mrs Graham, Miss Granville, one Mrs Clements, and myself – four dull women, without so much as one cavalier to attend us – went to Mr Conolly's house, called Castle Town, 'tis not in his possession at present, but will be so after his aunt's death.

It is a large heavy building, a vast deal of room in it, but not laid out with a good taste, the furniture good, but not disposed to the best advantage, the situation very fine, and the country about extremely pleasant – some wood and pretty winding rivers. Our *sleepy* lover was yesterday dubbed a knight, and to-day I have promised to give him the meeting at the Graham's, where I shall dine, but I am afraid *Sir Edward Pierce* will hardly think it worth his while to make up for the neglects of *Captain Pierce!* Our parliament was dismissed yesterday. The town will now grow idle – most people talk of going into the country.

The Duke [of Dorset] goes to England the 27th of April, but first he makes a visit to Plattin [Meath], and I doubt the Duchess goes, it will put my cousins in a fuss, and give them very little pleasure, for they are as awkward as ever at entertaining strangers; and I am afraid they will insist upon my going with them but I had rather be excused.   i pp342–43

Here she enjoys herself with the Wesleys, who were to remain her great friends, and others of that extended family circle of the Donnellans.

Dublin, 30 March 1732

This has been a week of great mirth and jollity; on Monday Phill and I went to the ridotto with Mrs Wesley, where we met with no disturbance; it began with a concert of music, the Duke, Duchess, and Lady Caroline were there; they went away when the music was over, and after some hideous minuets, we went to country dances. Mr Wesley was my partner, there were twenty couple, four dances were as much as my spirits would bear. We got home by a little after twelve. On Tuesday we had a party more to my *goût*. Mr Wesley in the days of yore, (before he had his great fortune), [Richard Colley before inheriting the Dangan estate] had a little house about three miles out of town called Butlers Town, – the situation of it very fine, something like Roskrow [Cornwall], but nearer the sea. It is now in possession of a near relation of his, Mr Kit Ussher [cousin of the Donnellans], a very sensible, plain, good humoured man: his wife is a poor little meek woman that never makes or mars sport.

To this place the old jaunting set went, about two o'clock, where we had cold fowl, lamb, pigeon pye, Dutch beef, tongue, cockells, sallad, much variety of liquors, and the finest syllabub that ever was tasted. When we had devoured as much as possible, we all adjourned to Mr Wesley's, where I was placed at the harpsichord, and after jangling a little, Mr Wesley took his fiddle and played to his daughters' dancing. Those children grow prettier and more agreeable every day than the other, and remember you very well. We mustered up five couple and danced two hours; the master of house fiddled and danced the whole time; then we went to supper, and had a profusion of "*peck and booz*" (terms for meat and drink) and extravagance of mirth. We parted at half an hour after one.

Yesterday, we had an entertainment of another sort, and very agreeable in its way, – an assembly at Mrs Butler's, a lady I have mentioned in some of my former letters, cards of all sorts; I played two pools at commerce: when that was over, at ten o'clock was placed on little tables before the company as they sat, a large Japan board with plates of all sorts of cold meat neatly cut, and sweetmeats wet and dry, with chocolate, sago, jelly, and salvers of all sorts of wine. While we were eating, fiddles were sent for, (a sudden thought). We began before eleven and held briskly to it till half an hour after two. Phill was not idle; she danced with her cousin Will (Usher), and I with Mr Butler: we were eight couple of *as clever dancers* as ever eye beheld, though *I say it that should not.*

To-day we are to dine at the college with Mr Lloyd, a clergyman, a great friend of the Bishop's [Clayton], a worthy, agreeable, well-behaved young man; he has a living near Killala, and is to be with us there. (Remember his name and character, because I shall speak of him sometimes). We shall be very merry in a quiet free way to-day, and come home soberly at eleven: nobody is allow'd to stay in the college after that hour.   i pp345–46

Mary went to Killala with the Claytons and despite the remoteness was busy with country social life.

Killala, 4 July 1732

As I was yesterday sitting on a haycock, thinking intensely of her that gives the relish to all my pleasures, and as a reward for so faithfully performing my duty, my dearest sister's letter was brought to me. As for the riddle, I own my ignorance, I cannot find it out; pray always send me the explanations with your riddles, for I am dullness itself.

Just as I came was I dragged out, to go to the grotto: I resisted as much as I could, that I might bestow all the evening on you, but company being here, I was afraid they might be affronted if I shut myself up, and country ladies, you know, are *tetchy things*.

I have now snatched up my pen in great haste, much afraid I shall not have time to finish my letter before the postman sounds his horn.   i p364

Killala, 7 August 1732

It is comical that I, who am removed to one of the remotest parts of Hibernia, should be sending you news from your neighbourhood, but sometimes foreign papers inform one more exactly of our own affairs than domestic ones.   i pp367–68

Dublin, 4 January 1732/3

The last time I writ to you was from Plattin [her cousin Graham's house in Meath] on this day sen'night [week]. I told you we were to have a ball, and a ball we had; nine couple of as clever dancers (though I say it that should not) as ever tripped. The knight and I were partners, we began at seven: danced thirty-six dances with only resting once, supped at twelve, every one by their partner, at a long table which was handsomely filled with all manner of cold meat, sweetmeats, creams, and jellies. Two or three of the young ladies sung. I was asked for my song, and gave them "*Hopd she*" ["Hopped she"]; that occasioned some mirth. At two we went to dancing again; most of the ladies determined not to leave Plattin till day-break, they having three miles to go home, so we danced on till we were not able to dance any longer. Sir Thomas Pendergast is an excellent dancer – dances with great spirit, and in very good time. We did not go to bed till past eight, the company staid all that time, but part of the morning was spent in little plays.

Here Mary refers to the game of commerce in which barter or exchange was the chief feature.

Yesterday Mrs Clayton had an assembly; a great many ladies, few gentlemen. I had a commerce table of *absolute beauties*: I divided them, or rather tied them together, like a black ribbon in a garland of flowers, for I am in mourning for Lord Villiers. I am very glad to find you keep up to a good spirit at Gloucester; long may it last!

To-day I dine at Mr Stanley Monck's (*my lord* that *might* have been) [a cousin who had proposed to Mary and been refused]. In the evening we are to have a merry tribe at home to eat oysters – Miss Usher, her cousin Miss Ormsby, Miss Kelly, and Miss Bush [her friend Letty], whose sketch I sent you, but there's something about the mouth that does her great injustice, for she has graces and sweetness which does not appear in her shadow; but she did it for you, and I would send it: the nose and eyes resemble her.

Mrs Wesley and those sweet girls are in town; I have not yet seen them. Mr Wesley is at Dangan with his Xtmas companions; we shall go to him some time in February. We had a notable masquerade among the servants at Phellin [Plattin ?] that entertained us mightily. Lord George Sackville dressed himself up in women's clothes, and played his part very archly; he is a comical spark.   i pp390–94

Dublin, 24 January 1732/3

I gave you an account of the ball we are to have, of which there are three Kings and three Queens, viz; Lord Montjoy, Mr Thomson, Mr Usher, Miss Pennyfather, Miss Biddy Southwell, and Mrs Pendarves [herself]. Yesterday we spent at home, had a *petite* assembly, which we among ourselves call a "ridotto", because at ten o'clock we have a very pretty tray brought in, with chocolate, mulled wine, cakes, sweetmeats, and comfits; cold partridge, chicken, lamb, ham, tongue, all set out prettily and ready to pick at.   i p397

Dublin, 20 February 1732/3

The town of Dublin begins to look a little pert again, people have shook off their colds, and are now making parties for plays, assemblies. Tonight we are all to go to Mrs Southby's assembly, a *charity affair*, a poor woman under the same circumstances as Mrs Hine. To-morrow we shall spend at Mrs Hamilton's, Thursday at Dr Delany's, Friday we are to have a great many people with us by way of a private assembly, and Saturday we are to have the black-coated gentry [clergy], and on Monday we go to the play; time, you see, does not lie heavy on our hands. We shall go to Dangan about the middle of March, and stay there a fortnight. In my last letter I writ to you to get me a *good maid* if you can. Mr Usher is to call on us at one o' the clock to take the air; afterwards we are to go home and dine with him, the hour draws near and I am not yet dressed, so farewell.   i p401

Dangan, 5 April 1733

I hope your journey to the Bath will not be put off, or at least that you will take a jaunt with Mrs Foley [family friend of the Granvilles] to Herefordshire, which indeed, I

Mary's uncle,
George Granville,
Lord Lansdowne.

believe will be the pleasantest of the two; though why should I think you grown as dull as I am – you have many years to come before you arrive at my station. I own I have now lost so much the relish of a public life, that I prefer the conversation of an indifferent friend or acquaintance to the hurry that necessarily attends all crowded places; but I will give you to your five-and-thirtieth year before you may say that. I must finish, they say, so adieu. My humble duty to my mother, and kind service as due elsewhere.   i p407

THE DELANYS AND THEIR SOCIETY

Mary returned to Ireland after her marriage to Patrick Delany in 1743. He had become dean of Down through her efforts and family influence. They enjoyed a varied social life and were important enough to invite the viceroy to visit. The informal social life centring round her close friends and their busy occupations with Delville and the deanery gradually absorbed them.

Dublin, 12 July 1744

I am now in Dames Street waiting for the raree show of the city militia, who are all in their regimentals, and, they say, make a most gallant show; but I am willing to secure a real pleasure to myself, therefore take this interval to write to my dear sister in the midst of so great a noise and hurry of people and coaches that I hardly know what I write. Before I left Delville this morning I wrote to my mother, and have directed it to Gloucester, supposing her by this time settled there, and I hope you are on the wing to Welsbourne. Last Sunday I made my first appearance at St Warbor's [Werburg's] church.

I have been three times called from my letter to look at the militia, and really they are a noble sight, very well-looking men in regimentals; three regiments well mounted and three of foot. It is a satisfaction to see so many brave men well prepared to defend us in case we stand in need of their assistance; but if the news is true of Prince Charles of Lorraine's victory over the French and Hessians they may sheath their swords in peace. My head turns round with the tumult, and I am obliged to defer my description of the gardens till I have a better opportunity.   ii pp307–308

Although from a family who were prominent in politics, the Lansdownes and the Carterets, Mary did not take a detailed interest in politics, although she mentions some of the great commotions of the time, like the '45 rebellion when she wanted to reassure her sister that Ireland was quiet. She was however absorbed in the more informal politics of society and patronage.

Delville, 3 October 1745

That you might know we are very quiet, and I hope likely to continue so, if the good news that came express yesterday to our Lord Lieutenant be true, of the rebels' defeat in Scotland. Ireland has been formerly a place of great disturbance and confusion on these occasions, but not for many years; people are in general very well affected towards the present government, and even the papists who are not in number what they were, seem to know their happiness in a quiet possession of what they have, so that had England been so unhappy as to have struggled under a civil war, we should have been the quietest part of his Majesty's dominions. At present the storm seems to be abated, and I hope in God, the next news we have from England will be of its being entirely quelled.

When I consider how great calamity a civil war is, we cannot be too thankful that a timely stop is put to it.   ii p391

Delville, 15 October 1745

We are very impatient to know what is doing in the north. I thank God we are very quiet, and hope the packets when they come, will bring us the comfortable news of the rebels being dispersed. I dread our being further engaged in a civil war, and think our last accounts were no way satisfactory. Various are the reports: the last was that Edinburgh was burnt to ashes!

Last Friday was the King's coronation. I went to the Castle morning and night. There was a ball, but *no good dancing*; and I hope *for our credit* Mrs Fortescue [formerly Miss Wesley] will come and grace the balls. Mrs Chenevix, the Bishop of Killaloe's wife, and I have agreed to go to the birthday in Irish stuffs. Lady Grandison [a cousin] and Lady Betty Mason [her eldest daughter who inherited the Grandison title] are come to Dublin, which I am very glad of; it is a great pleasure to meet with an old acquaintance. Lady Grandison is an agreeable woman and was always very obliging to me. Next Friday I go to court with [the] Miss McDermots [the dean's converts, their story is recounted later]; Lord and Lady Chesterfield [lord lieutenant and his lady] have heard their story, and are prepared to receive them with distinction, which indeed they very well deserve.   ii pp393–94

Delville, 22 October 1745

Yesterday we were honoured with a visit from our Viceroy and Queen [the Chesterfields]; they sent over early in the morning to know if we were disengaged, as they would breakfast. To work went all my maids, stripping covers off the chairs, sweeping, dusting, and by eleven my house was as spruce as a cabinet of curiosities, and well bestowed on their Excellencies, who commended and admired, and were as polite as possible. They came soon after eleven in their travelling coach, with only two footmen; Mr Bristol (Dash's uncle) and Mrs Chenevix in the coach with them. They were first carried into the drawing-room, examined every room in my apartments above, delighted with the situation, liked the furniture, but were impatient to see my own works; upon which the Dean conducted them into the Minerva, where I had two tables covered with all sorts of breakfast. When breakfast was over they made me play on the harpsichord, which I did with a very ill grace. When that was done we went into the garden and walked over every inch of it; they seemed much surprised with the variety they found there, and could not have said more civil things had it been my Lord Cobham's Stowe! They staid till near two, and my Lord Lieut and the Dean had a great deal of conversation, which I believe was mutually agreeable; we are going this morning to court to return thanks for the honour they did us, and the hour calls upon me to dress.   ii pp395–96

Delville, 30 November 1745

We were invited to dine at the Castle yesterday, and were received with great politeness and good humour: nobody there, but ourselves: as they said they "wished to have us alone, that they might enjoy our company without interruption." My Lord Chesterfield was in high spirits after dinner, which was small and very good; coffee was then set on the table, and the Dean and my Lord Lieutenant fell into a very entertaining and agreeable conversation, chiefly of poets and poetry. There is no entertainment equal to that of hearing two very ingenious men talk on agreeable subjects. We stayed till near seven, and came home well pleased with the entertainment of the day, and not at all mortified with the good fortune of others.

The Dean has always one happy and never failing satisfaction in his own way of thinking – which is a firm conviction that all things are ordered by a wise disposer, who knows best what is good for us.   ii pp402–403

Delville, 21 December 1745

I don't find that the troubles of the times [the '45 rebellion] have given any check to gay doings in this part of the world. The castle is crowded twice a week; plays, assembly, and drums, are as much frequented as ever. I must own this may be a right policy to keep up the hopes of people, but I am surprised that their spirits should hold out; and I cannot but think, under the terrible apprehensions of losing our liberty and our property, it would be more becoming to *abate* our diversions, especially as we have reason to think that the great irreligion and luxury of the times have brought our present calamities on us.   ii p406

Although she began to prefer home to gaieties abroad especially in the winter months, she puts a good case for society here.

Delville, 1 February 1745/6

Three days together spent abroad is being a downright rake, but the sobriety of my own dwelling is much pleasanter to me than all the flirtations of the world; though the society I will always keep up to the *best of my power*, as it is a duty incumbent on us to live sociably, and it is necessary to keep up good humour and benevolence in ourselves, or the qualities of the heart contract and grow useless, as our limbs would do without any proper exercise. On Thursday we kept home and fast; the Dean, his niece, and the servants went to church.   ii p418

Delville was about a mile from the centre of Dublin, near enough to visit, and far enough to be away from the hurly burly. Lord Chesterfield left Dublin at the end of April 1746, having maintained a lavish viceregal court. It was the custom to take leave of the departing lord lieutenant but Lord Chesterfield evidently wished to make a personal farewell to his friends at Delville.

Delville, 11 April 1746

Now everybody is going out of town, the sun shines, and they come in swarms to take leave and *bask in our sunshine*, which the smoke of Dublin will not allow of. I was last night the greatest of rakes; went to take my leave at the Castle, was crowded to pieces; did not come home till twelve o'clock, fatigued to death; slept well and refreshed myself with walking half an hour after breakfast;   ii pp434–35

Delville, 26 April 1746

I told you a long story about an invitation, but it was all a mistake and misunderstand-ing, which has occasioned me no small hurry, for on Monday morning Mrs Chenevix (whom I went to see) told me that the Lord Lieutenant designed dining with us on Wednesday, and held himself engaged. We were to dine at the Bishop of Clogher's [the Claytons], and just as we sat down to dine the Bishop of Waterford came, and told us that his Excellency would dine with us the next day. I immediately dispatched a messenger to Delville, with a note to my housekeeper, to tell her she must prepare the dinner for next day of seven and nine, and a dessert, and I was obliged, as soon as I had dined, to go to the Castle, and ask Lady Chesterfield, but she had refused the Primate and therefore could not come to me, which she seemed sincerely to regret. The Dean went that evening to my Ld L. to know at what hour he would dine, and to desire him to bring whom he pleased. Lord Lieut. said he feared he had made some mistake about the day; but he was glad to seize the first day for the fear the wind would change. Home we went at eight, and it cost me about an hour or two thinking; but my dinner turned out very well, the particulars of which, if you think it worth your while, you shall have when we meet. He came at three, said he had reserved us for the bon bouche, was extremely civil, agreeable, and cheerful, and staid till nearly eight. ii pp435–36

Delville, 20 June 1747

Last Sunday I spent at home, as I generally do. In the afternoon came some ladies of the neighbourhood, and Dowager Lady Kildare; on Monday Bushe and I made visits in Dublin, furiously drest out in all our airs! I caught a little cold, and kept at home quietly all Tuesday; four gentlemen of the college came and dined here, and not one day have I yet sat down to dinner with a less addition. On Wednesday two friends of Bushe's, and old acquaintances of mine dined here – Mrs Preston and Mrs Dillon, two sisters, and two young she Dillons. Mrs Dillon went by the name of "Beauty divine" when I came first to Ireland; fifteen years have faded her bloom, but not ruffled the sweetness of her countenance, which is still pretty. Mrs Preston is plain in her person, but a sensible, friendly, good woman; I have promised to make her a visit of a few days this summer [at Swainstown in Meath] when D.D. returns, it lies in his road from the north, and I shall meet him there.   ii p467

Lord Chesterfield was succeeded by his half-brother, William Stanhope, earl of Harrington.

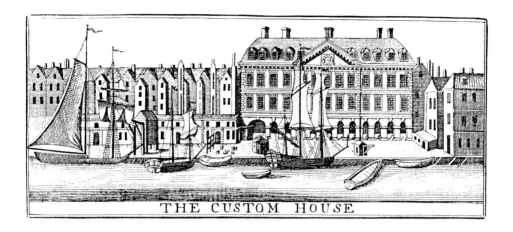

THE CUSTOM HOUSE

THE THOLSEL

Dublin buildings, 1766.

Delville, 28 October 1747

I had breakfast prepared in the drawing-room; the L.L. came with Sir John Cope and the Captain of the Guard in waiting, at half an hour after eleven; the Dean met him at the street-door and I at the bottom of the stairs; when he came in the drawing-room and saw Miss Bushe, he asked me if he had ever seen that lady? I told him her name, and that her ill health would not allow her to pay her respects to him at the Castle, upon which he very politely saluted her; he seemed much pleased with the place.

The Dean was in good spirits, and exerted himself to entertain him, so that it made the time pass easy and agreeably. He walked into all my rooms on that floor, commended everything, and said he must see the garden. About one we walked into the garden but Sir J. Cope whispered me and begged I would *not let him walk much*, for he had not ventured to walk at all since his coming to Ireland; he walked as far as to see the compass of the garden, and then we insisted upon his returning, which he did; when he came back we conducted him to the Minerva [a room off the library], and he seemed very glad of a seat. He was much amused with the medley of gimcracks that it contains, and at half an hour after two left us.

This evening I go to town to make my compliments to my Lord Lieutenant for the honour he did us. There hath not been a drawing-room since he was here, for last Friday (the usual Castle-day), was a festival that nothing could put by, and that always occasions a prodigious rout and confusion at the Castle – the anniversary of

Fireworks at St Stephen's Green, 1748.

the Irish rebellion. There is open house kept that day, and a vast dessert, and after the dinner is over the common people are let in to carry off all that remains both of dinner and dessert; you may imagine what a notable scramblement it occasions. ii pp480–81

Scandalous news was often exchanged between the sisters.

Delville, 22 December 1747

In return for your account of Mr Creswell I can send you two stories that will match it pretty well. One is of a young lady, youngest daughter to a Captain Johnston here, a very pretty girl just sixteen, who ran away on Friday night with Sir Robert King, a vile young rake of a considerable fortune in this country. They went off on Friday night: the father pursued and overtook them on Saturday morning, held a pistol at the knight's head, swore he would shoot him through the head if he did not instantly marry his daughter, which rather than die he consented to do. A parson was ready and called in, but Sir R. K's servants rushed in at the same time, gave him a pistol, and an opportunity of escaping, which he did, and left the forlorn damsel to return with her father. They all appeared at church in Dublin on Sunday morning, and the girl appears at all public places as unconcerned and brazen as if she had acted the most prudent part in the world.

The other story is indeed much more notorious and shocking. You don't know any of the people, so I shall not name names, but a gentleman's daughter who has for several years borne an extremely good character, about twenty-six years of age, has managed her father's house with great prudence, and always shewn a great tenderness for him on all occasions, has gone off with the schoolmaster of the parish, a clergyman who has been married several years, and his wife a very good kind of woman! He *now says* he never was married to her, and accuses her with carrying on an intrigue with the lady's father and brother that has run away with him! These are sad strokes in a family! how much less *is the death* of a dear friend to be lamented than such wicked conduct!   ii pp482–83

Here Mrs Delany gives her sister a pithy judgement on the Miss Gunnings. They were a famous pair of beauties, daughters of an impoverished gentleman from Roscommon, and were notoriously silly. They are said to have borrowed their presentation dresses from the actress Peg Woffington, but they managed to make a good impression on the viceroy Lord Harrington who was one of their first patrons. Maria married the earl of Coventry, her sister Elizabeth married firstly the duke of Hamilton, and secondly the duke of Argyll.

Delville, 8 June 1750

All you have heard of the Miss Gunnings *is true*, except their having a fortune, but I am afraid they have a *greater* want than that, which is *discretion*!   ii p553

Mrs Delany was always trying to promote her friends' interests and had found a tutor for a spoiled heir apparent.

Delville, 16 June 1750

Thursday we dined at Pickerstown, about four miles off, Mr Cavendish's and Lady Meade; it is with them Mr M. is fixed to take care of Sir John Meade, a fine spoiled boy of six years old; Mr M. looks wretchedly, and is fallen away to a shadow; I fear he will never recover his constitution. He is now in a very easy situation, and much esteemed. He says though Sir J. Meade has been extremely indulged and little contradicted, that he is naturally good-natured and tractable; and Lady Meade is so wise as to give him full authority over the child: we were 17 or 18 in company, and had a *vast dinner*, and *such* a *vast turbot* as I never saw for size.

The Delanys mixed with those in high legal office like Henry Singleton, lord chief justice of the Common Pleas in Ireland, 1740 to 1753, and later master of the rolls. Here she takes charge of decorating a cold bath house.

Yesterday we dined at Lord Chief Justice Singleton's at Drumcondra, a mile off. Our company were his brother and sister Fowkes (who keeps his house, for he is a bachelor) and their son and daughter. Mr and Mrs Foster, and the *grand connoisseur*, Mr Bristowe. After tea and coffee I walked out with the gentlemen; the ladies not able to be of our party. Lord Chief Justice is very busy adding to his house and altering his gardens; Mr Bristowe has the entire direction of all, but I cannot say he has shown so much real judgment as *conceit* in what he has done. In one part of the garden there is a cold bath that opens with an arch like a cave, this is put under my care to adorn and make something of, and I have presumed to undertake it. When finished I'll send you a little sketch of it.   ii pp554–55

Delville, 17 June 1750

To-day we dine at Lord Chief Justice Singleton's at Drumcondra. He has given Mr Bristowe *full dominion* over house and gardens, and like a conceited connoisseur he is doing *strange things*, building an absurd room, turning fine wild evergreens *out of the garden, cutting down* full grown elms and *planting twigs*! D.D. has no patience with him, and I shall be under some difficulty to-day to know *how* to commend any-thing, which is what I wish to do. I am called upon to dress. I have the pleasure of Miss Bushe's company with me at present; but we part when I go to the north. ii p557

When she was not in the deanery of Down for the summer, she often organised excursions and parties which included prominent ecclesiastics such as Pri-mate George Stone, and, occasionally, 'most unreasonably indulged children'

Delville, 7 July 1750

Thursday, had made a party to breakfast again at Lucan, ditto, party to dine at Castletown, Mrs Conolly's which we did; and there also dined the Primate, the Archibishop of Cashell, Lord George Sackville, Mrs Marley, and as many as made up our dinner company nineteen.   ii p567

Delville, 28 September 1750

Saturday morning. My company came – not all that I expected; and when they were gone D.D. and I enjoyed a *tête-à-tête* evening. Sir J. Meade is heir to a great estate, a child of six years old, *most unreasonably indulged* – a fine sensible boy, but under no sort of command. I had 20 frights for my china, shells and books: his little fingers seized everything with such impetuosity that I was ready to box him; had I been his mama I should have been *most heartily ashamed of him*. With pleasure I recollected that my little nephews would have been much scandalised at his behaviour, and wished them here to set him a good example. His sister, a girl about ten, is already a fine affected lady, knows everything, and pretends to ridicule, such airs! Well, thought I, my Pauline [Mary Dewes, her sister's child] will not be such a forward, pert thing! that's my comfort!

Lady Meade is a well-behaved, handsome woman, *not* bred up with *elegant politeness*, but *civil*, and does not want for understanding: so is it not amazing she cannot see the wrong behaviour of her children, and how insupportably troublesome they are? Mr Mount is better, and extremely well treated by Mr Cavendish and Lady Meade, but his task with the young gentleman is a difficult one, though he seems to understand the sort of charge he has undertaken very well.   ii p597

View of riverside at Lucan, by Mary Delany, 4 September 1752.

Delville, 20 October 1750

Last Monday we dined by invitation at Lord Grandison's; they are in high joy and spirits. The little Mason is a fine thriving child, and I hope will live. Bushe met me there, and there was a Mrs Wogan, sister to Lord Kilmare [Kenmare], I believe bred abroad, a Roman Catholic; she is one of the largest women of her age that I ever saw; she looks about 30, but has a charming sweet face. She gave me an account of part of her brother's estate in the province of Munster, the islands of Killarney, which are covered with bays, myrtles and arbutus trees; the echoes are so remarkable among the rocks in that river, that people every year go there to try them, and if you fire a gun, the echoes return the sound one after another like the going off of loud thunder; they say one can have no notion of the effect of music there, such as trumpets, French horns and hautboys. I am very desirous of seeing this *enchanted place*, but it lies entirely out of my way.

In her eagerness to finish her shellwork, she delayed her duties as hostess.

Tuesday I staid at home, worked hard in the morning, and had no interruptions – that was comfortable. Thursday the Bishop of Kildare (Fletcher by name), his sister, Dr Ledwytche and his lady, and Mr Greene dined here. I was in the morning so eager at my work that half my company came before I had begun to dress, but it was to put on the finishing shell that made me so earnest, and I shewed them my work as my excuse.   ii pp605–606

Delville, 10 December 1750

Last Monday we dined at the Bishop of Derry's (Bernard), Mrs Stone and Mrs McAulay of the party. I was very well entertained with looking over the Bishop's pictures: he has a very good collection, by above 200 different masters' hands, original pictures, well preserved and in good order; not many Italian, but the greatest variety of Dutch and Flemish I ever saw in one collection. It is an agreeable house to go to, the Bishop hearty and good-natured, Mrs Bernard sensible and clever, and very easy, and besides, a library well furnished with portfolios of fine drawings and prints, with which they seem pleased to entertain their friends.   ii p625

The Delanys were staunch members of the established church of Ireland and were naturally delighted when a conversion occurred.

Delville, 20 May 1745

I told you in one of my letters that Miss McDermots *had sent* to speak privately to D.D., and that I was in hopes it was on a religious account; thank God! so it has proved, and last Sunday they made their recantation in our church. They had not been at mass these twelve months and their brother died a Protestant. They had several conferences with the Dean, and he collected texts of Scripture for them.

What they most stuck at was transubstantiation, but I believe they have been thoroughly convinced of their error in that point. Miss McDermot said "though she had been so barbarously treated among the papists she should *not* leave them were not her reason thoroughly convinced of their errors." They dined with us on Sunday; the ceremony of their making their recantation is their reading a paper signed by them; the minister lays his hand on their head and receives them into the church as converts, and then prays for them, There is something very awful in it, and the poor ladies were under great confusion but behaved themselves very well, and seemed extremely glad when it was over. I thought they would have been here very private and quiet, but eight persons that I did *not expect* came to dinner beside themselves, still there could not be too many witnesses of so good an action. All the company came to church as well as to dinner, and we all went again in the afternoon; you can't think what a gay appearance we made as we walked through the garden to church attended by all the servants, who were pretty numerous.   ii pp346–47

Despite the penal laws which restricted Roman Catholics' rights, including rights over property and exercise of their faith, there were a number of Roman Catholics who were accepted in high society, like Mrs Wogan, and Miss Crilly, who was a member of a community of nuns.

Delville, 19 January 1750/51

On Thursday, Bushe went to see Lady Austin and Mrs Dillon and brought home, by appointment, Miss Crilly to dinner. And who is Miss Crilly? *say you.* Why, she is a *nun professed*, and lives at the Nunnery in King Street, Dublin; but nuns in this country have the liberty of going to see relatives and particular friends: this young woman is a relation of Mrs Forde's, and is just returned from France, where she has been ten years for the recovery of her health. She is an old acquaintance of D.D.'s, is extremely sprightly, civil, and entertaining, was in raptures with everything at Delville, and so *acknowledging* that I should desire her acquaintance, that she overwhelmed me with her civilities. After dinner we carried her home, and she entreated me to go in, that some of her sisterhood might gratify their curiosity by seeing me; we drank tea with them, saw their chapel, and I played on the organ: they wear no particular habit, only a black stuff nightgown and plain linen. I should like them *much better in their habit*; Bushe was very droll amongst them all, and said a thousand comical things, which they seemed not at all offended at. They have a handsome parlour to receive their company in, and no grates belonging to them [very often nuns could only be viewed from behind grilles or bars]: the chapel is pretty, the altar mightily decorated with candlesticks, gilding, little statues, but terribly bad pictures; a crucifix about a foot and a half high stands on the table, which is well done, and was taken at Vigo; on one side of the chapel is a small one with an altar dedicated to St Antony.   iii p9

Delville, 13 April 1751

To-morrow – here flew in *my nun* Miss Crilly: sprightly and agreeable as she is, I wish she had staid away an hour longer – she has overwhelmed me with praise and compliments. I must *break her* of that abundance of French civility, it *quite confounds me*, set that aside, and she is an agreeable entertaining creature, and seems to have good principles and pretty sentiments. She has been confined with sickness and devotion, and I don't call upon her so often as I should like to do, as people are so offended here if *these nuns* are much taken notice of, that I should be thought *disaffected.*   iii p38

Sometimes Mary did not restrain her impatience, even with company present.

Delville, 9 February 1750/51

Your letter of the 25 January I received last Sunday evening; I had company with me – some ladies of our town of Glasnevin – and when it was brought in, and one from my brother, I laid them on the table before me, expressing joy at the receipt of them, and the stupid Goths never said, "Pray open your letters", or anything civil about them. I staid a full minute for that compliment, and my patience would hold out no longer; so I said, "Pray excuse me, I must read my letters, as I expect some news of consequence." So, opened and read them from end to end. Bushe was so good as to entertain them but I huffed her after they were gone, for not encouraging me to open the letters sooner.   iii p13

Delville, 23 March 1750/51

In the evening came Lady Blaney and her two daughters, the Miss Murrays; *she* is very agreeable, not quite unaffected, but sensible, and has seen a good deal of the world.

Wednesday we dined at Mount Eccles with Lady Austin and Mrs Dillon, and found a happy man there; young Mr Preston, who has obtained consent from all sides to marry his pretty cousin [Ally Dillon]. Love has improved his appearance, and those who know him well say he is a very worthy man: his father settles in present £400 a year, and more after his death, and they are to live part of the year with him and part with Mrs Dillon, who has taken a very pretty house in Dublin. The pleasure of the day was damped to me by parting with Bushe, who has business to settle in Dublin, and goes to Mrs Bushe for the summer on Easter Monday.   iii pp28–29

Her companion on this occasion was Mrs Clayton, married to Robert, who had just become bishop of Clogher. In 1751 he published an essay attacking the doctrine of the Trinity thus causing controversy by his unitarian views. Mary was always irritated by Katherine Clayton's airs and graces.

Delville, 2 November 1751

I suppose you expect some account of the birthday: I went to *Madam* [Clayton] in my coach at one o'clock; she was in her sedan, with her three footmen in Saxon green, with orange-coloured cockades, marched in state, I humbly followed. A stop kept me about half an hour on the way; she got to the Castle without interruptions, and went on into the drawing-room directly. Can you tell *why* she desired me to go with her? I can. She was superb in brown and gold, and diamonds; I was clad in the purple and white silk I bought when last year in England; and my littleness set off her greatness! These *odd fancies* made me laugh, and not a bit angry: only rather self-satisfied, that I feel myself above doing the things which make the actor so despicable. The Duke and Duchess of Dorset came into the drawing-room at half an hour after one, very

Bishop Robert Clayton and his wife Katherine by James Latham (1696-1747).

graceful and princely. The Duchess had a blue paduasoy [Italian silk], embroidered very richly with gold, and done here; there was a great deal of handsome finery. The two best-dressed women there were Mrs Pomeroy and Miss Colley her sister, (who is come to spend the winter in Dublin) though not fine; and they had no *frippery whims in their heads*, which now prevail so much that *everybody looks mad*! At two all the company went and took their places in the ball-room, which is very fine, much better than that at St James's, and Dubourg [violinist head of the viceroy's musicians], who is master of the band of music, gave us the birthday song. I can't say much in commendation of it, as it was not great enough for a crowd, pretty pastoral music, which has no effect in so large an assemnly. I did not get to my Lord Grandison's dinner till half an hour after four; the ball I would have nothing to do with, and am glad I was so prudent, as they say it was insufferably crowded.

Monday, we dined at Portico. Tuesday, Pomeroy and Colley dine here: and this day se'night [week] we are to spend at the Bishop of Derry's, a day of *virtu* – in the morning prints, drawings, pictures; in the evening music.   iii pp51–52

In 1750 Lionel Sackville, duke of Dorset, returned again as lord lieutenant.

Delville, 7 November 1751

I have had a slight cold, but am quite well again: I got it last Monday in a cold shop staring at my Lord Lieutenant's parading – a custom always observed the 4th of November, King William's birthday, whose memory is *idolized* here almost to superstition. The Duke's equipage; and the nobility that attended him, were very fine, and all the horses decked out with orange-coloured ribbons: there is a statue of King William erected in a large space before the Parliament-House, and they tour round that statue and round Stephen's Green.   iii p54

Delville, 28 December 1751

Monday we dined at *Porticorareo*; met by the Bishop of Derry, and his agreeable wife Mrs Bernard; Dubourg there, two other violins, and Mr Smith for the harpsichord, all in good humour; Miss Bushe was of our party, and I brought her away with me, and she spends her Xtmas here, which I will prolong as much as I can. We have staid at home ever since, as my company like staying at home better than going abroad, and that suits my inclination extremely, for with such agreeable guests as I have, I never wish for any engagements abroad.   iii p68

George Stone, the archbishop of Armagh, lived at Leixlip Castle from 1752 and entertained in a princely fashion.

Delville, 26 January 1752

Last Saturday we were invited to the Primate's to hear music. D.D., Donnellan, and I went a little before 7; it was the Duke of Dorset's birthday, and the entertainment given in honour of it. A fine dinner was given to a number of the principal men. A Perigord pie had been sent for on the occasion, to be directed to a merchant in Dublin; the pie came when the merchant was in the country, and his wife, supposing it a present from one of her husband's correspondents abroad, invited several of her particular friends to eat up this rare pie the very day the Primate gave his entertainment. That morning, after all the company was engaged, the Primate's *maitre d'hotel*, who had enquired often after it in vain, once more called and *got the pie*, and the poor merchant's wife looked very silly when her company came who were forced to sit down to a homespun dinner, and give up their foreign rarity. I own *I am sorry* they *did not eat it!* such expensive rarities *do not become the table of a prelate*, who ought rather to be given to hospitality than to ape the fantastical luxuriances of fashionable tables. iii pp80–81

Delville, 7 February 1752

The grand ball was given last Wednesday, to the great contentment of the best company of both sexes. The men were gallant, the ladies were courteous! I enclose you Mr Falkner's account of it, but must add that the musicians and singers were dressed like Arcadian shepherds and shepherdesses, and placed among the rocks. If tea, coffee, or chocolate were wanting, you held your cup to a leaf of a tree, and it was filled; and whatever you wanted to eat or drink, was immediately found on a rock, or on a branch, or in the hollow of a tree. The waiters were all in whimsical dress, and every lady as she entered the room had a fine bouquet presented to her. The whole was extremely well conducted; no confusion; and the ladies say, never was there seen so enchanting a place; but a few dissenters have the assurance to say, it was no better than a puppet-show.

I am now in a run of visiting. I have lain by all winter, and now weddings and deaths call on me for ceremonials. Don [Phil] and I made fourteen visits last Thursday in the afternoon, and propose doing near as much this day.   iii pp85–86

As she grew older, Mary created her own agreeable social circle and preferred that company to grander society.

Delville, 22 February 1752

Wednesday, Lord Mornington and his family dined here, much enquiry after you. Thursday we spent a very agreeable day at the Bishop of Derry's, I like Mrs Bernard extremely, and her sister Mrs Stone, though a plain gruff sort of a woman, [both sisters of the Primate, George Stone] but they have both very good understandings and not the least elated with their extraordinary good fortune. Yesterday we spent at the Grandisons – too much form and company to be agreeable; Lord and Lady Fitzwilliam, Lady Bell and Mr Monck, were there, though the entertainment was chiefly for *their tenant* Mrs Donnellan. It ended with a drum [a fashionable assembly of company in the evening], and as soon as the card-tables were settled we withdrew; to-day we regale ourselves with a quiet day at home, in which all are perfectly agreed. iii p94

Delville, 11 April 1752

Some day next week, if the weather is good, we have thought of asking the Duke and Duchess of Dorset to breakfast. Dinners are grown such luxurious feasts in this country that we do not pretend to show away with such magnificence, and our viceroy loves magnificence *too well* to be pleased with our way of entertaining company. I own I think there is a time of life as well as a station when *very gaudy* entertainments are as unbecoming, as pink colour and pompadours! Apropos [a] *drum ecclesiastic* in Stephen's Green beats for company next Monday; Miss Brown [Mrs Clayton's niece] told me she had sent out three packs of cards with invitations from her aunt, but we can't with prudence go after having kept house above a week, though we are in the list.   iii pp110–11

Delville, 12 May 1752

I am glad my brother [Bernard Granville] looks so well, and hope his looks are as honest as his heart; if he is still with you my kindest love to him. And now for my journal. On Thursday last, Lady Lambard (as I told you before, I believe) and Lady Drogheda came, and puffed me up with their praises of everything within and without doors; whilst we were in the garden a violent storm of thunder, lightning, and hail drove us into the Beggar's Hut [a garden feature] for shelter. In the afternoon we went to Finglass, and drank coffee with the agreeable sisters [Forth and Hamilton]. Friday dined at Mr Pomeroy's, – first made visits. Were met there by the Bishop of Elphin and his family, and Miss Colley, who is grown a shrivelled crab! Her sister Pomeroy is *as sweet* as she is *sour*, and has a very good-humoured well-behaved husband; they have a pretty little boy, whom they doat on. She lost a fine girl last year.

On Saturday the Lord Lieut and Lady Lieut [duke and duchess of Dorset], and Lord George Sackville, and the Primate breakfast here; and on the Tuesday following we set out for the county of Wicklow, and propose returning on Saturday. As to my hurries they are just beginning, and *alas!* for *want* of *the prize* the end which this year *was* to have bestowed on me, packing and travelling seem formidable undertakings. All things remain as I have already told you, only I have the additional hurry of going to the drawing-room morning and evening to-morrow, D.D. has asked a dozen people here to dinner to-day, which honour I could have spared, as I want to keep my house for Saturday, though I have too much regard for *les petits soins* of those I love not to value every mark of affection; but if people only keep upon the *great road of loving*, and neglect the little paths of friendship, many delicate pleasures are lost. iii pp119–120

Richard Pococke (1704–65), came to Ireland as chaplain to Lord Chesterfield, and then acquired high office in the Church of Ireland, eventually becoming bishop of Ossory, then bishop of Meath. He travelled widely in the near east between 1737 and 1742. Mary had already met this scholarly clergyman when he was archdeacon at St Patrick's cathedral.

Delville, 22 April 1752

Next Tuesday we are to dine at the Bishop of Clogher's [the Claytons] and go in the afternoon to an Egyptian drum (I suppose) at Dr Pocock's. Instead of spreading his table with cards, I hope he designs to cover them with drawers of curiosities, and instead of the tittle-tattle of the town to give us some philosophical lectures! It would be pleasant enough to see the surprise of the smart beaux and belles when they observe such an entertainment prepared for them; and instead of the rooms being decorated with china, japan, indian paper, and looking-glasses, to observe nothing but Egyptian deities on pedestals, tables covered with precious fragments such as toes and fingers, lumps of stone that have neither shape nor beauty of colour. Turkish robes hanging on pegs, travelling kitchen utensils, and a medley that would make much too large a catalogue for my paper to contain.   iii p112

Delville, 30 April 1752

I am, I thank God! very well, and as a proof was yesterday at Dr Pocock's drum. The Dean and I dined at the Bishop of Clogher's, and went from thence, it being in the neighbourhood. His house (meaning the Mufti's) is very pleasant; he has a large room on the ground-floor of thirty-one feet long, filled with his curiosities. It opens into a very pretty garden, gaily filled with flowers. Our company was Lord and Lady Grandison, Lord and Lady Fitzwilliam, and Lord and Lady Cavan, Lord and Lady Strangford, Countess of Drogheda, Bishop of Clogher, [and his wife] Mrs Clayton, and self; more company was expected, but as it was my second day of being abroad I would not stay late. Poor Donnellan could not be of the party; she has been tortured with the tooth-ache, and yesterday had the tooth drawn. She is still uneasy, and her cheek much swelled, but I believe it is only the effect of the terrible wrench. iii pp113–14

Delville, 19 June 1752

Yesterday Mrs A. Don [Phil whose name was Anne] and Gran [Anne's maid] were engaged to spend the day at Selbridge [Celbridge], Mr Marlay's [bishop of Dromore], three miles beyond Mr Vesey's of Lucan. I made them set me down there, and found them in the midst of their haymakers. Lord and Lady Kildare, Miss Macartney, Mrs Lushington, Mr Ponsonby, and Mr Centleger [St Leger] dined there. As I know them all they did not frighten me, though I should have been better pleased to have had Mrs Vesey to myself, but the day passed pleasantly enough. D.D. was so busy at home with his books and haymakers he could not go; no news of our law yet, though we expected it to come this week. I must finish to-morrow.

I am pleased with Lady Georgiana Cowper for remembering her god-daughter [Mary Dewes], and thank you for all your Bath news.

The Mr Usher we went to see is a Mr Christopher Usher, cousin to my old aquaintance [and dancing partner] Will who has been dead these six years [the Ushers were cousins of the Donnellans].   iii p133

Lotteries, then as now in Ireland, were a great way of raising money for specific objects and ladies of Mary's standing were instrumental in getting them under way. It was a favourite way of exercising charity.

Delville, 2 September 1752

We are going to have a lottery here for the settling the poor French Protestants amongst us; it will be a very charitable good work and an advantageous lottery to those who will put in; recommend it, as it may be of use.   iii p156

Mrs Conolly, described here, was originally a Miss Conyngham, and wife of William Conolly, speaker of the Irish houses of commons, property magnate, who built the superb Italianate house Castletown (Conolly) near Celbridge.

Delville, 26 September 1752

We have lost *our great* Mrs Conolly. She died last Friday and is a general loss; her table was open to all her friends of all ranks, and her purse to the poor. She was I think in her ninetieth year. She has been drooping for some years, but never so ill as to shut out company; she rose constantly at eight, and by eleven was seated in her drawing room, and received visits till 3 o'clock, at which hour she punctually dined, and generally had *two tables* of eight or ten people each: her own table served with *seven* and *seven* and *a dessert*, and two substantial dishes on the side-table; and if the greatest person in the kingdom dined with her she never altered her bill of fare. As soon as dinner was over, she took the ladies to the drawing room and left the gentlemen to finish as they pleased. She sat down in her grey cloth great chair and took a nap, whilst the company chatted to one another, which lulled her to sleep. Tea and coffee came exactly at half an hour after five, she then waked, and as soon as tea was over, a party of whist was made for her till ten, then everybody retired. She had prayers every day at twelve, and when the weather was good took the air, but has never made a visit since Mr Conolly died. She was clever at business, wrote all her own letters, and could read a newspaper by candlelight without spectacles. She was a plain and vulgar woman in her manner, but she had *very valuable* qualities. For about a month past she has had frequent fainting fits, that alarmed those about her. On Friday morning her nephew Mr Conolly and heir to her great fortune breakfasted with her, and she as well or better than she had been for some time. After breakfast she said she "wished to lie down" which she did; in half an hour she desired they would turn her, without making any complaint, and in turning her from one side to the other she died as quietly as if she had only fallen asleep! What a blessed ending to a well-spent life! Nothing else is talked of now with us.   iii pp158–59

Mount Panther, 20 October 1752

I am afraid Mrs Conolly has not shewn such justice and judgment in the disposition of her fortune as could be wished. She has left Mr Connolly (her husband's nephew and heir to a vast fortune) £10,000, to Colt Cunningham a small estate of hers in Wales, but to her sister, servant and poor, very inconsiderable legacies, but Mr Connolly, who is a very generous good man, will, they say, make up her deficiencies. iii pp166–67

Here she describes her neighbours in County Down who lived in Castlewellan. Lady Anne was a daughter to Marcus Beresford, earl of Tyrone, and was married to William Annesley. He was related to the 6th earl of Anglesey who was reputed to have committed bigamy when he married Juliana Donovan in 1741.

Delville, 4 November 1752

Lady Anne Annesley is daughter to Lord Tyrone of this kingdom, married to a near relative of Lord Anglesey's. They are very rich and know it, and spend their lives *in increasing not enjoying* their good fortune; but he is a very honest man in all his dealings, still would be more agreeable as well as more useful if he thought *less* of his possessions. His lady suits him exactly; she does not want sense, and is comical enough in a *satirical* way (which I don't love), but they are very civil neighbours to us in the country [County Down].   iii p170

Lady Rawdon, whom Mary mentions here, was born into the intellectual Hastings family, who were significant in the development of early Methodism.

Delville, 26 January 1753

This I began yesterday. This morning have been in Dublin; sat an hour or more with Mrs Hamilton, went afterwards to visit Lady Rawdon, Lady Betty Hastings that was; she was so desirous of my acquaintance (I don't know why) as to make me the first visit; she is modest and civil in her manner, neither handsome nor genteel.   iii p199

Although there is no suggestion that Mary was a close friend of the idealist philosopher George Berkeley, she had come in contact with his family.

Viscountess Catherine Sudley, daughter of William Annesley, and Lady Anne Beresford, m. 1760 (see page 231), by William Watson (d. 1765).

Delville, 23 January 1753

The newspapers say the Bishop of Cloyne [George Berkeley] is dead; there is (if so) *a great man* gone. His country people are much disobliged at his settling his son at Oxford, and think that an university that trained him up was worthy of his son; I wish Oxford was enough in your neighbourhood for you to offer some consolation to his widow, who is an excellent woman and your old acquaintance.   iii pp197–98

Thomas Tickell (1685–1740), the poet and literary executor of the essayist Joseph Addison, had lived in Glasnevin and his widow was on calling terms with the Delanys.

Delville, 17 February 1753

Last Wednesday Bushe and Miss Anne Hamilton spent the day with me. One evening last week Mrs Tickel made me a visit: she is an original, she talks and cries, and laughs as fast as she can, ringing the changes as Mrs Griffiths used to do; but what makes it surprising, is that she really has sense and wit, but her passions are strong, and her spirits volatile! She entertains me like a good actor that performs an odd part. iii pp205–206

Delville, 24 February 1753

Lady Rawdon pleases here very well; she is very gay, and I believe the more so for the confinement she had at home: a moderate indulgence of pleasure makes it a thing of less consequence than when people are totally denied it. Lord Rawdon is a good-natured man, but reckoned near, and is too apt to talk like a traveller.   iii p208

Delville, 21 April 1753

Mr Mount [tutor to the Meades?] is in pretty good health; he has nothing to support him but a small income which is returned him out of England, arising, I think, from some houses in Westminster; for the salary of his place has run on to pay his debts, and if justice has been done him he expects that is now nearly done: if he meets with no advancement this year here, I believe that next he will go to England. On Monday next Mrs Bushe and I design to make him a visit, and he is to give us cold gammon, and I shall carry cold beef, and make a merry day of it. Tuesday we spend at the Bishop of Derry's, which is always a pleasant day.   iii p222

Despite her opinions about the necessity for social life, Mary was quite glad to rest from it occasionally.

Delville, 29 May 1753

Saturday was a sweet solitary day, for as well as I love society, a day sometimes entirely to one's self is very pleasant, and I wonder at people who think it a melancholy thing to spend a day alone: it is like a pause in music, which when properly introduced gives a grace to the whole piece.   iii pp231–32

When she was in England on a protracted visit she still enjoyed the company of her Irish circle in Bath, then a fashionable watering place. The new viceroy in Ireland was John Russell, 4th duke of Bedford, who, with his wife, kept up great state.

Bath, 4 September 1757

Here are swarms of Hibernians. I thought a Parliament winter, and a new Lord and Lady Lieutenant would have kept them at home. I must go to the Rooms (which begin on Monday) *for privacy*, for if I stay at home I may have a drum every night. Mrs Fielding is here, and has taken a lodging across the water at Bathwick; she and Mrs Forth dined with me last Friday. After dinner came two Irish ladies, Mrs Greene, and her fair daughter, Lady Falkland.   iii p464

Back in Ireland she meets with some of those who made their wealth out of property development in Dublin. Luke Gardiner was deputy vice treasurer of Ireland and developer of the north side of eighteenth century Dublin.

Delville, 5 May 1759

"Not hear of Mr and Mrs Clements!" Why she is finer than the finest lady in England. Dress, furniture, house, equipage – *excelling all! Mr Clements is – her husband!* They set out in life very young and very humble, though both of good families; he was a favourite of the famous Luke Gardiner's, and has gathered together by degrees an immense fortune, if one may judge by the magnificence of his living; and what is quite surprizing, they are both very moderate in their understanding, and yet there is a cleverness and elegance in everything about them that is beyond what could be expected; they are now gone to their house in the [Phoenix] park, about four miles from hence – three from Dublin; they keep Wednesdays.   iii pp551–52

Mary was sympathetic to learning in women, although she herself had no pretensions about the extent of her own knowledge.

Delville, 5 May 1759

I called on Lady Rawdon. She is very sensible, well bred, and agreeable. She told me she had heard her brother Lord Huntingdon was going to be married to Lady Harriet Bentinck, but she "feared it would be too great a honour and happiness for him to expect." I could not make her the compliment of *wishing* it to be *true*, unless I had thought him as deserving as his sister, and then I should very sincerely; for I believe she is a very worthy woman, an excellent wife and mother. She reads a vast deal and has a surprizing knowledge of history. I much regret I did not apply myself more to it in my younger years, particularly the history of my own country; but I find it now pleasanter to read than I used to do, I believe it is being more sensible of the importance of it. In the course of conversation with Lady Rawdon she told me that she "had been assured by a person she thought must know, that the Duchess of Portland kept her daughters at such a distance, that even now they are not permitted to

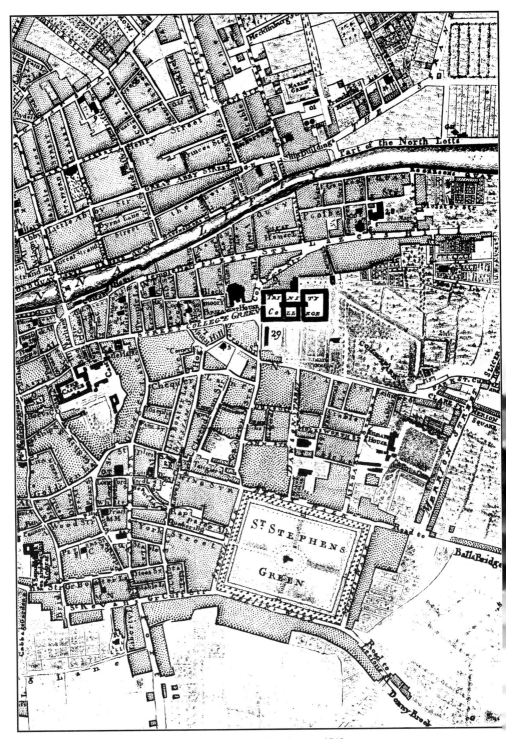

Part of map of Dublin by J. Rocque, 1765.

dine at table with her." *You know how untrue that is!* It is surprizing the delight that people have in *propagating lies!*   iii pp552–53

Delville, 12 May 1759

Tuesday, Lord Rawdon and Mr Comin, (a clergyman of extraordinary learning, and a very agreeable as well as good man) dined here; friends at Finglass met them. iii p553

Delville, 22 September 1759

Monday, we carried Mr Sandford to Mrs Clement's Lodge in Phoenix Park, found her *at breakfast*, was first denied, but on hearing our names let us in. We eat a second breakfast, and walked all over her house; she *very fine*, and very civil, but it rained so violently we could not see her improvements abroad. Before we came away a pine-apple was brought in ready pared and cut, all served in fine old china. We hastened home without going to the camp, that is an entertainment still in store. On Tuesday we set out as soon as breakfast was over to Ballydoyle strand, just by the Hill of Howth, which I have described to you, and Mr Sandford was quite delighted *with a sight so new, a sight so gay!* We picked up a great many common shells, and came home to dinner.

Lord Charlemont, made earl in 1763 for his services during the attempted invasion by the French, was a scholar and traveller of note, and later came to live in Ireland, building a small but incomparably beautiful villa at Marino, his small estate outside Dublin, as well as playing an important part in the Volunteer movement in the 1780s.

Thursday, Lord Charlemont, his brother and sisters, dined here. He is perfectly recovered, and a very agreeable (ugly) man – sensible, lively, and polite. I wish he would fall in love with Miss Mary Hamilton [daughter of her great friend Mrs Henry Hamilton], as she would make him a very proper wife.   iii pp565–66

John Russell, 4th duke of Bedford, came to Ireland as viceroy in 1757, and entertained handsomely at the Castle. This was against a background of harvest failures in 1757 and 1758, and an attempted French invasion by the French naval commander Thurot who actually entered Belfast Lough as far as Carrickfergus in 1759 but was repulsed. In that year there were riots in Dublin because of difficulties in the Irish parliament and fears about an act of union.

Delville, 13 October 1759

D.D. went yesterday to the Castle to pay his devoirs, but *no Castle* – the Duke's levée not yet fixed – but the Primate desired D.D. would meet him at the Castle chapel to-morrow and he would present him after chapel.   iii p571

Delville, 3 November 1759

The Castle produced me no entertainment. Our cousin [the Duchess] looks *as yellow as a kite's foot*, and *very stately* in her drawing-room, though at other times very condescending, and will go to anybody that will give her cards and supper. I am sure I am not one of those; she dines every Sunday with Lady Barrymore on her own dinner. In the afternoon his Excellency comes, and cards and supper finish the day: such examples are *unnecessary!*   iii p572

There were rumours of more French invasions and three Dublin banks closed because of a run on reserves. However Mrs Delany put her faith in the continuity of patronage.

Delville, 10 November 1759

We are now so stout about the French, that we seem to bid them defiance should they land among us, which now I believe they hardly will: if they do, they say we have 14,000 regular troops *ready* to receive them; but this day is given to *song and dance*, great doing and finery expected at the birthday. I could not bring myself however to mix with such a crowd, having in truth no business there; though I don't design to *exclude* myself from the Castle, and I think it wrong to give up powerful acquaintance, even when they are not very valuable, they may be of use some way to somebody or other.   iii p575

In these troubled days of rumours of union, alarms about invasions, and growing discontent in the rural areas Mary reports on the doings of the Irish parliament, though in the same breath she mentions her godson Garrett Wesley's Musical Academy, an ensemble of amateur players who put on concerts for charity.

Delville, 24 November, 1759

The Musical Academy has not yet made half so much *noise*, though it is opened, as the House of Commons, where there was so great a mob assembled one day this week, apprehending the Union Bill was to be brought into the House, that the Speaker [John Ponsonby, speaker 1756–71] and the great Secretary (now Master of the Rolls) Mr Rigby, were frightened out of their wits, and forced to harangue the mob. They had prepared a gallows for Mr Rigby, if he had not *assured them he was on their side!* This makes diversion for some, and matter of boast to others, who like these daring spirits; for my own part, I either am so little of a patriot, or understand the matter so little, that I am rather shocked at these tumults, and wish for more peaceable proceedings, and thank God for my pleasant, tranquil situation; but by the time I get an account of these turbulent matters the fury of their spirit is a little evaporated. iii p577

Delville, 15 December 1759

I have heard nothing lately of Lord and Lady Rawdon, but fear no happiness can be

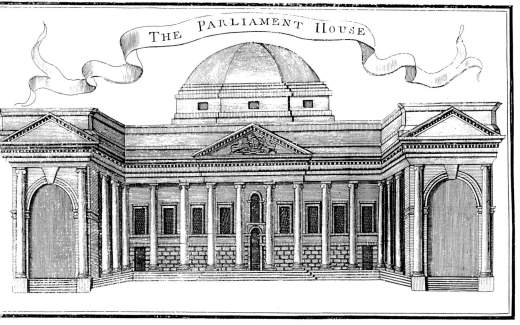

Parliament buildings, 1766.

expected where the dispositions are so different. Sally and I have been visiting Lady Annesley; Lady Tyrone her mother, Lady Jane Cary her sister, all living within ten yards of each other, – enviable happiness! And though they are not refined in their sentiments, they have *a jolly sort* of family love for one another, that makes them feel the comfort of being so near.   iii p579

Delville, 2 February 1760

And what a wretched end Lady Coventry makes after her short-lived reign of beauty [one of the famous Miss Gunnings]. Not contented with the *extraordinary share* providence had bestowed on her, she presumptuously and vainly thought to mend it, and by that means they say has destroyed her life; for Dr Taylor says the white she made use of for her face and neck was rank poison; I wish it may be a warning to her imitators.   iii p584

Delville, 24 April 1760

I fancy Mr Dunbar is mistaken about his ward Mr Dill. I never heard he had any attachment to Mademoiselle Le Gondez; though her beauty might well warrant it. If that is the case, he is a *woeful lover*, for she is *engaged* to a son of Lord Tyrone's, and they are to be married when he has finished his studies at the Temple. His mother, who has a great estate, settles fifteen hundred a year on him at his marriage. Mademoiselle has no fortune; a near relation of Lady Rawdon's, of a considerable family, bred a Roman Catholic, and was going into a nunnery sore against her will. When Lord and Lady Rawdon were abroad, they rescued her with the consent of her parents, and on their promise not to endeavour to change her religion, and as they had no fortune, they were glad to put her into such good hands: last year Mademoiselle Le Gondez renounced the Romish religion and came into our church. They say it was the Archbishop of Dublin who made her a convert, Lord and Lady Rawdon were no way whatever accessary to it.   iii pp587–88

Delville, 8 May 1760

Friday *morning* I dressed and went to her Grace of Bedford's morning drawing-room. Waited with many very fine ladies in *beaten silver*, and glittering with jewels, till half an hour after three: then the door was opened, and the word "*approach*" was given. I stalked in with the train, made a low curtsey, sat down, was asked how Lady Weymouth did? As I went away I said (I believe coldly enough), "*I hope I shall have the honour of seeing your Grace at Delville to breakfast.*" She said, "I don't know how I can get at you, but should be glad to wait upon you if I could." I answered, "*I am but just come from thence, and am returning home;*" and I *could* have added, "where company have waited dinner for me above an hour!"   iii p591

Mary to her niece Mary Dewes
1 September 1760

Last Saturday, we dined at Viscountess Grandison's at Clontarf, three miles from hence by the seaside; it is the only place we have *dined* at, but she came here and would not be refused: I have always avoided dining in Dublin, it is so hot and close there. Next Thursday, Mrs Gustavus Hamilton [married to the eldest son of her great friend Mrs Henry Hamilton] and her two little girls come here to stay some days, whilst Mr G. Hamilton goes to visit his living.   iii pp600–601

When her sister was ill, the Delanys came over to England, to be with her, and to see some of their English friends.

Mary to her niece Mary Dewes
Bulstrode, 2 January 1761

The Bishop of Ossory [the orientalist Richard Pococke] has been here ever since Monday; he goes away to-morrow. We lose not much entertainment, for he is the *dullest man* that *ever travelled*; but he is a good man, and he has promised to get some of the Giant's Causeway for the Duchess of Portland, which rejoices her extremely. Many materials are still wanting for the cave, which has a large mouth, and swallows a vast deal [refers to the making of a grotto].   iii pp626–27

After her sister's death in 1761, the Delanys lived a quieter life. Their home circle which included the Sandfords, and their friends formed their chief society, although Mary still followed the gossip of the salons. Her correspondents were now her niece and family, and friends from the duchess of Bulstrode's circle like Viscountess Andover.

Mary to Viscountess Andover
Delville, 8 June 1765

Weddings are going forward, some *wise* some *other wise*. Miss Monck, Lady Bell's daughter, to be married to the Earl of Tyrone, a man of more intrinsic worth than he appears to be, and she is much commended for good nature and not wanting sense, among her acquaintance; no beauty between them, but very good fortune. As it will fix them in this country, I think it will be agreeable to *all* parties.   iv pp50–51

Because of the Dean's increasing age, their social life quietened down. After 1768, she remained in England and gradually resumed a busy life based round her interests and her circle of friends particularly the duchess of Portland.

JONATHAN SWIFT, DEAN OF ST PATRICK'S (1667–1745)

During her first visit to Ireland Mary met the great dean of St Patrick's, Jonathan Swift, with whom she afterwards entered into correspondence. We are not sure whether the acquaintance was completely enjoyable for Mary; she seems to have far preferred the Dean's friend, Patrick Delany, but she certainly realized that it was an honour to know so illustrious a man. Swift himself seems to have seen in her a link with his old friends and English patrons, like her uncle George Lord Lansdowne, and her cousin Lord Carteret. He was growing older in the knowledge that all his great gifts for incisive political writing and satire would not further his position. Stella, or Hesther Johnson, had died in 1728; Vanessa, or Esther van Homrigh, had died of consumption earlier in 1723. Swift still enjoyed the company of attractive and intelligent young women, making several new friends like Letitia Pilkington, the writer, and Mary Barber, the poetess, whose reputation he helped forward.

Mary describes the company at dinner where she met the great dean. Miss Frances Kelly, daughter of a Jacobite Dennis Kelly, was a famous beauty and much admired by Swift; John Boyle, 5th earl of Orrery, was a regular companion at the Thursday night dinners held at Delville, and Dr Helsham was the original partner with whom Dr Delany bought Delville and a fellow at Trinity College, Dublin. The Donnellans were a well known Dublin and Trinity family whom she knew from London society. Dr Christopher Donnellan was a favourite brother of her great friend Anne or Philomel, and, after his death, she endowed some lectures at Trinity College in his honour. Mary's host at dinner was Dr Delany.

Along with actor impresario Thomas Sheridan, Patrick Delany was one of Jonathan Swift's greatest friends, and particularly valuable because he lived in Ireland. In the 1730s Swift had given up hope of advancement in England and maintained his friendships through correspondence. He described Patrick Delany

Jonathan Swift (1667-1745), Dean of St Patrick's Cathedral, by Rupert Barber (fl. 1736-72).

to Alexander Pope in one of his letters as "a man of the easyest and best conversation I ever met with in this Island, a very good list'ner, a right reasoner, neither too silent, nor talkative, and never positive."

Dublin, 24 January 1732/3

On Thursday Phill and I dined at Dr Delany's; there we met Miss Kelly, Lord Orrery, the Dean of St Patrick's, Mr Kit Donellan, Dr Helsham – a very ingenious entertaining man. In such company you may believe time passed away very pleasantly. Swift is a very *odd companion* (if that expression is not too familiar for so extraordinary a genius); he talks a great deal and does not require many answers; he has infinite spirits, and says abundance of good things in his common way of discourse. Miss Kelly's beauty and good humour have gained an entire conquest over him, and I come in only *a little by the by.*

Lord Orrery is very gentle in his manner, and mighty polite; he only dined with us, for he is in the hands of lawyers and was obliged to give us all up for those vultures: the rest of us staid the evening. We are initiated of that *witty club*, and Thursday is the day of meeting.

This morning I had appointed to take the air with Miss Kelly, and came to her for that purpose, but by the time I came here, it rained and spoiled our sport. She kept me to dinner; Donellan came to us, and I am now writing at Kelly's desk. God bless you my dearest sister, and adieu, for I can write no more! All the while I have been writing, Don and Kelly have read with an audible voice Hans Carvell and some other pretty things of that kind, and how can one help listening? but I would stop my ears had I anything to say that would be entertaining. My humble duty to my mother, and service to all friends.   i pp396–97

Dublin, 20 February 1732/3

I have not been again in company with Dr Swift, but I don't fear having my vanity raised by anything he can say. You have used me so much to praise, that I think I am proof against all that can be said from any other tongue; and indeed if I did not suppose you partial to me, I should by this time have been monstrously conceited of my own perfections. Next Thursday we are to dine at Dr Delany's; it has been twice put off on account of the violent colds that everybody in some degree has shared; I hope their fury is abated, though *we* have not had much reason to complain.

The Dean of St Patrick's answered my Lord Orrery's verses by a letter in prose, which Mrs Barber saw, and says it is very pretty. He is in love with Miss Kelly *at present*. He [the dean] sent her some Spanish liquorish for her cold, and with it a fable very prettily applied of Lycoris. His works are going to be published, collected by themselves, all his verse and prose, four volumes. They are only printed in Ireland; I have subscribed to them.   i pp398–400

Lord Orrery's first wife, Lady Henrietta Hamilton, had died in August, 1732, so he was free to enjoy the beautiful (but ill) Miss Kelly's company. Her illness was to prove fatal, for she died in October 1733.

Dublin, [undated c.February 1733]

I have given up the trial with Kelly, her beauty and assiduity has distanced me, and I will not attempt a second heat. At present she is disabled, poor thing, for she is confined to her bed with a pleuratic disorder, but the Dean attends her bedside: his heart must be old and cold indeed if that did not conquer. But Dr Delany will make a *more desirable friend*, for he has all the qualities requisite for friendship – zeal, tenderness, and application ; I know you would like him, because he is worthy.

Oh, I forgot to tell you my Lord Orrery was at Dr Delany's the last time we dined there, and that he only looked at and talked with Miss Kelly, a most formidable young woman; but she has touched me in a tenderest part, for she has *so entirely* gained Mrs Donellan, that without joking she has made me uneasy, but what does all this serve to show? why to show me my dear sister's love in all its value, that never has been turned from me by anybody.

The Dean of St Patrick's is writing a poem on poetry. Dr Delany has seen what is done of it, he says *'tis like himself,* but he gives us no hopes of seeing it yet awhile. Mr Pope I find has undertaken to lash the age; I believe he will be tired before they are reformed. He says he *"will spare neither friend nor foe"* so that declaring oneself for him, will not secure us from a stroke.   i pp402–404

Dangan, 5 April 1733

The day before we came out of town, we dined at Doctor Delany's, and met the usual company. The Dean of St Patrick's was there, in very good humour, he calls himself "my master," and corrects me when I speak bad English, or do not pronounce my words distinctly. I wish he lived in England, I should not only have a great deal of entertainment from him, but improvement. I am in great hopes Mrs Barber will be well enough to travel with us; she will be an excellent companion for us, for she has constant spirits and good-humour.   i p407

When Mary returned to England she corresponded with Swift. These letters betray a certain awkwardness on her part, probably because she was too selfconscious with such a correspondent.

Mary to Dean Swift
London, 29 May 1733

Sir, You will find to your cost that a woman's pen, when encouraged, is as bad as a woman's tongue; blame yourself, not me; had I never known the pleasure of receiving a letter from you, I should not have persecuted you now. I think (a little to justify this bold attack) that I am obliged by all the rules of civility, to give you an account of the letter you charged me with. I delivered it into my Lord Bathurst's hands, he read it before me; I looked silly upon his asking me what you meant by the Fosset affair? and I was obliged to explain it to him in my own defence, which gave him the diversion you designed it should. We then talked of your vineyard [Swift's garden in the Liberties of Dublin], he seemed pleased with every subject that related to you, and I was very ready to indulge him that way. I did not forget to brag of your favours to me: if you intended I should keep them secret, I have spoiled all, for I have not an acquaintance of any worth that I have not told how happy I have been in your company. Everybody loves to be envied, and this is the only way I have of raising people's envy; I hope, sir, you will forgive me, and let me know if I have *behaved myself right*. I think I can hardly do wrong as long as I am, sir, your most obliged and most obedient servant, M. Pendarves. Mrs Donellan is much your humble servant, and as vain of your favours as I am.   i pp414–15

However, she encouraged him to continue improving her English style.

Mary to Dean Swift
Gloucester, 21 July 1738

Sir, May I say without offending you, that I was overjoyed at the honour you did me in answering my letter? and do not call me formal, when I assure you that I think myself made happy by such a distinction. It was stupidity in me not to let you know where to address to me, but I do not repent of it; I have by that means tried your zeal, but I am afraid your good-breeding more than inclination procured me that favour. I am resolved to be even with you for what you say about my writing, and will write henceforward to you as carelessly as I can; and if it is not legible thank yourself, I do not wonder at the envy of the ladies, when you are pleased to speak of me with some regard: I give them leave to exercise their malice on an occasion that does me so much honour. I protest I am not afraid of you, and would appear quite natural to you in hopes of your rewarding my openness and sincerity, by correcting what you disapprove of; and since I have not now an opportunity of receiving your favours of pinching and beating, make me amends by *chiding me* for every word that is *false* spelt, and for my *bad English*. You see what you are like to suffer: if this promises you too much trouble, do not give me so much encouragement in your next letter, for upon something in your last I have almost persuaded myself, that by your assistance, and my own earnest desire, I may in time become worthy of your care. Vanity stands at my elbow all this while, and animates me by a thousand agreeable promises: without her encouragement I should never have presumed to correspond with the Dean of St Patrick's. Some say she is a mischievous companion; I swear she is a pleasant one. You must not be angry with me for keeping her company, for I had very little acquaintance with her till I had received some marks of your favour.

I wish you could make your words good, and that I *was* a "*sorceress*"; I should then set all my charms to work to bring you to England, and should expect a general thanksgiving for employing my spells to so good a purpose. *The syren* [Anne Donnellan alias Philomel] has lately been at Oxford: we parted very unwillingly, she is extremely obliged to you for remembering her so favourably. I am glad Mr Donellan pleases you; I know he has a high value for you, and I agree with you in thinking him a most deserving young man. My Lord Lansdowne is much at your service, laments the days that are past, and constantly drinks your health in champaign [champagne], as clear as your thoughts, and sparkling as your wit; Lord and Lady Carteret, and my Lady Worsley all talk kindly of you, and join their wishes to mine for your coming among us. I request it of you to make my humble service acceptable to those friends of yours that are so good as to remember me. I am, sir, your most obliged and faithful humble servant, M. Pendarves. Be pleased to direct for me at Mrs Granville's, Gloucester.   i pp415–17.

There was a truly country loving side to the fashionable Mary Pendarves as she was then, although her uncle teases her that it is only a whim.

George, Lord Lansdowne to his niece Mary
London, 8 August 1733

Mr dear niece, Your good sense will make all places agreeable to you, but with *your pardon*, notwithstanding all your fine rural descriptions, the *pleasures of courts*, and *the entertainments of the town* are more at the bottom of your heart; and it is fit they should be so for the sake of the public, qualified as you are to grace our assemblies. Nor can you ever *make me believe* you prefer the murmuring of a purling stream, to a quaver of Cuzzoni! Your friend the Reverend Dean [Swift] would tell you this is all "*widowe's cant*" and "*meer pruderie*". Widow! have a care; a matrimonial star is reigning over young and old, you may be caught before you are aware, and there is no resisting one's destiny.   i p418

Letters were shared between friends and in that way news travelled far.

Mary to Dean Swift
Gloucester, 24 October 1733

Sir, I cannot imagine how my Lord Orrery came by my last letter to you: I believe my good genius conveyed it into his hands, to make it of more consequence to you; if it had that effect, I wish this may meet with the same fortune. If I were writing to a common correspondent, I should now make a fine flourish to excuse myself for not sooner acknowledging the favour of your letter; but I must deal plainly with you, sir, and tell you (now do not be angry), that the fear of tiring you stopped my hand. I value your correspondence so highly, that I think of every way that may preserve it; and one is, not to be too troublesome. Now I cannot guess how you will take this last paragraph; but if it makes me appear affected or silly, I will endeavour not to offend in the same manner again. Some mortification of that kind is wanting to bring me to myself. Your ways of making compliments are dangerous snares, and I do not know how to guard against the pleasure they bring: to be remembered and regretted by you, are honours of a very delicate kind; I have been told, that unexpected good fortune is harder to bear well than adversity.

The cold weather, I suppose, has gathered together Dr Delany's set: the next time you meet, may I beg the favour to make my compliments acceptable? I recollect no entertainment with so much pleasure, as what I received from that company; it has made me very sincerely lament the many hours of my life that I have lost in insignificant conversation. A few days before I had your last letter, my sister and I made a visit to my Lord and Lady Bathurst at Cirencester. My Lord Bathurst was in great spirits; and though surrounded by candidates and voters against next parliament, made himself agreeable in spite of their clamour: we did not forget to talk of Naboth's vineyard [Swift's walled garden in the Liberties of Dublin] and Delville [Dr Delany's villa at Glasnevin]. I have not seen him since, though he promised to return my visit. i pp420–21

St Patrick's Cathedral, Dublin, 1766.

Mary to Dean Swift
Little Brook Street, London, 9 September 1734

Sir, I find your correspondence is like the singing of the nightingale – no bird sings so sweetly, but the pleasure is quickly past; a month or two of harmony, and then we lose it till next spring. I wish your favours may as certainly return. I am at this time not only deprived of your letters, but of all other means of inquiring after your health, your friends and my correspondents being dispersed to their summer quarters, and know as little of you as I do. I have not forgot one mortifying article on this occasion, and if your design in neglecting me was to humble me, it has taken effect. Could I find out the means of being revenged I would most certainly put it in execution, but I have only the malice of an incensed, neglected woman, without the power of returning it. The last letter I writ to you was from Gloucester, about a twelvemonth ago, after that I went to Long Leat to my Lady Weymouth; came to town in January, where I have remained ever since, except a few weeks I spent at Sir John Stanley's at Northend, (the *Delville* of this part of the world). I hope Naboth's vineyard flourishes; it always has my good wishes, though I am not near enough to partake of its fruits.   i pp492–93

Dean Swift to Mary
Dublin, 7 October 1734

Madam, When I received the honor and happiness of your last letter (dated September 9), I was afflicted with a pair of disorders that usually seize me once a year, and with which I have been acquainted from my youth, but it is only of late years that they have begun to come together, although I should have been better contented with one at a time – these are *giddiness* and *deafness*, which usually last a month; the first tormenting my body, and the other making me incapable of conversing. In this juncture your letter found me: but I was able to read, though *not to hear*; neither did I value my deafness for three days, because your letter was my constant entertainment during that time; after which I grew sensibly better, and, although I was not abroad till yesterday, I find myself well enough to acknowledge the great favor you have done me, but cannot guess your motive for so much goodness. I guess that your *good genius*, accidentally meeting mine, was prevailed on to solicit your pity! Or, did you happen to be at leisure by the summer absence of your friends? Or, would you appear a constant nymph, when all my goddesses of much longer acquaintance have forsaken me, as it is reasonable they should? But the men are almost as bad as the ladies, and I cannot but think them in the right; for I cannot make shifts and lie rough, and be undone by starving in scanty lodgings, without horses, servants, or conveniences, as I used to do in London, with port wine, or perhaps Porter's ale, to save charges!

You dare not pretend to say that your town equals ours in hospitable evenings, with your *deep play* and no entertainment but a cup of chocolate, unless you have mended your manners. I will not declare your reasons for not taking a second trip over hither, because you have offered none but your royal will and pleasure; but if I were in the case of your friends here, with more life before me and better health, I would solicit

Mrs Kelly, sister-in-law of Swift's 'Blue-eyed nymph' (Irish School, 18th century).

an act of parliament to prevent your coming among us; or, at least to make it high treason in you ever to leave us.

In the meantime, I wish you were forced over by debts or want, because we would gladly agree to a contribution for life, dinners and suppers excluded, that are to go for nothing. I speak for the public good of this country; because a pernicious heresy prevails here among the men, that it is the duty of your sex to be fools in every article except what is merely domestic, and to do the ladies justice, there are very few of them without a good share of that heresy, except upon one article, that they have as *little* regard for *family business* as for the *improvement of their minds!* I have had for some time a design to write against this heresy, but have now laid those thoughts aside, for fear of making both sexes my enemies; however, if you will come over to my assistance, I will carry you about among our adversaries, and dare them to produce *one instance* where your *want of ignorance* makes you affected, pretending, conceited, disdainful, endeavouring to speak like a scholar, with twenty more faults objected by themselves, their lovers, or their husbands. But, I fear your case is desperate, for I know you never laugh at a jest before you understand it; and I much question whether you *understand a fan*, or have so good a fancy *at silks* as others; and your way of *spelling* would *not be intelligible.*

Therefore upon your arrival hither (which I expect in three packets at furthest), I will give you a licence to be as silly as you can possibly afford, one half-hour every week, to the heretics of each sex, to atone for which you are to keep one fasting-day at Doctor Delany's, or Dr Helsham's, and one at the Deanery. Nothing vexes me so much with relation to you, as that with all my disposition to find faults, I was never once able to fix upon anything that I could find amiss, although I watched you narrowly; for when I found we were to lose you soon, I kept my eyes and ears always upon you, in hopes that you would make some *boutade*. It is, you know, a French word, and signifies a sudden jerk from a horse's hinder feet which you did not expect, because you thought him for some months a sober animal, and this hath been my case with several ladies who I chose for friends; in a week, a month, or a year, hardly one of them failed to give me a *boutade*; therefore I command you will obey my orders, in coming over hither for one whole year; after which, upon the first *boutade you make*, I will give you my pass to be gone. If I have tired you, it is the effect of the great esteem I have for you, do but lessen your own merits, and I will shorten my letters in proportion.

If you will come among us, I engage your dreadful old beggarly western Parson to residence, otherwise we all resolve to send him over, which in our opinion the surest way to drive you hither, for you will be in more haste to fly from, than to follow even Mrs Donellan, when you keep out of sight; if she be among you, I desire she may know I am her true admirer and most humble servant.   i pp501–505

In the 1730s Dean Swift frequently lamented his loneliness and was often hurt by the refusal of his English friends to travel to Ireland. He declared he could not maintain his style of living in England and relied on them to visit him. His favourite Miss Kelly died of pleurisy in October 1733. However he continued to fraternise with promising young women like the poetess Mary Barber whom he encouraged to write, helping to get her volume of Poems on Several Occasions (1734) published, and he continued to write to Mary.

Dean Swift to Mary
Dublin, 22 February 1734/5

Madam, I have observed among my own sex, and particularly in myself, that those of us who grow most insignificant expect most civility, and give less than they did when they possibly were good for something. I am grown sickly, weak, lean, forgetful, peevish, spiritless, and for those very reasons expect that you, who have nothing to do but to be happy, should be entertaining me with your letters and civilities, although I never return either. Your last is dated above two months' ago, since which time (as well as a good while before) I never had one single hour of health or spirit to acknowledge it. *It is your fault*; why did you not come sooner into the world or let me come later? *It is your fault* for coming into Ireland at all; *it is your fault* for leaving it.

I confess your case is hard, for *if you return*, you are a great *fool* to come among *beggars and slaves*, and if you *do not*, you are a *great knave* in forsaking those you have seduced to admire you. The complaint you make of a disorder in one of your eyes will admit no raillery, it is what I was heartily afflicted to hear, but since you were able to write, I hope it hath entirely left you. I am often told that I am an ill judge of ladies' eyes, so that I shall make you an ill compliment by confessing that I read in yours all the accomplishments I found in your mind and conversation, and happened to agree in my thoughts with better judges. I only wish they could never shine out of Dublin, for then you would recover the only temporal blessings this town affords – I mean sociable dinners and cheerful evenings, which, without your assistance, we shall infallibly lose. For Dr Delany lives entirely at Delville, the town air will not agree with his lady, and in winter there is no seeing him or dining with him but by those who keep coaches, and they must return the moment after dinner. But I have chid him into taking a house just next to his, which will have three bed-chambers, where his winter visitants may lie, and a bed shall be fitted up for you.

Your false reasons for not coming hither are the same in one article for my not going among you, I mean the business of expense; but I can remove yours easily, it is but to stay with us always, and then you can live at least three times better than at home, where everything is thrice as dear, and your money 12 in the hundred better, whereas my sickness and years make it impossible for me to live at London. I must have three horses, as many servants, and a large house, neither can I live without constant wine, while my poor revenues are sinking every day. Well, madam, pray God bless you wherever you go or reside! may you be ever as you are, agreeable to every Killala curate and Dublin dean, for I disdain to mention temporal folks *without* gowns and cassocks. A year or two ago I would have put the whole into English verse and applied it to you, but my rhyming is fled with my health, and what is more to be pitied is even my vein of satire upon ladies is lost. Dear madam, believe me to be, with the truest respect and esteem, your most obedient humble servant J. Swift.
i p522–25

Mary to Dean Swift
London, 16 May 1735

Sir, You have never yet put it in my power to accuse you of want of civility; for since my acquaintance with you, you have always paid me more than I expected: but I may sometimes tax you with want of kindness, which, to tell you the truth, I did for a month at least. At last I was informed your not writing to me was occasioned by your ill state of health: that changed my discontent, but did not lessen it, and I have not yet quite determined it in my mind, whether I would have you sick or negligent of me; they are both great evils, and hard to choose out of – I heartily wish neither may happen.

I am sorry the sociable Thursdays, that used to bring together so many agreeable friends at Dr Delany's, are broken up: though Delville has its beauties, yet it is more out of the way than Stafford street. I believe you have had a quiet winter in Dublin; not so has it been with us in London.   i p538–39

Dean Swift to Mary
Dublin, 29 January 1735/6

Madam, I had indeed some intention to go to Bath, but I had neither health nor leisure for such a journey; those times are past with me, and I am older by fourscore years since the first time I had the honour to see you. I got a giddiness by raw fruit when I was a lad in England, which I never could be wholly rid of, and it is now too late, so that I confine myself entirely to a domestic life. I am visited seldom, but visit much seldomer. I dine alone like a king, having few acquaintances, and those lessening daily. This town is not what you left it, and I impute the cause altogether to your absence. I fear if your sister mends, as I pray God she will, it is rather due to the journey than the Bath water.

I must despise a lady who takes me for a pedant, and you have made me half angry with so many lines in your letter which look like a kind of apology for writing to me. Besides, to say the truth, the ladies in general are *extremely mended* both in writing and reading since I was young, only it is to be hoped that in proper time *gaming and dressing*, with some other accomplishments, may reduce them to their native ignorance. A woman of quality, who had *excellent* good sense, was formerly my correspondent, but she scrawled and spelt like a Wapping wench, having been brought up in a court at a time before reading was thought of any use to a female; and I knew *several* others of *very high quality* with the same defect.

Dr Delany hath long ago given up his house in town. His Dublin friends seldom visit him till the swallows come in. He is too far from town for a winter visit, and too near for staying a night in the country manner; neither is his house large enough; it minds me of what I have heard the late Duchess complain, that Sion House was "a hobbedehoy, neither town nor country."   i pp550,551,552

Dr Delany to Mary
8 February 1735/6
extract from unpublished manuscript, Newport Library Gwent.

The Dean will not go to Bath. He is, if possible, a more domestic animal than I am. I wait to see him and the swallows together. I have scarce room to beg my best respects to my most valuable friend Mrs Barber as to beg you to believe me to be, with the greatest esteem your most obliged and obedient humble servant Patrick Delany.

Mary to Dean Swift
London, 22 April 1736

Mrs Donellan, I am afraid, is so well treated in Ireland, that I much despair of seeing her here; and how or when I shall be able to come to her I cannot yet determine. She is so good to me in her letters, as always to mention you. I hope I shall hear from you soon; you owe me that pleasure, for the concern I was under when I heard you were ill. I am, sir, your faithful and obliged humble servant, M. Pendarves. P.S. I beg my compliments, to all friends that remember me, but particularly to Dr Delany. i p555

Mary to Dean Swift
London, 2 September 1736

Sir, I never will accept of the writ of ease you threaten me with; do not flatter yourself with any such hopes: I receive too many advantages from your letters to drop a correspondence of such consequence to me. I am really grieved that you are so much persecuted with a giddiness in your head; the Bath and travelling would certainly be of use to you. Your want of spirits is a new complaint, and what will not only afflict your particular friends, but every one has the happiness of your acquaintance. I am uneasy to know how you do, and have no other means for that satisfaction but from your own hand; most of my Dublin correspondents being removed to Cork, to Wicklow mountains, and the Lord knows where. I should have made this enquiry sooner, but that I have this summer undertaken a work that has given me full employment, which is *making a grotto* in Sir John Stanley's garden at North End, and it is chiefly composed of shells I had from Ireland. My life, for two months past, has been very like a hermit's; I have had all the comforts of life but society, and have found living quite alone a pleasanter thing than I imagined.

Painting and music have had their share in my amusements, I rose between five and six, and went to bed at eleven. I would not tell you so much about myself, if I had anything to tell you of other people; I came to town the night before last, but if it does not, a few days hence, appear better to me than at present, I shall return to my solitary cell; Sir John Stanley has been all the summer at Tunbridge. I suppose you may have heard of Mr Pope's accident, which had liked to have proved a very fatal one. He was leading a young lady into a boat from his own stairs, her foot missed the side of the boat, she fell into the water, and pulled Mr Pope after her: the boat slipped away, and they were immediately out of their depth, and it was with some difficulty they were saved. The young lady's name is Talbot; she is as remarkable for being a handsome woman, as Mr Pope is for wit; I think I cannot give you a higher notion of her beauty, unless I had *named you* instead of *him*. I shall be impatient till I hear from you again; being, with great sincerity, sir, your most faithful, humble servant, M. Pendarves.

Dr Delany to Mary
[Delville] 26 January 1739
extract from unpublished manuscript, Newport Central Library, Gwent.

The Dean is as you hear wholly retired and I can't tell you that my quitting the town may partly be the occasion of it. But it was time to quit the town when the fine spirits that made it agreeable had departed it. So that he had no loss but what I feel would double regret. But after all there is a season in realizing [it is] wise to retire and I am sorry to tell you that season is come with the Dean.

Swift died on 19 October 1745. He had spent the previous three years in the care of guardians appointed by a commission of lunacy, having quarrelled with most of his friends, and enjoying only intermittent lucidity. This was a sad and terrible end for one of the blazing intellects of the eighteenth century.

Delville, 16 November 1745

Pray have you ever read the four sermons by Swift that were published last year? They are very fine and worth the reading. Have your read Bishop Sherlock's sermon on the rebellion? It is charming. There is just published a humorous pamphlet of Swift's, I think called "Advice to Servants;" it is said to be below his genius, but comical – I have not yet seen it. Surely I wrote you word a month ago of his death. It was a happy release to him (I hope), for he was reduced to such a miserable state of idiotism that he was a shocking object; though in his person a very venerable figure, with long silver hair and a comely countenance, for being grown fat the hard lines, which gave him a harsh look before, were filled up.   ii p397–98

Jonathan Swift (Irish School, 18th century).

Lord Orrery's "Remarks" were published six years after Swift's death and painted a critical portrait of a churlish, splenetic character which the Delanys much resented.

Delville, 30 November 1751

The remarks of Lord Orrery on Dr Swift are published, and have made me very angry; they are much commended, said to be very entertaining, but I am so angry at the unfriendly, ungenerous manner of Swift's being treated by one who calls him his friend, that it quite prejudices me against the book, and casts a cloud over all its merit; *every failing is exposed, every fault is magnified, every virtue almost either tarnished or concealed!* I have not time to tell you my particular objections, which are indeed very numerous. But one thing I must observe, that Lord Orrery makes *no mention* of Swift's singular, wise, and extensive charities, yet calls himself his *"friend"*! He tells of his resentment, with the strongest reflection on his pride at his sister's marrying a tradesman, but does not tell you he allowed her £25 a-year to his death, yet calls himself his friend! He calls his being "void of all envy" *"pride of his own superior talents"*, yet calls himself his *"friend"*! Such a friend that, Brutus-like, gives the deepest and the surest wound. I am so angry *I can't keep within bounds*, and I am afraid I shall take off your pleasure in reading a book which I believe may be very agreeable to those who have no regard for the memory of the Dean of St Patrick; and I fear there are too many truths in the book; but they do not become my Lord Orrery to publish them, who was *admitted at all times*, and saw him in his *most unguarded moments*. iii p64

This prompted Patrick Delany to make a defence, although in this corre-spondence it looks as though her friend Sally Chapone might also have undertaken one. Mary refers here to Samuel Richardson, printer and novel-ist, who was a friend of the Chapones.

Delville, 14 December 1751

I have this day begun a letter to Richardson; but have laid it by for fear of not having time to write this. Your judgement of Lord Orrery I hope is a just one, because it entirely agrees with my own, but I am indeed so vexed with him about his manner of treating Swift, that I *can hardly* allow him *any merit*. I must write, and provoke or intreat Sally to *take him in hand*, and expose this coxcomb of a *"friend"*, as he pre-sumes to call himself. If magnifying *all* his *known* faults, exposing some never known, charging others falsely, turning his *best* virtues into pride, and many sneering in-sinuations cast into the bargain, is being a *"friend"*, then Lord Orrery is a friend in-deed! I am serious in what I say about Sally's *answering this book*; but she must be for ever concealed, and not discover the author to be *a woman*. The first leisure hour I have I will tell her my mind freely, and very likely she will be with you at the time. iii p65

Delville 3 January 1751/2

All your observations on Swift are very just, and do credit to your taste and judgment. I hear Lord Orrery is going to be answered; I wish those that do it may know enough of Swift to justify him properly. What Lord Orrery says of Vanessa is *barbarous*. The paragraph you mention about learning is *downright nonsense*; even his fondness to his son appears to me forced, and the conclusion of most of his letters extremely so. iii p73

Delville, 18 January 1751/2

The following epigram is now handed about on Lord Orrery's remarks on Swift –

> A sore disease this scribbling – is,
> His Lordship of his pliny vain,
> Turns Madam Pilkington in – es,
> And now attacks the Irish Dean.
> *Libel* his *friend* when *laid in ground*
> Pray good Sir you may spare your hints,
> His *parallel* I'm sure is found,
> For what *he* writes, *George Faulkner* prints,
> Had Swift provoked to this behaviour,
> Sure *after death* resentment cools,
> And his last act bespoke *their* favour,
> *He founded hospitals for fools.*   iii p79

Delville 18 January 1751/2

There is now in hand, and soon will be published, a Life of Dr Swift, in which the world will see the difference between *true* and *false friends*. The manuscript is to be shown to D.D before it is sent to the press.   iii p80

The dean is credited with publishing a defence of his friend Swift in 1754. Mary here implies that he did not wish to be acknowledged as the author.

Delville 18 June 1754

Politics, thank God! subside, and the present conversation runs on a book just published, the author unknown: "Observations on Lord Orrery's Life of Swift". I hear it very much commended, and D.D. has been applied to, to know how he likes it, and if the facts are true, which *you* may imagine has given *us some sport*. I am glad to find it so well received; it is you remember never to be owned. Everybody thinks his Lordship is very gently treated.   iii p279

Delville, 13 July 1754

The "Observations on Lord Orrery", lately published, is much talked of and commended here, but Swift was more loved and known here than in England! iii p286

Delville, 20 July 1754

Everybody thinks the author of the "*Observations on Lord Orrery*" has treated *him* with great lenity and good manners, and gives no reasonable offence even to the person it is addressed to; it is generally thought to be D.D., but nobody owns it. iii p287

Later Mary was very annoyed by the publication of a volume of Swift's correspondence in which her letters were reproduced.

Mary to the Viscountess Andover
Delville, 4 September 1766

I am *sick* with the account of Swift's last volume! The publisher has *done basely* for he promised a friend of mine who insisted on the letters of Mrs Pendarves [her previous married name] being delivered to him, that if any were found, they should be. It is a serious vexation.   iv p77

In later life, when she was taken up by Hannah More and Fanny Burney, afterwards Madam D'Arblay, they spoke reverently of her as Swift's Mrs Delany.

CHAPTER 3

FRIENDS

Mrs Delany was a sociable person and a loyal friend. Because she was an inveterate letterwriter, because she was hospitable and enjoyed company, she created a large circle of friends for herself, many of whom were shared by her sister, her great childhood friend Sally Kirkham, afterwards Chapone, and later, her friend, Margaret, duchess of Portland. This chapter is divided into sections dealing with the different groups of friends. The social circles of eighteenth century Ireland were very small, and intermeshing. Friendship was largely restricted to those of similar class, very often bounded by family ties as well as by education.

CHAPONE SANDFORD CIRCLE

Her oldest friend was Sally [Sarah] Kirkham from early days in Gloucestershire. Sally was the daughter of a local clergyman, Lionel Kirkham of Stanton. Her brother was the Reverend Robert Kirkham, one of the preacher John Wesley's followers at Oxford. She was something of an intellectual when she married Mr Chapone, and had a large family. Her son John married the writer, Hester Mulso, a well known "bluestocking" and one of Samuel Richardson's protegees or "nightingales". Her own daughter, Sally Chapone, was a dear goddaughter of Mary's and spent much time with the Delanys. This first mention of Sally Chapone, Mary's goddaughter, is during her first trip to Ireland.

Killala, 13 August 1732

I hope Sally finds a great deal of comfort from her fair companion whose person you commend: if she has a mind capable of improvement she has now a fair opportunity of cultivating it to the utmost advantage. I am glad our goddaughter is such a lively creature, and gives you reason to think she *will* have her *mother's wit*. I hope Mr Gore has accommodated his affairs to Mr Kirkham's satisfaction: they say he is a good sort of a young man, but I question if he is unprejudiced enough to relish the conversation of our friend – his life has not been spent with women of *her turn*; so much for Sally, I delight to talk of her! Mr Gore could not say more of the Bishop of Killala's, than they deserve [the Claytons with whom Mary was staying]. The Bishop seems to be one of the best of men, so even-tempered and obliging, everybody is at liberty to do what they like, and he is never so well pleased as when his company is diverted. Mrs Clayton has also her charms, and Phill's you are acquainted with better than I can describe. Miss Forth is also a very agreeable creature.   i pp371–72

After her marriage to Patrick Delany, Mary exerted herself to do something for the Chapones.

Delville, 19 January 1744/5

If *we* are promoted I hope in time something may be done for Mr Chapon, but at present D.D. has old friends and relations to provide for that claim the first right to his interest. The Chapons talk of sending Harry to study in our college [Trinity], – I think if they can afford to bring him up in that way, it will be better and cheaper than the universities of England; here he may be maintained and educated in that way for 40 pounds a year, and be upon the same footing as the best gentlemen's sons. ii p338

One of the Chapone sons made his way to the West Indies, the other sought employment nearer home.

Delville, 30 June 1750

I believe by the account Dr Barber has sent his wife of Harry Chapon, that he is in effect agent victualler, for he says "his place is now five hundred pounds a year". I am the more pleased with this news as I think my recommending him by word of mouth to my Lord Gower has been of service to him. I hope Jack will find Jamaica as profitable as Hal has done: and that they will be enabled to make the latter days of their parents comfortable, and provide well for their sisters, who otherwise I think have a melancholy prospect, for all young women bred to idleness and with a relish to the gaieties of the world, are much to be lamented. I have not heard from Mrs Chapon since I wrote to her by Dr Barber.   ii p560

Delville, 23 March 1750/51

I had a letter to finish to Lord North, to recommend Jack Chapone for a stewardship on Lord Dartmouth's estate, had written it very fair, instead of throwing sand, threw the ink over it! no time to write it and to complete my work over again, so scraped the ink off as well as I could, and made my apology in a postscript.   iii p28

Her kindness was appreciated by the young Chapone who sent presents home from the West Indies.

Delville, 2 April 1752

I have had great pleasure in Mr Emerson's account of Harry Chapone [sent off to the West Indies]; he is so well beloved that he has not an enemy in the island, and bears in every respect a most extraordinary character. His income there he believes is a thousand pounds a year; this sounds a great deal but is not more than equivalent to half, as it is a most extravagant place. Harry C. has sent us a present of sweetmeats, pickles, and half a hogshead of old rum. Mr Emerson has brought me some shells, but he has not yet got them out of the ship.   iii p108

Sally Chapone, Mary's god-daughter.

The Delanys were delighted when Sally Chapone came to live with them in 1754. The dean had a young clergyman helping him called Sandford.

Delville, 22 June 1754

I did not tell you how well I like Sandford. The young gentleman is *still more* to be liked, and his *respectful, tender* behaviour to our Sally is very remarkable, and yet I believe he does not design it should be so, *her's* towards him was quite easy and proper.   iii pp278–79

The courtship between Mr Sandford and Miss Chapone was long, complicated by a lack of fortune and a difficult Sandford father.

Lucan, 28 June 1754

I am no less happy with *my brown maid* [nickname for Sally Chapone], who likes the new scenes she is engaged in; nothing can give more pleasure than to see those obliged whom one wishes to oblige. I almost heartily wish Mr S[andford] in circumstances to declare the sentiments of his heart, which yet he has not done; but it is very plain what they are. I have had some conversation with my young friend on the subject: she is as innocent as *Emily*, and as sensible, delicate, and generous as *Harriet*.

Sally is fallen deperately in love with that river [the Liffey], but how she will be able to deal with such a whimsical lover I can't tell.. What do you imagine her gentleness will be able to do with so changeable a lover? She sees all this, and yet admires him more and more!   iii pp280–81

Delville, 13 July 1754

I have also great satisfaction in our god-daughter. What a pleasure it is to have the children of the friends of our youth so ready to enter into a friendship with us! I think such a union mutually advantageous; the young friend's vivacity and the old friend's experience and seriousness make an agreeable mixture, if mutual complacency be *properly observed.*   iii p285

Mr Sandford was related to the Wards who were neighbours in County Down.

Delville, 22 June 1759

I am very much afraid Mr Sandford is ill; I wrote to him on the death of Mr Chapone to give him an account of his friend, and have not heard since; Judge Ward's death I fear is a great loss to him.   iii p555

Delville, 7 July 1759

D.D. has a great mind to make Mr Sandford his librarian and household chaplain; but he fears what is convenient to him to offer Mr Sandford is not worth his acceptance; and *if the little friend* [another patron] gives more, it cannot be desired that he should quit his present situation.   iii p557

Mary was obliged to cancel her visit to County Down to nurse Sally .

Delville, 16 July 1759

Our amiable god-daughter has been so extremely ill, that I sent on Friday night for Dr Quin, who is a very sensible, good physician, and an ingenious and agreeable man. Had an emetic in case it should be wanted; but he desired it might not be given till next morning, and when he came he would not venture to give it, but said she *must be blooded*; no marks appeared till Saturday night, and the doctor pronounced it the small pox with every favourable symptom. Mrs Hamilton of Finglass has offered (and I gladly accept) her assistance to nurse. She has had a great deal of experience, with her children and friends, and has *sense and spirit*, which will be useful to all, and a great relief to my mind, when I can't be in the way myself. Smith and William are gone to the north. D.D. follows, please God, to-morrow, and has been so good as to insist upon my staying and taking care of Sally; indeed, as she has no mother or sister to take care of her, I think it is a *duty incumbent on me.* Thus far yesterday: everything goes on as well as can be. The Dean set out at 5 this morning. I have sent *Smith and John to take care of him*, but it is *not easy to me.*   iii pp558–59

Delville, 18 July 1759

This is the eighth day. Mrs Hamilton lies in a little bed in the dressing-room next to

Sally, and will not suffer me to sit up beyond my usual hour. As she is very watchful, and never goes to bed when at home and alone before two o'clock, it makes me comply easily. The nursekeeper also is a very sober, good sort of woman, and used to tend in the small pox, but it is too critical a distemper to trust entirely to any nurse-keeper till after the turn. I gained some experience with the Lady Bentincks. As soon as Sally is quite safe I shall set about abundance of business, and am to have painters, whitewashers, and the addition to the library to be opened, and all the books new arranged; by that time I hope the Dean will have a librarian, which is much wanted, for he has a *very good* collection of books, but they are in great disorder. iii pp559–60

Delville, 20 January 1760

Mr Sandford seems inclined to undertake our young cousin [tutoring job], and has taken it into consideration, if Lady Grandison can be prevailed on to make the situation as desirable really as it appears to be; but if he is to be the slave of a silly woman and a teazing child, and not allowed a proper authority, it *would be insupportable* to one of his delicacy in mind and body, for his health is very indifferent. Master Villiers is between nine and ten years of age; not a dull boy, but humoured to the last degree. He will be Earl of Grandison after his grandfather's and mother's death, which is the reason he is called Villiers and not Mason.   iii pp581–82

Delville, 14 May 1760

I believe we shall lose our librarian. He has had a *sort of an invitation* from his *father*, which he ought not to neglect; but as his temper is so very variable, he may receive in a post or two a contradiction to it. I own I wish he was at home, and shall encourage his going, though his company has been extremely agreeable. Nothing could be more obliging or more useful than he has made himself to D.D.; he is now very busy making a catalogue of our books, and the library is in very good order, which was a great work and required skill to accomplish.   iii pp592–93

At last the long betrothed couple were free to marry.

Mary to her niece Mary Dewes
Delville, 6 October 1764

According to my promise I shall give my dearest niece an account of our wedding, which I am sure will be a satisfaction to all our kind friends, now assembled at Calwich. It has been currently reported for some time that Dr Sandford and Miss Chapone were privately married some months ago, a report which, if it reached the old gentleman's ears, might have been of bad consequence as it must then have been *before* his consent had been obtained; for which reason the Dean thought it best the marriage should *not* be in a very private way, and we prevailed on Mrs Sandford to admit some of her friends. The Dean of Down desired he might be her father and give her away. Mr Gustavus Hamilton performed the office [Mrs Henry Hamilton's eldest son]. Mrs Preston could not be here, Mr Preston was, and Mrs Gustavus Hamilton, Miss Hamilton, (Mrs Preston's sister,) and Mr T. Hamilton's sister were bridemaids,

Mr Sackville Hamilton and his brother (the lieutenant) bridemen. This was our company. All met here at eleven; the sun shone bright, and we proceeded in order through the garden to church; when we returned, breakfast was prepared in the drawing room, every countenance cheerful. The Dean gave Dr Sandford a pair of gold buttons in the morning before he went to church with these lines.

> I'm an emblem of marriage, of two I make one,
> Both useful together, both useless alone.
> Then may yours, like to mine, for ever remain
> A polished, a precious, and permanent chain!

When breakfast was over the company dispersed for a little while, some to different rooms, some to the garden, and breakfast things removed, all met again and music took place. I tried and recollected some of my old tunes to set the rest agoing, then the Mr Hamiltons brought fiddle and flute and played some very pretty sonatas together. Mrs G. Hamilton plays very agreeably on the harpsichord, but particularly excels in country dances and minuets, which she plays so distinctly, and in such firm good time that it supplied the place of an excellent fiddler. Dinner at four.

Here's my bill of fare:– turbot and soles, remove ham. Force meat, 2 partridges, 2 grouse. Pies. Rabbits and Onions, sweetbreads and crumbs.
Salmigundi. Soup. Boiled chicken. Collop veal and olives. Pease. Cream Pudding. Plumb crocant. Chine of mutton. Turkey in jelly. Hare. Lobster Fricassee. Desert – nine things, six of them fruit out of our own garden, and a plate of fine alpine strawberries.

These particulars may be impertinent, but it is doing as I would be done by; and between real friends no circumstance is ever trivial. Coffee and tea at seven, one cribbage table in a corner of the room which is pretty large, and three couple of dancers to Mrs Hamilton's playing. At half an hour after nine the prayer bell rang and we went to chapel, after that a salver with bridal cake ready in the parlour, the coaches at the door and the company went away at ten. We had a quiet supper by ourselves, a party quaree yesterday, and to-day so much company that I have hardly time to add everybody's compliments.   iv pp25–27

Mary continued to try and find a position for Dr Sandford through her friends and in the meantime, the growing Sandford family lived with the Delanys at Delville. Mary's godson, Thomas Sandford, the eldest child, had a beautiful quilt made for him which is preserved in the Ulster Museum collection.

Mary to Viscountess Andover
Delville, 3 June 1766

I have another great care upon my spirits, which is my dear Mrs Sandford, now at the end of her reckoning of a second child. Increasing cares to one of so delicate a constitution are hard to sustain, and notwithstanding Dr Sandford's great merit and

Part of the quilt, made by Mary Delany and presented to Thomas Sandford, on the day of his birth, 1765.

good recommendations, nothing hath yet been done for him. Political embarrassments turn the stream of preferments into another channel than that of rewarding merit or obliging particular friends – it is happy to be connected with those that are free from such engagements. I have been told that Lord Donegal has several considerable livings on his estate, and from his Lordship's and Lady Donegal's disposition, favour for those that are truly worthy and unfortunate might be obtained, if such a solicitor as dear Lady Andover would undertake the cause. I am afraid I am very presuming in making such a request, and beg if it will in the least embarrass you that it may drop here. I know the great regard and friendship you have for Lady Donegal may make it a tender point, but if it can be done without distressing you, I shall be obliged and made happy beyond expression.   iv pp60–61

Mary to her brother Bernard Granville
Delville, 3 July 1766

Last Tuesday morning Mrs Sandford was brought to bed of another fine boy, and though she had kept us in expectation for above a fortnight every day, at last was too quick for the necessary attendants. Thank God she is in a fair way at present; but she gave me no small hurry of the spirits. The same day I received a letter from the Duchess of Portland, with an account of Lady Weymouth's being brought to bed of *two* dead children [wife of a favourite cousin] which added a little to my flutter, and prevented my writing till to-day.   iv p64

Mary to Viscountess Andover
Delville, 15 July 1766

How excessive good your ladyship has been to recommend my petition to Lord Donegal in so kind a manner. I cannot, notwithstanding the cautious answer, give up the cause, and especially as you are so good as to say you will, when an opportunity offers, renew the conversation. I should imagine it impossible to resist what Lady Andover pleaded for, and indeed this is a very extraordinary case, and I think at the same time that it would do honour to the patronized it will to the patron. Much of my own happiness depends upon it, as *my influence* has drawn them into their present encumbered circumstances, making no doubt at the time that the old gentleman would have allowed them something till fortune did better for them.   iv pp67–68

Mary to her nephew Bernard Dewes
Delville, 16 October 1766

Mrs Sandford but so so; she misses you extremely, though her ill health did not permit her to have as much of your company as she wished to have enjoyed. Your friend Dr Sandford has had a long and severe fit of the asthma, and is still very bad, though he goes about, and is now gone with his wife and Tommy [eldest boy and Mrs Delany's godson] to take the air. Tommy as lovely as when you saw him, and every day increases that pleasure which you so justly observe "must attend the progressive improvement of his understanding"; he can, when he pleases walk the length of the drawing room, balancing his little arms like a rope-dancer. Danny [second son, afterwards Bishop of Edinburgh] grows very sprightly and loses everyday something of the golden hue he possessed when you were here, and is a very pretty little babe. iv p86

The next year (1767) Mary mentions "Dr Sandford at his living", so, at long last they were financially secure. When she left Ireland, Mary left all the packing up of Delville to the Sandfords and continued to keep up a correspondence with them. In her will she made specific bequests to them.

DONNELLAN FAMILY

The Donnellan family were responsible for inviting Mary to Ireland. Their relations and connections were part of her circle in England and Ireland. They were descended from an illustrious Irish family, ancient princes in Connaught. As with most old Irish families who managed to maintain their position, some branches conformed to the established church and others retained the faith of their fathers. The Ballydonelan sept still owned an ancient family castle at Loughrea in Galway in the eighteenth century. Mary's friends were a younger branch of this family who had early been prominent in the Church of Ireland and also owned property in the Galway area. They were friends of the dean of St Patrick's, Jonathan Swift. Mary's friend Anne, or Philomel, was the daughter of

Nehemiah Donnellan, baron of the court of exchequer, and her mother was Martha, daughter of Christopher Usher, from another wellknown Dublin family with famous ecclesiastical connections. When Judge Donnellan died in 1705, Lady Donnellan married another lawyer called Percival and they lived in London. The family included two brothers, Christopher (Kit) who was a clergyman and Nehemiah (Nemmy).

Anne's sister Katherine was married to Robert Clayton (1695–1758), a re-markable man. A wellknown freethinker and considerably wealthy in his own right, he early came under the influence of Dr Samuel Clarke, a cleric of unitarian persuasion who had influence on Queen Caroline. Through this he gained royal patronage and became Bishop of Killala and Achonry in 1730, moving to Cork in 1735, and succeeding Bishop Stearne, scholar and philanthropist, in Clogher in 1745. The Claytons were magnificent hosts and entertained sumptuously.

Mary knew all the Donnellan circle well in England, and she first saw Dublin society from the Clayton's house, a mansion on St Stephen's Green (no. 80) designed and built by Richard Cassels in 1730.

Dublin, 22 September 1731

I must do justice to the good people I am with, and give you a notion of our way of living, and the friendliness I meet with. The Bishop and his lady, [the Claytons] you know, are agreeable, but were never so much so as in their own house, which indeed is *magnifique*, and they have a heart answerable to their fortune. They received me with real joy, which does not seem to allay upon our being longer together. The first day we came we were denied to all but particular friends. Mrs Usher and her son and daughter came; you were much inquired after, and heartily wished for. Alas! did I not join in that wish? The next day we dined at Mrs Usher's and *supped*, an established rule in this place, and were very handsomely entertained. Sunday we went to church, and in the evening saw all company that came, which was numerous, for Mrs Clayton is extremely liked, and visited by everybody. Yesterday we were at the same sport, and this morning we are to go to the Duchess of Dorset's to pay our court.

So much for our company – now for our habitation! Stephen's Green is where this house stands; the chief front of it is like Devonshire House. The apartments are handsome and furnished with gold-coloured damask – virtues, and busts and pictures that the Bishop brought with him from Italy. A universal cheerfulness reigns in the house. They keep a very handsome table, six dishes of meat are constantly at dinner, and six plates at supper.   i pp288–89

Dublin, 21 October 1731

Yesterday, being Wednesday, Mrs Clayton opened her apartment and admitted all her acquaintance. I will describe to you how they are disposed and furnished. First there is a very good hall well filled with servants, then a room of eighteen foot square, wainscoted with oak, the panels all carved, and the doors and chimney finished with very fine high carving, the ceiling stucco, the window-curtains and chairs yellow Genoa damask, portraits and landscapes, very well done, round the room, marble tables between the windows, and looking glasses with gilt frames. The next room is twenty eight foot long and twenty-two broad, and is as finely adorned as damask, pictures and busts can make it, besides the floor being entirely covered with the finest Persian carpet that ever was seen. The bedchamber is large and handsome, all furnished with the same damask. There was an abundance of good and agreeable company; they went away about half an hour after ten, and so delighted with their reception that Mrs Clayton has promised to admit her friends every Wednesday. I preside at the commerce table.   i p305

In 1745 Robert Clayton became bishop of Clogher, a position Mary had hoped might go to her own Patrick Delany. The Claytons bought a large house near Lucan called St Woolstans at that time.

Delville, 15 October 1745

I have had a good deal of Mrs Clayton's company, she is in good spirits; their house is very magnificent, but *more for show* than *comfortable living*. I would not give my sweet Delville for it, no, nor for *any palace I ever yet saw*.   ii p394

Delville, 8 February 1745/6

To-morrow we are to have a houseful of our northern neighbours, and on Monday we

St Woolstan's, Co. Kildare, 1792, by Francis Wheatley (1747-1801).

dine at the Bishop of Clogher's. Mrs Clayton is to have a drum [party] in the evening
and we are invited to it. Their house is very proper for such an entertainment, and Mrs
Clayton very fit for the undertaking. She loves the show and homage of a rout
[fashionable assembly], has a very good address and is still as well inclined to all the
gaieties of life as she was at five-and-twenty; the Bishop loves to please and indulge
her, and is himself no way averse to the magnificence of life.   ii p422

Kit Donnellan died leaving a faulty will, which created family problems.

Delville, 26 January 1750/51

I had an account as soon as I was up of Dr Donnellan's death; he has been declining
for a year past, and about three months ago was so ill in the country that he was
thought in great danger; with much persuasion he was brought to town about six
weeks ago. I was asked to write to him as having some interest with him, which I did,
and he came to town soon after: he has grown worse every day, (his was a consump-
tive case) and last night, a quarter after 8, died. He was a very good man, and has
made a happy exchange, as his sickly life made him incapable of any earthly
enjoyment, but the poor will have reason to lament for him, and his death will be a sad
stroke to our poor Don. They had a warm friendship for each other, and very likely it
may hasten Mrs Percival's end, and that will be a sad addition to her distress. I wish
her sister may have the tenderness for her on this occasion she ought to have; for as
her affections will not be much touched, she will be more at liberty to offer consolation.   iii p10

Delville, 2 February 1750/51

Since my last letter to you, I have been much taken up with hearing different accounts
of Dr Donnellan's will; he left his sister A. Don fifteen hundred pounds, all his plate
and china. Two hundred pounds to each of our three hospitals in Dublin, and six
hundred pound to build a charity school at Inniscarra [Cork] (his living). The will
drawn up with his own hand, signed and dated; but as he has lately purchased a lease
of lives, which makes it *real* estate, from not being sufficiently witnessed *his fortune
goes to his brother*! If *he* has the honest and generous heart of my brother Dewes, he
will not take such an advantage, but he has not I fear; and I am much concerned, not
only that such good charities, and my friend Don should lose their right, but that it
may occasion a family dispute. I feel a good deal for poor Don, she had a particular
friendship for this brother, who was truly worthy of it, and her affections are very
warm.   iii pp11–12

*The Delanys enjoyed having Anne Donnellan's company in their home. She
was not called Philomel (Greek for nightingale) for nothing.*

Delville, 2 November 1751

I wish your house finished, as this is a bad time of year to be incumbered with
workmen. Monday, I went to Dublin, was two hours and a half choosing worsteds for
a friend in the north, who is working a *fright* of a carpet! Donnellan not well enough
to go out, spent the rest of the day in our comfortable home way. Every evening as

Miniature of Anne Donnellan by Rupert Barber, who lived beside the Delanys at Delville.

Wild rose, rosa canina, *by Mary Delany, 25 June 1777.*

soon as prayers are over we go to the harpsichord, and to my playing Donnellan hums over the oratorios; and though her voice has *not* the *force* it had, it is *very melodious*, and her taste and manner so different from anything I meet with here that it gives me great pleasure. Tuesday morning, Lady Blaney made us a visit. Wednesday, the birthday. I went with Mrs Clayton *at her request*, but *will not again* for reasons too long and impertinent to insert in a letter; dined at Lord Grandison's; finished at Mrs Hamilton's; home before nine.

Thursday, invitation to dine at Mrs Ormsby's (eldest daughter to Mr Donnellan); a family meeting, which when not cordial, are *the most disagreeable of all meetings*. Donnellan's heart was full, and her eyes ready to overflow all the day; they gave her an extravagant dinner, as Mr Donnellan did; and think to repay her for what they have withheld by this entertainment. Yesterday we spent a more agreeable day at Mr Hills, Mr and Mrs Curry [Corry], and Mr Leslie (all agreeable people) were all the party. The house is an extremely good and pleasant one; the dinner elegant and properly suited to the company – their plate in good taste, and very well attended. iii p50–51

Anne Donnellan brought her maid with her, Gran, whom Lady Llanover tells us wrote letters published under the title Martha of Calwich.

Delville, 16 November 1751

Gran is very comfortable with us here, and we won't part with her. She is called by the *Adversary* [Mrs Clayton] "*a Godi*", but they do her great wrong; she never makes *any improper advances*, and always dines and sups with Smith [the Delany's house-keeper]; and when we are alone we send to her to come to us *after* dinner and supper, which she does with great modesty, and I should *very willingly distinguish her more*, but Donnellan does not care I should.   iii p62–63

Delville, 14 December 1751

Don continues very well and very good, and makes my house very lively and entertaining; she is now gone to town, black-acreing [attending to business relating to property] to her lawyers. Where to fix for life? She is still at a loss. She is chagrined with her friends here, and afraid of the expensiveness of settling in London. iii p67

Robert Clayton was called the Cardinal by the Delanys, a reference to the magnificence of the Claytons' lifestyle.

Delville, 28 December 1751

Last Saturday Don and I dined at a Mr Croker's, a lawyer, married to a niece of the cardinal's; he manages Don's affairs, and I was clawed into the party out of civility, and could willingly have been excused. The Cardinal and his lady were there, and those meetings are *never right cordial*; however, the day past well enough: the worst part of the affair was that the Dean had so bad a cold he could not venture, and that was not quite easy to me, not being used to leave him when out of order. iii pp67–68

In 1751 Robert Clayton published an essay attacking the doctrine of the Trinity. Patrick Delany was not sympathetic to Robert Clayton's religious views, and they found the quarrel between the sisters Donnellan and Clayton upsetting.

Delville, 11 April 1752

I believe D.D. will answer the Bishop of Clogher's book on Spirit; he is highly offended with it, and so is every orthodox Christian. The Bishop of London said on hearing of it, "Why will that trifling *slight man* undertake such subjects!"   iii p111

Delville, 12 May 1752

Saturday morning Mrs C.[Clayton] and her flaunting niece came here very grave and reserved, asked her sister "when she went to England," who said "she could not tell". I lamented being obliged to leave her, by going into the north, upon which Mrs C. said to her sister: "*if I were you, I would go at the same time. What signifies your not having a house, can't you take a lodging?*" Such sisterhood! Oh how it makes me bless my happy lot! D.D. went to Dublin that morning, from thence to Finglass, and brought away Mrs H. and Forth to dinner; the day was charming, and we walked a great deal in the garden; after dinner came two coachfulls of company to drink tea, and by the time they were gone, I was as tired as if I had been threshing.
viii pp118–19

Dangan, 3 June 1752

I never knew a more provoking behaviour than Mrs C's has been, but I believe it has had one good effect, that it has made Don so indifferent, as to prevent her feeling any pain at parting; but how willingly would I feel the bitter pangs of parting rather than than dreadful indifference! As we came home, the Dean said, "Some sisters love *too much* and some *too little*".   iii p127

Mrs Delany was very sensitive about the Tenison lawsuit which at that time was not in their favour.

Delville, 30 December 1752

I have found my agreeable set of friends here most *particularly* kind to me, but *Mrs Clayton* has shewn *an indifference* that confirms my opinion of her having no real tenderness.   iii p190

Despite this lack of feeling, they were on calling terms.

Delville, 14 April 1753

Thursday morning Madame Clayton and her niece made us a visit, and we promised to dine there to-day. Have I really never told you that Miss Brown [the niece] is going to be married? and that after all her flirtations, coquetting, she is to have one of the prettiest sort of young men in Dublin – modest, sensible, sober, a clergyman with a living between seven and eight hundred a year, the Bishop of Derry's son and the Primate's nephew? Is it not strange he should fall desperately in love with one who is in *every respect his opposite?*   iii p221

Delville, 28 April 1753

Monday we spent at Mrs Hamilton's in Anne Street; in the evening came sailing in Mrs C.[Clayton] and her niece with all their colours flying, making full sail to a drum! Tuesday, dined at the Bishop of Derry's; met ditto company, who went to ditto in the evening. After she was gone Bushe and I staid an hour, and spent it more to our minds than when all the company were there. Can there be a more deplorable sight than to see a woman with brilliant parts, *qualified by nature* to make *not only* a rational but a *delightful companion*, so intoxicated by vanity and the love of pleasure as to sacrifice every valuable talent to it, and to be so far from being a desirable companion, that her levity sets her infinitely below the silly trifling girls she keeps company with. Youth and folly are excuses for an insignificant course of life; but sense and years to be so overtaken is indeed a severe reproach. Don't imagine, my dear sister, I am grown rigid and splenetic. I hope to avoid both, and will guard (as much as lies in my power) against them, and I am not for having women as they grow in years withdraw themselves entirely from the company of young people, but I would have them maintain such a dignity as shall make them respected, and have the *young* people *court their company*: much may be said on this copious subject, but I must proceed to my journal.   iii pp223–24

Bishop Clayton died in 1758 "of a nervous fever", possibly caused by a commission appointed to judge him for his heretical suggestion that the Athanasian and Nicene creeds be removed from the prayer book.

Delville, 24 March 1759

Whilst we were enjoying the fresh air Michael (my new footman) came running out of breath. "Madam, *Mrs Clayton* and Mrs Barnard the younger are come." We wished them at St Woolstans, as we were forced to give up our sweet prospect for a *very sour* aspect, for she was exceedingly cross, much offended at finding *Mrs F*.[Mrs Forth, one of Mrs Forth Hamilton's sisters], here, and said "*if they* did not *live with me* she should *never* see them." Why does she not then go to Finglass, or send her coach for them? they have no equipage, nor are they in the way of getting one; and there are no hackney coaches in the country. However, she made us diversion with recollecting, after she was gone, the many civil things she said to all the company; to be sure there must be an infinite deal of *verjuice* [sourness] in her composition!   iii p543

Delville, 31 March 1759

A propos, we dined last Thursday at Mrs C's., she was very lively. After dinner the discourse ran upon women living single: she said it was a foolish scheme, for *after forty* it was awkward because they *were insignificant*; and she spoke with great contempt of them. I was angry at the indignity, and said, but with great calmness, "*I wonder you should say so, for who makes better a figure, or lives more comfortably than your sister Donnellan, whose drawing-room is constantly filled with the best company,*

and whose conversation is much sought after?" It would have diverted you to have seen how blank she looked. "Oh! but," she added, "they grow jealous and suspicious." *"Not at all,"* said I, *"unless they were inclined to it when young."* How strange they should not love each other as we do? But they don't: that wicked fiend *Interest* blasts all felicity where he interposes, aided and abetted by another vile spirit, *Envy.*
iii pp544–45

Philomel Donnellan continued a close friend until Mary left Ireland, but Mary never became comfortable with Mrs Clayton who died in 1766.

THE DELVILLE CIRCLE

Mary's first visit to Dublin introduced her to a variety of congenial friends. Her great friend was Letitia Bushe, a talented artist, and a delightful companion. Mary had an immediate sympathy with her awkward plight. Smallpox was very widespread in the eighteenth century.

Dublin 25 November 1731

I eloped for an hour or two to make a visit to a young lady who is just recovered of the small-pox [Letty Bushe]. I think I never saw a prettier creature than she was before that malicious distemper seized her, a gay, good-humoured, innocent girl, without the least conceit of her beauty; her father has been dead about six months, a worthless man that has left a very uncertain fortune. She paints delightfully. All the men were dying whilst she was *in danger*, but, notwithstanding their admiration of her, not one of them will be generous enough to marry her while the lawsuit is pending; now indeed even their adoration will cease, they will not acknowledge her for a divinity since she is divested of those charms that occasioned their devotion.   i p316

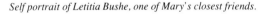

Self portrait of Letitia Bushe, one of Mary's closest friends.

Dublin, 9 December 1731

On Monday Miss Donellan and I went in the afternoon to Mrs Hamilton's [Elizabeth, daughter of Joshua Dawson, who was married to Henry Hamilton], Mrs Clayton staid at home with her love. We supped abroad and staid till near one, I never saw a couple I liked better; she says she never had the least wrangle with her husband in her life, for she always yields to him in great matters, and he never will dispute little things with her. If that state could be envied, I think it can only be when it is such as they make it. They are sensible, cheerful, well bred, and very friendly in their behaviour, have a small fortune, several children [who were to become popular visitors at Mary's home in later years], and live as comfortably as any people in Dublin.   i pp327–28

Dublin, 3 February 1731/32

Monday we spent at home; and in the evening had an assembly we spent at home; and in the evening had an assembly of our prettiest men – Mr Percival [cousin of the Donnellans], Mr Frank Hamilton (the clergyman) [later to marry Dorothea Forth], Mr Coot, Mr Will. Usher. We sang and talked, and were very good company. Tuesday were invited to eat oysters at Mr Pilkington's and went accordingly, every woman was to take a man. Mrs Clayton took Index; Mrs Don., Frank Hamilton; my man was to have been Mr Usher, but he basely deserted me; so by way of revenge, I seized on Phill's partner; secured him to myself the whole night and left her to take care of herself, which she knows how to do as well as any of them all, but nothing less serves her proud spirit than an *Archbishop* or a *general*! At present she *has the last* in her power, his fortune, quality, temper, unexceptionable, (this is no joke) while I must forsooth be contented with a poor curate!

  Miss Bush is abroad again and comes very often to us, she has lost her fine complexion, but her eyes have *not* received *any damage*, but are lively and sweet; she has many agreeable ways with her and would please you I am sure.   i pp335–36

One of the talented Forth sisters lived with Mrs Clayton for a time. They were from Red Wood in Offaly.

Dublin, 11 March 1733

Letty Bushe is a very good-humoured agreeable girl, with abundance of fancy; we never meet without giving the company a great deal of entertainment. I will tell you exactly how my acquaintance stand in my favour:

  I esteem Mrs Hamilton as a woman of excellent sense and conduct, and I would (were I under her circumstances of life) place her as *my pattern*, I like her company extremely; she is easy, unaffected, has read a good deal, and her memory serves her very well on all occasions. Miss Mary Forth (the young lady in the house with us) has a more exalted understanding and great quickness of parts, but I have often spoken of her, so I shall say no more, but that is almost impossible to know her and not have some degree of love for her. She has two sisters very different in their characters, the one older and the other younger than herself; the eldest, Miss Betty Forth, has more sense than comes to her share, but withall so fantastical, that 'tis not easy to describe her; she has a *great deal of wit*, but she must like her company prodigiously when she bestows any of it on them, unless she is angered, and then *nothing ever was so keen*. Miss Doll Forth, the youngest, does not want for understanding, though her sisters have the advantage of her on that side; she is good-humoured, and a good deal in the way of the world; her person rather pretty than otherwise, has a great deal of vivacity, and is very *ingenious* – 'tis she that paints *so well*. Kelly [much admired by Swift] comes here for ever, she has taken such a liking to Phill that she will *not live* without seeing her *once a-day*! She is very harmless, and not at all coquet; I thought her quite another creature before I was so well acquainted with her. She brings in all the wit that flies about, and now and then adds a little of her own. These are the women that we converse with most, and from the variety of characters can't fail of some diversion.   i pp340–41

Although Mary had doubted she would ever see such friends again, on her return to Ireland after marrying Dr Delany, many of her acquaintances from the first visit became the closest of friends and allies.

They included the Barbers, the children of Swift's protegee, the writer Mrs Barber: the Delanys' doctor as well as Rupert Barber, the enamellist, who was married to a niece of the Dean's and whose family lived literally at the bottom of the Delville garden. For a time there were the Greens, family of another Delany niece. There were also neighbours near Delville and friends from County Down who lived, according to the season, near Dublin like the Fordes and the Bayleys.

After her marriage her circle of friends in Dublin included the two Mrs Hamiltons. Her particular friend Elizabeth, the daughter of Joshua Dawson, member of parliament and man of property – he owned Sackville Street, now O'Connell Street – was married to Henry Hamilton and and their attractive children were often included in Delville parties. They included Gustavus, a clergyman, Sackville, afterwards secretary of state for Ireland, and Mary who married Mr Preston of Swainstown, became friends later on. Dorothy Forth had married the younger son of the 6th earl of Abercorn in 1733, the Reverend Francis Hamilton who lived in Dunleer, on the road to the deanery of Down. She was a talented painter and needlewoman and had two sons and a daughter. When she was widowed in 1746 she made her home in Finglas, near Glasnevin. The "ingenious" Letty Bushe who made a second home with the Delanys was another of the Alliance. This was the name for the happy combination of friends. They painted together, chatted and decorated together, walked and played together. Of them all, Letty Bushe became a particular favourite.

Delville, 28 June 1744

We did not come directly to Delville it being so late, but packed away bag and baggage and went to Mrs Forde's, who expected us to lie at her house: she is a very wellbred, friendly, agreeable woman, and I was perfectly easy with her and had a most comfortable bed.   ii pp305–306

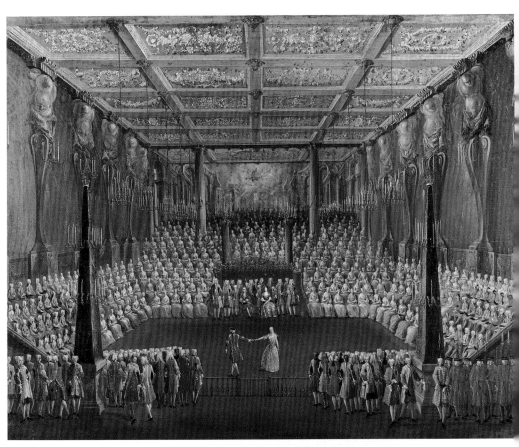

State ball at Dublin Castle, 4 November 1731 (see page 28); painted by William Van der Hagen.

Detail of court dress, embroidered by Mary Delany.

Delville, 19 July 1744

I am afraid this will prove an incomprehensible description; but if it does but whet your desire of seeing it, that is sufficient for me. Monday I invited all the Barber race, and our good old friend [Mary Barber the writer and friend of Swift], though she had the gout upon her and was forced to be lifted out upon men's shoulders, came, and was delighted with my new room, and seemed very happy to see me mistress of this charming place. She has a true sense of your worth, and we never meet but she talks incessantly of the "*lovely pearly Dewes*" [a pet name for the Dewes family]. Poor Mira (Barber) is a melancholy drooping young woman, and I wish a prospect of her being well settled; but I hear of none.   ii p316

Delville, 3 January 1744/5

The ingenious and agreeable Letty is still with me, thanks to the winds that have kept back her clothes, as soon as they arrive away she flies into the country sixty miles off to Lady Anne Magill, a sister of Lord Darnley's. She will be a great loss to me; she is one of the few who is perfectly qualified for an agreeable companion in a domestic way; her sweetness of temper makes her give into all one's ways as if she chose to do whatever is proposed; her other agreeable and engaging talents you have long been acquainted with; she paints for me in the morning and draws in the evening, which with reading, prating, walking, backgammon and puss in the corner employ the hours of the day and evening so fully that we do not feel how fast they fly. Our concerts are begun again and are to be continued every Tuesday.   ii pp333–34

As a clergyman's wife she was obliged to consider the calendar of the Church of Ireland which set out fast days as well as feast days. Over the years she made it a custom to celebrate around the twelfth day of Christmas, Epiphany, with the children of her close friends at Delville. To this informal dance, or hop, she invited one of her Monck cousins, nicknamed Bell, from Charleville, the Hamilton children and several of the Dean's nieces.

Delville 10 January, 1744/5

Our little hop which I promised Bell was appointed for Wednesday, but that proving the fast-day, it is to be this evening; the dancers are to be your humble servant and Mrs Hamilton's eldest son (very sober, well-behaved youth) his sister and Mr Ford; how the rest will be coupled I can't tell; but these are the rest of the hoppers – two Mr Swifts, young men of this village, Mr Parker, and a younger son of Mrs Hamilton's; Miss Delany, Mrs Barber (the Dean's niece), Miss Parker, Miss Green, we begin at five and end at nine, tea, coffee, and cold supper and beds for those that will accept of them.

Saturday: 12 January

The little rout [fashionable evening assembly] is over; we had four hours of smart, clever dancing; and broke off a quarter before nine; supped, and were all quiet in our nests by twelve, and the Dean seemed as well pleased with looking on as we were with our dancing.   ii pp335–36

Delville, 11 January 1745/6

Last twelfth-day I invited Mrs Hamilton's little family to choose King and Queen. The eldest daughter about nineteen, three boys, the eldest thirteen, and a little girl not yet five, a most delightful entertaining child. She was Queen, and entered into the part as well as Garrick could have done. I sent them home loaded with plum-cake, and in fine spirits.   ii p412

Some of their northern neighbours wintered in Dublin.

Delville, 1 February 1745/6

Last Monday we dined at Mrs Frank Hamilton's; the Bishop of Clogher's [the Claytons] people were there and Miss Forth; on Tuesday we dined at Dr Clarke's in the college, and met Mrs Forde's family; and on Wednesday we dine at Mr Bayley's, our neighbour at Holly Mount [Edward Bayley, Treasurer of Down].   ii p418

Elizabeth Vesey, daughter of William Brownlow and Elizabeth Hamilton, daughter of the 6th earl of Abercorn, was a great friend of the Delanys. She eventually earned a reputation for herself as a hostess of the Blue Stocking Circle: in the mid eighteenth century, this was a nickname for those holding parties for serious conversation, in London, not the slighting term as used later. She married Agmondisham Vesey, an Irish M.P., of Lucan House which they later replaced as a Palladian villa in the 1770s. At this date their innovations were confined to a cold bath, a house in the grounds with a cold plunge bath, with an ante room in which to entertain. Together the friends visited Luttrellstown, an ancient Norman castle of the Pale, still owned by members of the Luttrell family in the eighteenth century.

Delville, 7 July 1745

Last Sunday the Veseys engaged us to breakfast and dine with them at Lucan; Mrs F. Hamilton [her husband was a cousin of Mrs Vesey] of our party; her *wit and sprightliness* make her a good addition on such occasions. D.D. gave us prayers in the chapel, as soon as they were over we set out in open landau to Luttrell's town (2 miles from Lucan); the road by the river side, on the other had, high banks covered with trees; it is a fine place, and I think I have described it to you in some of my former letters. We dined very agreeably at the cold bath.   ii p567

The scientific evidence for vaccination against smallpox using cowpox was not published till the end of the eighteenth century although the technique of inoculating people with material from a mild case of smallpox in the hope of preventing the onset of the serious form of the disease was practised before this. It was a disagreeable and dangerous business at this very early date, but such were the fears of smallpox that Mrs Forth Hamilton was prepared to let her children undergo the trial.

Delville, 26 May 1747

We were invited to dine on Friday with the Fordes, and went, and in the evening I called upon the two Mrs Hamiltons and Miss Forth, and found all well. But Mrs Forth Hamilton is now under an anxiety I am sure you will feel for – her two children were inoculated last Friday morning. I hope they will do well, and that joy may restore her to a happy state she has not known for some time.

On Sunday went to church, had a table-full of old acquaintance, in the afternoon went to church again, and found ladies at home on my return.   ii p460

To celebrate her wedding anniversary, a party was planned in the Delany's new ninepin alley which she and the Dean built at Delville soon after arriving in Ireland.

Delville, 6 June 1747

I should have mentioned to you my pretty birthday present before but that I thought D.D. had told you what it was. [Her birthday was 12 May]. It was a pair of 3-drop amethyst earrings, set round with diamonds: I shall wear them on Tuesday next (the *9th of June*), with the pearl necklace; we have invited all our good friends, the Barbers and Mr and Mrs Greene, to make merry with us that day, and have got my pretty ninepin alley in order for their entertainment. I wish poor Dowager Barber [Mary, the poetess, friend of Swift] could make one amongst us; but alas! she scarcely ever rises out of her bed, though I think on the whole she looks and is better than when I left her last year. Mrs F. Hamilton's children are in a very fair way [after their inoculations]. Bushe is gone to spend the day with them, and we dine with Mr and Mr Lawe [of Leixlip].   ii pp462–63

Delville, 20 August 1748

I found all the Barbers well; and *Quadruple Alliance* – (Mrs F. Hamilton, Miss Forth, and Miss Anne Hamilton) dined and spent the day with me on Thursday and we drank tea in the new part of the study. Yesterday morning they breakfasted with me, with the agreeable addition of *my* Mrs Hamilton, and staid till near three. My orange-trees come on finely; there is but one that has failed, and four of them bore prodigiously. ii p499

Their home circle enlarged to include more connections and their life was at times very busy with their entertainment as well as their domestic chores. The dean also maintained his connection with Trinity. They visited their neighbours nearby: Carton, home of the Fitzgeralds, which had been recently rebuilt and enlarged by Richard Cassels. Emily Kildare, afterwards duchess of Leinster, had two sisters, Caroline who married Henry Fox, and Louisa who married Tom Conolly of Castletown.

Delville, 6 June 1750

Monday, Mrs F. Hamilton passed the day with me. Tuesday, we went (D.D.,B., and me) to Lucan to breakfast; D.D. went to Leixlip, two miles further, to see the Primate [George Stone], and Mrs Vesey carried Bushe and I to Carrtown [Carton] to see Lady Kildare and Lady C. Fox; nobody at home but the Dowager; dined with the Veseys.

Wednesday I travelled all over Dublin shopping, bespeaking paper for hangings, linen for beds, and a thousand things too tedious to be here inserted. Thursday, D.D. went to Dublin by 7 and attended the college examinations for fellowships; sent a *how de'e* to Mrs Fortescue (eldest daughter of Wesleys), just brought to bed of another son, and to Miss Wesley who is to be married as soon as her sister's month is up. Visited Mrs Smith of the north, Mrs Helsham, Mrs Burghs, Lady Meade and Lady Blessington, four of the five at home. This morning before nine came Mrs F. Ham., Mrs Forth, Miss Anne Hamilton, and the two young Hamiltons; we have breakfasted and walked all over the garden, and I have stole away to finish my letter with a promise (this being a *jubilee day*) of playing to them on the harpsicord as soon as I have done. Tomorrow, Dr Mathews and his family [neighbours from Down] and Mrs Marlay [wife of the Bishop of Dromore] dine here; Tuesday, Mr and Mrs Ellis and Mrs Agar; Wednesday, Capt. Forde and his lady; Thursday we dine three miles

View of Castletown House in the early 1800s by J.P. Neale.

off, at Mr Cavendish's and Lady Meade's with whom Mr Mount lives.
ii pp552–53

Here she visits the Veseys; their cold bath house was used on this occasion
for entertaining not for bathing.

Delville, 30 June 1750

On Monday Mrs F. Hamilton, Bushe, D.D. and I went to breakfast at Lucan, left this
at half an hour after 7, and called for Mrs H. at Usher's Key. Found breakfast
prepared for us in Mrs Vesey's dairy, and the table *strewed with roses*; just as we
were in the midst of our repast came in Lady Caroline Fox, Mr Fox, Mrs Sandford
and Master Fox – a fine rude boy, spoiled both by father and mother; Mr Fox is a
sensible, agreeable man, Lady C.F. humdrum. At 2, the supernumeraries went away;
we dined in the cold bath – I mean in its antichamber; it was as pleasant as a rainy day
could be when we wanted to roam about. The cold bath is as far from their house as
Mrs Whyte's is from you; the coach carried us, and brought us back to the house for
tea and coffee. They are pretty people to be with, no ceremony, everybody does what
they please.   ii p563

All her close friends were enlisted when special household reorganisation
was under way.

Delville, 22 September 1750

Last Sunday Dr Barber and his agreeable, gentle, wife dined here; I saw nobody else,
except one. (What a fib I was going to tell – I was at church, and *saw a full congre-*
gation) and in the afternoon Mr Parker and his sister came, and drank tea, and supped
with us. On Monday two Mrs Hamilton's, Bushe, Miss Hamilton, Mr Sackville
Hamilton, came to breakfast. As soon as that was done, I *set them all to work*; gave each
a dusting-cloth, brush, sponge and bowl of water, and set them to cleaning my
picture-frames. Bushe undertook cleaning the pictures, and egging them out, whilst
the *carpenters and I fixed up the shelves for* my books and china: everybody that
popped their head in, was *seized to work*; no idler was admitted: a very merry working morning it was, and my dressing-room is very spruce and handsome.

   I have pulled my old lustre [a light holder made of shells] to pieces, and am going
to make one just like the Duchess's. Tuesday we dined at Mrs Forde's, and found the
good old lady pretty well. Wednesday, dined at my Mrs Hamilton's, met by the other,
and L.B., and spent the day very agreeably. Miss Hamilton sung very prettily your
favorite songs of the Messiah, accompanied by her brother, Mr Sackville Hamilton,
on the violin: she has a sweet-toned voice and good ear, but wants a little management of it.   ii pp592–93

Mary to her brother Bernard Granville
Delville, 22 September 1750

I have been in such a hurry ever since I came home that I have not had leisure to
answer my dear brother's kind letter. I have been very well since my leaving the

North, though I have no reason to think the place disagreed with me, as I had not been well some time before I went, but I thank God it is all over. Mrs F. Hamilton has just finished a little piece of flowers and butterflies for Mrs H. Hamilton that is *really exquisite*; they are a pretty set of people that would please you extremely and are sincere sensible friends.   ii pp593–94

Delville, 28 September 1750

Mrs F. Hamilton, her son and daughter, walked from Dublin this morning, and we have been this hour past in the garden; she *never* will come into the house till the bell rings for prayers, for fear of *interrupting my affairs*. As soon as breakfast is over, to work we shall go.   ii pp597–98

Delville, 20 October 1750

Yesterday, to Lucan to *breakfast* with the Veseys; it was clear and pleasant, and the autumn scene rich and beautiful, and in no place it appears with more beauty than at Lucan – the banks of the river being covered with wood. We got home half an hour after 3.   ii p606

The Delanys felt quite happy to roam around the countryside without fear of attack.

Delville 10 December 1750

We had a pleasant jaunt on Saturday. Went to Lucan to breakfast, found Veseys up to the chin in business, hanging pictures and settling other decorations: all of us engaged in their business, staid to dinner, and till 7 in the evening, came home by a charming moonlight. A comfortable circumstance belonging to this country is, that the roads are *so good and free from robbers*, that we may drive safely any hour of the night. ii p626

Delville, February 1751/52

Mrs F. Hamilton is going to settle at Finglass, a village a mile beyond this: she has taken a house there in order to have her son go to a very good school that is in that town, as he has for some years had a private tutor at home and is far advanced in his learning, but she does not propose keeping him longer than three or four years there.

I hope he will answer her expectations and reward her great care of him, as *for his sake* she breaks up a pretty agreeable way she was settled in, a very good house and pleasant situation for a very confined place in a country town that he may board with her; he is a fine boy but requires management.   iii p16

As well as working together, Mary and her friends often attended fund raising events such as those arranged by Dr Bartholomew Mosse to raise money for the hospital he built – the Rotunda.

Cowslip, primula veris, *April 1775*.

Delville, February 1751/52

Bushe painted, and I finished the drawing of Calwich; my drawings have gone on slowly this year: I have had so much painting that I had not time for both. Went to Dr Moss's *gratis breakfast*, Mrs F. Hamilton with us (N.B., when I say "Mrs Hamilton goes with us on this party or that" you may conclude, without my making any distinction, that it is Mrs *F.H.* for my *other friend* ventures *not* to such places. iii p18

Mary often planned entertainment for her friends' children.

Delville 16 March 1750/51

Monday, the Veseys left us, and we were dull as cats and mute as fish.
iii pp27–28

Delvillle, 23 March 1750/51

On Monday, madam, I give a sumptuous ball! Seven couple of young things! Oh that my little *dew-drops* [her sister's children] were here to hop about with them! All the Hamilton young things, and some of their acquaintance to make the set up; the ball begins at eleven in the *morning* and to last till half an hour after two; then dinner, and if not tired an hour's dancing after dinner.   iii p29

Delville, 30 March 1751

I told you I was to have a tiny ball on Monday; my company came at eleven exactly, as appointed; the fiddlers here before them. They had all breakfasted and were eager to begin, which they did *immediately*. Seven couples, I never saw happier set of dancers. I had all ages, from twenty-one to eight years old, Miss Anne Hamilton, the eldest; and to keep her in countenance and *to gratify ourselves*, Mrs F. Ham. and I made a couple for *above half* their dances. At one o'clock they found prepared for them in my dressing-room green tea, and orange-tea, and cakes of all kinds. In half an hour they returned to their dancing till half an hour after two, and they rested till dinner. I had one table which held eleven, and another of eight. The two Mrs Hamiltons and Bushe were all the company besides the dancers. At five o'clock the fiddlers struck up again, and for two hours more they danced as briskly as if they had *not danced at all*. At 7 I *made them leave off* and gave them tea, and played to them on the harpsichord till they were cool enough to venture home.   iii p31

As well as her friends and their families, she also had her godchildren, all of whom she regarded with affection and interest. Some, as we have seen with Sally Chapone, were very special. The Wesleys with whom she had been friendly from her London society years remained on good terms and her godson Garrett Wesley, whose exploits in navigation are recorded in chapter 4 was often entertained and his career scrutinised. He became 2nd baron Mornington and later 1st earl of Mornington in 1760.

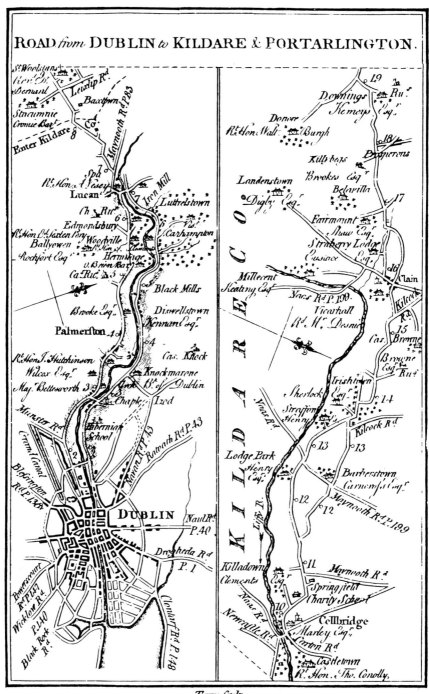

Map by Taylor and Skinner, 1778.

Delville, 15 February 1752

When I came down this morning who should I find in my dressing room but my godson Wesley. We have just breakfasted; I have given him my book of views to look over, and Donnellan is tuning her nightingale pipes.   iii p86

When the Tenison lawsuit took an unsatisfactory turn, Mrs Delany's spirits were quite dampened and her friends rallied round her.

Dublin, 11 August 1752

My kind and affectionate friends the Hamiltons, Bushe, and Forth, have shown all the kind concern and attention to me imaginable. I must not omit Mrs Vesey, who has shown me a particular regard; but for the rest of my acquaintance I keep from them as much as I can, as I have much business to think of and can at this time receive no pleasure but from discharging my duty to the best of my power: cheering one of the most worthy husbands in the world, and gratefully receiving the kindness of those friends who I know sincerely love me.   iii pp145–46

The Dean and his lady got comfort from the company of particular friends. They also got advice from the primate, who was George Stone (1708–64). He first came to Ireland as the chaplain of the duke of Dorset, and rose rapidly in importance. He was very powerful at this time, taking an active part in politics, to the extent of being considered virtual dictator of Ireland in 1753. He maintained that he had injured his constitution by sitting up late and rising early to do the business of government in Ireland. In 1752 he moved to Leixlip Castle (then owned by William Conolly), a Norman castle with eighteenth century additions, overlooking the river Liffey and close by Lucan, home of the Veseys.

Lucan, 26 August 1752

We came here on Tuesday to dinner. There is no house in Ireland I like so well to be in for any time except my own. Mr and Mrs Vesey are very friendly and perfectly easy, so we have no sort of restraint, but say and do just what we like; but I had no great inclination to come. I had begun to dead colour my picture, and am not much now entertained with company; but D.D. thought it would amuse me to come to this pleasant place, and as it happens I am glad we did. We are within half a mile of the Primate's. D.D. went yesterday morning to pay his duty to him, and he received him with much kindness, and gave him an opportunity of talking over his affairs to him, in such a manner that I hope it may be of some use to him.   iii pp151–52

Delville, 2 September 1752

We staid at Lucan from Tuesday till Saturday, the weather too bad to enjoy that fine place in perfection; but it is as agreeable within doors as without – perfect ease and freedom, and books and prints innumerable. I should have been glad to have seen

Honeysuckle, lonicera periclynemum *by Mary Delany.*

nobody except themselves, but that was impossible. Mrs Stone, the Primate's sister, and Lady Blaney and her daughters (all at present at the Primate's house at Leixlip, a mile and a half from Lucan) came to see me on Wednesday in the afternoon. In the morning D.D. went to see the Primate, who expressed great concern at the perplexity of his affairs, but hoped the worst was over.   iii p154

Delville, 26 September 1752

And to-morrow morning, please God, we set forward for Mount Panther; the weather is better, and I think the bustle of the journey will do us both good, and help to unbend our thoughts from the one thing at present of consequence to us as to worldly matters. This day the Dean spends with Mr Stannard, one of his council, and Miss Forde [Charity Forde, daughter of Matthew Forde, and Christian Graham, a cousin of Mrs Delany's, was a favourite young neighbour in County Down] is to come to me; we shall be very differently occupied: he deep in law-matters taking council – I deep in love-matters *giving council*! I wish I were as able a council as the person D.D. has to consult, for the point is as arduous in its way: she is a very pretty, sensible girl: her *heart* I believe *deeply engaged*, with the approbation of her friends, but there are rubs in the way which require some prudence to remove, and as you don't know the parties I can't explain to you without engaging is too long a story at this time.   iii p157

Mary's counselling of "Cherry" or Charity Forde's love affair seems to have helped the young couple arrive at a happy conclusion.

Delville, 15 December 1752

I have spent this week idly enough, Monday went to Dublin to see Mrs Hamilton and other friends returned to dinner. We are now reading Anne of Austria, by *Madame de Motteville*; she is entertaining and authentic, has a good heart, and though not very methodical is very intelligible in all her accounts. My young friend Miss Forde, who I told you was to be married to Mr Price, Mrs Conway's nephew, will be very soon married: wedding clothes are bought; – they are to be asked in the church – Lord Limerick's daughter was – and so it will now be *the fashion*, and *I think a very good one*: Miss Hamilton [Anne, eldest daughter of Mrs H. Hamilton] was married last Monday to Mr Jocelyn, the Lord Chancellor's son.   iii pp183–84

Letty Bushe was a constant visitor to Delville and her predicament illustrates the precarious position single gentlewomen endured, without family, fortune or trade to support them.

Delville, 30 December 1752

I have found my agreeable set of friends here most particularly kind to me. Bushe is still with me; she wishes she could board for two or three years at a farmer's in Welsbourn [near Anne Dewes], if any such there be that could undertake it; I say there *is not*, that I know of – is there? I believe she is not quite in earnest, but she *does love England* and wishes to settle there, at which her friends here are a little angry; and indeed I *think* her *wrong*, for her fortune is very small and must answer here better than it would there; and as she has been used to a pretty way of easy living amongst her friends (who are glad to have so agreeable a companion), she would not easily be reconciled to the narrow limits of boarding in any farmer's house. iii p190

Delville, 17 February 1753

I am happy to find the children are so fond and affectionate to one another; I hope the seed is sown in good ground, and will in time produce a fair crop of friendship. We spend our evenings much as you do, and send for our neighbour Barbers in the evening; Rupy [the enamellist] reads to us, and our niece helps me in any work I am in haste about. They have a little girl about ten years old, who though not a pretty child, being sadly marked with the small pox, is tractable and handy, and intelligent; she winds worsted and thread, and runs messages, and is much pleased to be employed, and Rupy is really a very sensible young man. Old Mrs B. [the poetess and protegee of Swift] is better; she always speaks of you with great regard and gratitude. She has given me two very fine gold medals of Queen Anne, one of them was Swift's legacy to her. After supper we play a pool at commerce; I think it prudent in a moderate degree to encourage in young people an inclination to any innocent amusement, and am happy when I find they have a turn for any art or science; the mind is active, and cannot always bend to deep study and business, and too often bad company and bad ways are the relaxations sought; to guard against that, nothing is so likely as any amusement that will not tire, and that requires application to bring to any perfection, and of course must prevent that idleness which *at best* makes them *very insignificant.*   iii pp206–207

Trinity College, Dublin from Brooking's map of Dublin, 1728.

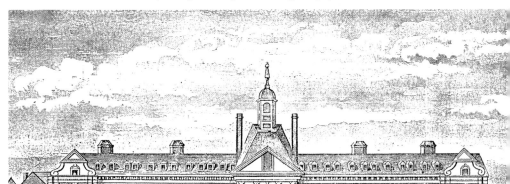

Delville, 14 April 1753

The Dean left me last Tuesday, and the bad weather makes his absence doubly mournful to me, but he would not consent to my going, and has promised to be back in three weeks. I had a letter from him last night from Newry, within 14 miles of Mount Panther. Thank God, he got safe so far! Poor old Mrs Barber has been extremely ill; not so much bodily pain, for she says she has none, but her mind much disturbed. Dr Barber has put on blisters on her legs, and she rested better last night, and is pretty well composed to-day.   iii pp220–21

Here Mrs Delany introduces us to Mrs Montgomery who was married to a fellow of Trinity, Dr Clements. The rules of the college enjoined all fellows to celibacy but by the mid eighteenth century breaches in the regulations were sometimes overlooked.

Delville, 28 April 1753

On Wednesday morning we made a visit to Finglass, tempted Mrs Hamilton to go with us to Dublin to pick up a good old cousin of hers, who wished to spend a day with us at Delville. Just as we were setting out (Mrs Forth not daring to be of our jumbling party, we left her behind) Mrs Montgomery came with an intention, I believe, of spending the day; she is a very agreeable woman, and her story remarkable – too long for a letter. Her friend Dr Clements was with her, and I prevailed on them to give us the meeting at Delville. They promised, and we pursued our first design, and carried off Mrs Hamilton, picked up Mrs Pen. Forde, and the day passed very pleasantly.   iii pp224–25

She explains the situation later to her sister.

Mount Panther, 28 August 1758

Mr Clements and Mrs Montgomery have been married privately many years, but they are *only called friends*, – her fortune *small, his nothing* (if he gave up his fellowships and other advantages that are considerable in the college); *the circumstances* they are under are well known to everybody, but as *they* are both very agreeable they are winked at.   iii p507

While the Dean was in the north, Mary kept good company with her friends.

Delville, 29 May 1753

Sunday I kept as usual, Bush came and spent the day with me; she would fain have staid with me in D.D.'s absence, but I have so many things to settle in my house, and lost some time by my cold, which confined me above a week, that every hour now is full of business, and so adieu for to-night. I see some trolloping interruption coming in the shape of a milliner, waddling up the portico walk where I am seated, and so good night. D.D. I thank God, is very well, and got safely to his journey's end again on Friday. He went 70 miles in two days, with a hired pair of horses to his chaise 40

William Connolly, M.P., of Castletown, Ireland's greatest Palladian house (Irish School, 18th century).

West prospect of Giant's Causeway by Susannah Drury, c. 1739.

miles of the way, the rest with his own pair. If we can bring our coach we will. My cook-maid is not worth transporting. D.D. leaves Mount Panther, if nothing unforseen prevents him, on Whitsun Monday.

Went to town at eleven, made morning visits, dined at the Bishop of Clogher's [the Claytons] – the wedding is to be in the country about three weeks hence [their niece was getting married]. In the afternoon walked to Archdeacon Pocock's [famous traveller and orientalist], to see some specimens of the Giants' Causeway; it is a wonderful natural curiosity, which we will talk over. To-morrow and Saturday I propose painting, to finish the picture I began some time ago for the Duchess of Portland, that it may be dry before I go. Impatience increases with approaching pleasure. I count minutes now, which is a foolish way if one could help it, as it makes the time appear so much longer.   iii p232

After this visit to England, she brought back her goddaughter Sally Chapone to live with them.

Delville, 18 June 1754

I am glad you did not come over with me; I never had so rough and so disagreeable a passage: thank God it was short, and we are all very well after it. I think D.D. much better than he has been yet, and the sweetness and business of his garden has cheered him extremely. Our god-daughter [Sally Chapone] is pretty well, still in a whirl and *an amaze*; she is writing to Kitty. I have introduced her already to most of my intimates, went yesterday morning to Mrs H. and Mrs Forth, of Finglass, dined at Mrs Forde's, drank tea at Mrs Hamilton's in Anne Street, and there met Mrs C.[Clayton], who has quite disgusted me with her indifference about her sister. The Dean has fixed his time for the north, to the 2nd of July, to come back in August. Nothing yet done in our affairs [lawsuits].   iii p278

Delville, 26 July 1754

On Tuesday Mr and Mrs [Cromwell] Price of Holly Mount [near Downpatrick] spent the day here. Dined yesterday at Mrs Forde's, and brought away L. Bushe, who came from Mrs Bushe's at Kilfane on purpose to see me.   iii p288

Her friend Letty Bushe died before 1759, perhaps in 1758. There are no letters describing the sad occasion. Although she lost some friends, the children of others were taken into the family circle, the Hamiltons in particular. Note Mrs Delany's reservations about unusual learning amongst young women.

Delville, 5 January 1759

To-morrow is post-day, but as I expect a rout of Hamiltons to breakfast, and choose king and queen (an *annual custom here ever since my possession*), I am sure I shall have little time for writing. Sally and Miss Hamilton are our readers. Dr Lawson's Treatise on Oratory is our present morning book; it is very clear and entertaining. Dr Lawson is one of the senior Fellows of the college, a very ingenious man and eminent preacher, but I fear he is no more; the last account was that the physicians had given him over. Have you read the new play, Cleone? It is very touching, and has many prettinesses in it, but a critic's eye perhaps may see great faults: tell me how you like it? if Dodsley is really the author, he is a very extraordinary man.

We separate after dinner till tea calls us together at half an hour after six, and then Homer's Iliad takes place; Miss Hamilton reads the notes and translates all the Greek words and passages as she goes along, with so much ease that the first day she read (till I looked over her and saw the Greek characters) I thought they *had been* all translated! The Dean now makes her read the Greek first, and so we have the pleasure of hearing that fine-sounding language, not without some mortification at not under-standing it; she is very bashful and modest with her learning, but in some points I believe it has been a disadvantage to her, and taken her off from an attention to little polishings of behaviour that are very becoming to all ages and should not be overlooked. Our present works as follows: I am working the cover of a stool, Mrs Hamilton is working a rose in the back of the chenille chair, she has already done a marygold and convolvulus. I send in the box *a cup that was dear Mrs Bushe's*, which I am sure you will value, *a few ordinary shells* that I picked up at the Giants' Cause-way and Magilligan strand, and the *prints of the Giants' Causeway* for Lady Anne Coventry, which I beg her acceptance of.   iii pp533–54

Garrett Wesley, 2nd lord Mornington, Mary Delany's godson, was very musical and founded a chamber ensemble which included many talented amateur musicians and which was known as the Musical Academy. She recounts the story of his rejection by Louisa, younger daughter of the Duke of Richmond, in favour of Tom Conolly, whom she married in 1758. Garrett then proposed to Miss Hill of Belvoir, near Belfast.

Delville, 27 January 1759

I have communicated to Sally the death of her uncle, R.B. The death of the Princess of Orange has put us all in mourning.

I am amazed you did not know that Lord Mornington had made his addresses to Lady Louisa Lennox, young Lady Kildare's sister, a pretty girl about sixteen. He was well received, and much encouraged by all the family, and no appearance of dislike in the young lady; but before an answer was positively given, Mr Conolly, with double his fortune, (and perhaps about half his merit), offered himself, and was accepted; the answer to Lord Mornington was, that "the young lady had an unsurmountable dislike to him."

However, his heart had no great part in the affair, he liked her, *and the alliance*. If any wound was made, Miss Hill *has cured* it by making a deeper one; settlements are drawing up and the clothes bought, and the whole family as happy as truly they have reason to be. She is eldest daughter to Mr Hill [Arthur Hill, later 1st viscount Dungannon] of Belvoir, at whose house we were in our way to the Giants' Causeway; she has six thousand pound, and the family estate settled on her in case her brother has no children; Lord Mornington settles £1400 a year jointure on her, with five hundred a year pin money; his estate is now eight thousand pounds a year, and it will be ten in two or three years more.   iii pp535–36

*Here she recounts an awkward social encounter at a performance of William
Congreve's tragedy The Mourning Bride.*

Delville, 3 February 1759

Mrs Delany, with ditto company, [Mrs Hamilton and her daughter, and Sally Chapone]
went to the Mourning Bride to see the new playhouse, and Mrs Fitzhenry performed
the part of Zara, which I think she does incomparably! The house is very handsome
and well lighted, and there I saw Lady Kildare and her two blooming sisters – Lady
Louisa Conolly (the bride) and Lady Sarah Lenox, who I think the prettiest of the
two. Lord Mornington was at the play, and looked *as solemn* as one should suppose
the young lady he is engaged to would have done! They are to be married next
Tuesday. When their great invitations are over they shall have a quiet one at Delville;
Lord Mornington has acted very generously on the occasion. When he made his
proposal, Mr Hill told him he did him and his daughter a great deal of honour, but that
he could not pretend to give his daughter a fortune any way suitable to his Lordship's
estate without injuring his other daughters: Lord Mornington said he did *not* desire *any
fortune*, but would settle £1600 a year jointure on Miss Hill, and five hundred a year
pin money; and if she had any fortune, desired it might be laid out in jewels for her. I
hope she will prove deserving of this pretty behaviour, and make him happy: he is a
very good young man on the whole; but where is the perfect creature?
iii pp538–39

Mary did not approve wholeheartedly of her godson's match.

Delville, 10 March 1759

Thursday, Lord and Lady Mornington dined with us, but I did not pretend to give
them a wedding entertainment; my dessert was all Smith's fancy, and *very pretty* and
much set off by some fine china, part of my dear Bushe's legacy. Lord Mornington
seems *very happy* as well as his Lady, a pair of good-humoured young things, but I
think her education not finished enough for her to make any considerable figure, nor
her judgment sufficient to get the better of some disadvantages he has had in his
education.   iii p540

Mrs Delany had an aristocratic and fine tuned sense of manners.

Delville, 14 April 1759

I believe Mrs Hill has been very careful in the common way of the education of her
daughters; they are in very good order, and civil. What I think L.M. may be wanting
in, is what very few people have attained at her age, who have not some real
superiority of understanding and a little experience of the manners of the world: nor
could she learn from her mother that politeness of behaviour and address, which is
not only *just but bright*. She is pretty, excessively good-natured, and happy in her
present situation; but I own I think my godson required a wife that knew more the
punctilios of *good breeding*, as he is *much wanting* in them *himself*, and those things

should not be wanting to men of rank and fortune: indeed, *I carry it farther* and I think that nobody can do so much good in the world who is *not* well bred as those that *are*! iii pp546–47

Delville, 17 March 1759

Miss Mary Hamilton is still with me; she is a sort of girl you would like extremely; she is very sensible, extremely lively and modest, with a great deal of Mary's drollery. I am sorry Lord Mornington did not fix here instead of where he has done – there is no comparison in the good sense and clever education of one to what the other has had; but these things are ordered all for the best, though they may not appear so to our short sight.

Sometimes there was sad news of her friends.

You have often heard me mention Mrs O'Hara, a blind lady, a very sensible agreeable woman, sister to Lord Tyrawley – had his wit, but not his wickedness, for she was a very religious, good woman; she had a servant, Mrs Outing, who had lived with her many years, and she always said she should not survive her. Mrs Outing died last Friday, and Mrs O'Hara on Monday morning, seemingly not in a worse state of health than she had been in for a year past, and the apothecary who attended them both died on Tuesday! a mournful tale this of mortality if we look no farther than this world! I shall miss Mrs O'Hara extremely; she was always at home and very partial to me, and I don't know anybody that was more constantly entertaining. iii pp540–41,542

Many of her friend's children were finding partners.

Delville, 24 March 1759

Last Monday Mr and Mrs [Edward] Bayly [neighbours in county Down], Miss B, and Miss Newcomb, a relation that lives with them, dined here, and they brought with them Mr Butler, son to Sir Richard Butler, a young gentleman of a very good character, well enough in his person, genteel and civil in his behaviour. He is to be married to Miss Bayly; Mr Bayly gives her 7000 pounds; Mr Butler has at present of his own a thousand pound a year, his father's estate reckoned three thousand a year. Lady Butler is very eager for the match, Sir Richard is somewhat of an old hunks, and demurs about settlements. I hope it will be a match, as the young people like one another. Thursday we walked in the garden and fed the robins, – several of them eat out of D.D.'s hand.   iii pp542–43

She followed the careers of her younger friends with interest. Sackville Hamilton afterwards became secretary of state for Ireland.

Delville, 20 April 1759

Easter Sunday, after the satisfaction of joining with a very full congregation in all the duties of the day, we had only family friends to dine with us. Mr Sackville Hamilton came, drank tea and supped with us, went away at eleven by a bright moon-light. He is by much the prettiest gentleman in Ireland, sensible and polite. He has got an employment in the custom-house, about £200 a year; the salary used to be but fourscore, but he has made himself so useful in the place he is in, that the salary has been augmented as a reward to his industry; no news yet from Mr Harry Hamilton now at Halifax, which occasions much anxiety in the family. On Monday Lord Shelburne and his sister, Lady Arabella, dined here, and were much pleased with everything (they are the pink of compliment), but especially with my *bow window* closet, and the day was favourable. Wednesday and Thursday, I painted.   iii p548

Here Mrs Delany describes their quieter social life at Delville. She is still an interested observer of court and church advancement.

Mary to her nephew, Court Dewes at Oxford
Delville, 7 December 1764

The season of the year confines us at home pretty much, and the badness of the weather cools the courage of our visitors, who would otherwise afford us more tittle tattle than we can now pick up. The Primate's [Archbishop Stone] unexpected recovery has caused very different emotions; among his intimates great joy, the contrary to those who were in expectation of succeeding him. I, *who feel* family attachments very powerfully, am glad he is well again, though as a Prelate and a Prime Minister, perhaps he *might have* done better, but that is *not certain.*
iv pp39–40

Her lively and constant interest in family and friends was to remain a vital thread in her later life.

CHAPTER 4

TRAVELS

Mary Pendarves, as she was still, first came to Ireland in 1731. Her purpose was distraction from an unhappy relationship with Lord Baltimore, a suitor who had overstepped the limits of discretion in his ardour, and whose intentions seem to have been far from honourable. The invitation to visit Ireland came from the Donnellan family amongst whom was her great friend, Anne, known as Philomel or Phil, often referred to as Mrs Donnellan or Don. There were several Donnellan brothers, including one who had an estate at Loughrea, near Nenagh, County Tipperary, and a sister, Katherine, who was married to the wealthy ecclesiastic, Robert Clayton. It was through this family that Mary made her debut in Ireland although she had her own connections. Through her aunt Stanley she was related to the Moncks of Charleville, and through her uncle Lansdowne she had cousins near Drogheda, the Grahams of Platten or Plattin.

In the eighteenth century travelling required a sense of adventure as well as purpose and single ladies had to travel in company. She consulted her family over her visit to Ireland even at her age (31 years). Mary appears to have enjoyed travelling and endured the hazards and discomforts of bad roads, bad weather, and uncertain itineraries with equanimity. She travelled for pleasure and her remarks about the countryside wherever she went do not betray an enquiring interest in the different localities. Her observations are confined to narrative descriptions of the estates and landscapes which impressed her.

The journey to Ireland required more stamina than most because of the distance and the boat journey which was always unpredictable because of the weather. While waiting for the boat she and her companions made an excursion to the Grosvenor estate.

Chester, 10 September 1731

Philomel [Anne Donnellan] whose conversation, you know is not inferior to her voice, exerts herself, and is an excellent traveller. Our spiritual guide takes abundance of care of us, and by way of variety we have a *pretty butterfly* man now and then – Mr Gore, son to Judge Gore, of Ireland and heir to a great estate. Mr Donellan, his sister and I breakfast together on coffee and parapyclites [a sort of biscuit]. At dinner-time our company meet and we pay a shilling a head for our meal and find our own wine; we are very well provided for; our supper we have by ourselves. We amuse ourselves with working, reading and walking and in the evening play a pool at picket [a card game].

We have secured places in the "Pretty Betty". The best cabin Mrs Donellan and I have taken to ourselves, and are to pay five guineas, but I believe it will be some days before we shall go away. Yesterday morning Mr Gore tempted us to go to Sir Richard

Grosvenor's; the day favoured us, and we were mightily pleased with the place; the gardens are laid out in the old-fashioned taste with cut work parterres and wilderness enclosed in hedges; the ground lies extremely well to the house, and every way there is a fine prospect. I have not seen an inland situation that I like so well. We were offered fruit and wine, though Sir Richard was not there. We might be entertained with assemblys and plays, but we do not think it worth our while to shine at Chester.
i pp286–87

TOUR OF THE WEST OF IRELAND

For the first months she stayed in Dublin, enjoying a lively social life and meeting friends and relations.

Then commenced a tour of the west of Ireland with the Claytons and others, including one of the Forth ladies with whom a warm friendship was to develop, and a couple of clergy visiting their western parishes. The Claytons were visiting their episcopal seat in Mayo. Like most travellers, they broke their journey with friends, among whom were the Wesleys of Dangan: this was the family into which the famous duke of Wellington was eventually born. Once in the west, they were given hospitality in all the big houses of the district.

Dangan, Meath, 27 May 1732

We left Dublin last Thursday at twelve o'clock, stopped at a place called the Pace, where we bated ourselves and our horses. Miss Kelly [object of Swift's admiration] and Letty [Letitia] Bushe [afterwards one of Mary's greatest friends] accompanied us so far on our journey in a chaise, Mr Usher, Nemmy Donellan and Mr Lloyd on horseback; those that we were to leave behind had most sorrowful faces. Phillis's love and mine (that is Miss Kelly and Letty Bushe) played their parts very handsomely, and I should have been very glad could they have proceeded on the journey with us, but that was not practicable, so part we must, and did; at five o'clock I went in a chaise with my Lord Bishop; the evening was very pleasant, and the road very good.

Mr Wesley took a walk to meet us two mile from his house; we got to our journey's end about eight o'clock, were received with a very hearty welcome; we shall not stay here longer than the latter end of next week. Our young men are not with us now, but are expected today. The house is very large, handsome, and convenient, the situation not very pleasant, the country being flat about it, and great want of trees. Mr Wesley is making great improvements of planting trees and making canals. You know the good people so well that belong to this place that there is no occasion for me to say how agreeable they make their house, and they never fail of obliging me enquiring after my dearest sister. The sweet little girls remember you and all your pretty ways. Miss Wesley does the honours of the house as well as if she was a woman. We live magnificently, and at the same time without ceremony. There is a charming large hall with an organ and harpsichord, where all the company meet when they have a mind to be together, and where music, dancing, shuttlecock, draughts, and prayers, take their turn. Our hours for eating are ten, three, and ten again.   i pp348–49

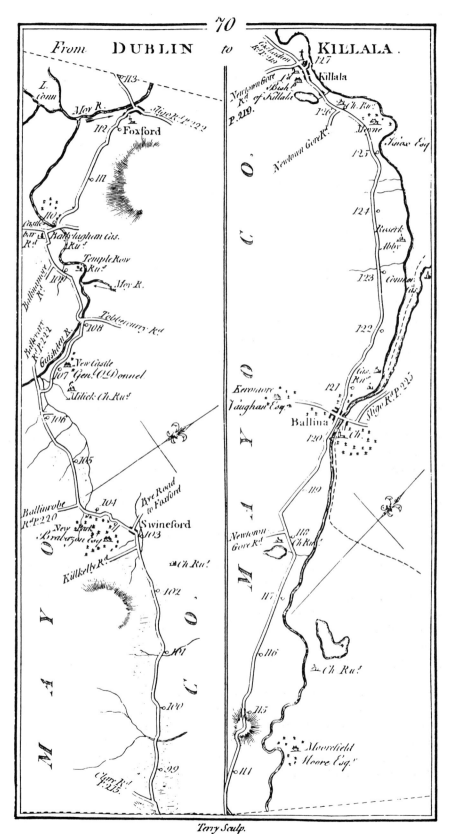

From DUBLIN to KILLALA.

Terry Sculp.

Map by Taylor and Skinner, 1778.

Not all the houses Mary visited were grand, and sometimes they were not within reach of friends with whom to stay. In this letter she makes one of her very few remarks about the ordinary people of Ireland, noticing the poverty of their general circumstances.

Newtown Gore, 12 June 1732

We went a-fishing to the most beautiful river that ever was seen, full of islands delightfully wooded. We landed on one of the islands belonging to the gentleman that carried us there – Mr Mahone [probably of Castlegar, Ahascragh, County Galway]. A cloth was immediately spread on the grass under the shade of the trees, and within view of the winding of the river, great variety of provisions was produced. We sat ourselves down and partook very plentifully and merrily of the good cheer before us; our sweet Phill supplied the place of nightingales, and the weather favoured us. I often sighed that you were not there to share so agreeable an entertainment, for I think I have not met with anything since my being in Ireland that I have liked so well.

We staid on the water till eight o'clock, then went to a cabin, which is such a thing as this thatched. It belongs to a gentleman of fifteen hundred pounds a year, who spends most part of his time and fortune in that place; the situation is pretty, being just by the river side, but the house is *worse* than I have represented. He keeps a man cook, and has given entertainment of twenty dishes of meat! The people of this country don't seem solicitous of having *good dwellings* or more furniture than is absolutely necessary – *hardly so much*, but they make it up in *eating and drinking*! I have not seen less than fourteen dishes of meat for dinner, and seven for supper, during my peregrination; and they not only treat us at their houses magnificently, but if we are to go to an inn, they constantly provide us with a basket crammed with good things; *no people can be more hospitable or obliging* and there is not only great abundance but great order and neatness. All this by way of digression. We went to the above-mentioned cabin, where we had tea, wine, bread and butter, and might have had a supper would we have accepted of it. At nine we mounted our chaises and returned to Mr Mahone's where we had spent Saturday, Sunday and Monday.

On Tuesday we proceeded on our journey; that night lay at Tuam [County Galway] where we had a very tolerable inn, where Mr Loyd met us; his living is near Killala and he is to be all the summer with us, which I am glad of, for he is a very good-humoured, well behaved man. From Tuam we went to Mr Bingham's, the name of the place Castlebar, where we staid Thursday and Friday. The house is a good old house, and Mr Bingham [ancestor to the earls of Lucan] is improving about it, so that in time it will be a very pretty place, there are very pretty shady lanes about it, at the end of them a wood; at some distance from the house there is a *lough*, which in our language is a lake.

The face of the country has very much improved since we left Mr Mahone's, bogs less frequent, and pretty woods and water have supplied their place – a good exchange you'll say. The country of Ireland has no fault but want of inhabitants to cultivate it; the mountains and noble *loughs*, of which there are abundance, make a fine variety, but they *cut down all their woods* instead of preserving them here. Mr Bingham and his lady are very agreeable people; he has been a great beau, and has seen a good deal of the world, is now turned perfect country gentleman, and affects bluntness and humour, which he manages so as to be very entertaining; Mrs Bingham is very civil, and a smart woman. We left them on Saturday morning, travelled that day over very high mountains – a pretty romantic road. The roads are much better in Ireland than England, mostly causeways, a little jumbling, but *very safe*. We arrived at this place on Saturday about nine o'clock; 'tis an old castle *patched up* and very irregular, but well fitted up, and good handsome rooms within [the sixteenth century tower house at Castle Gore had formerly belonged to the Bourkes]. The master of the house, Sir Arthur Gore, a jolly red-faced widower, has one daughter, a quiet thing that lives in the house with him; his dogs and horses are *as dear* to him as his children, his laugh is hearty, though his jests are coarse.

By the wall of this garden runs a river that ends in a lough [Lough Conn], we rowed all over it yesterday; 'tis bounded by vast mountains such as you never saw. As soon as I have finished this letter I must eat my breakfast, and then depart, for all things are ready. Phill hopes she shall find a letter from you at Killala; you may now direct your letters to me there; you need say no more than *for me "at Killala, in Ireland"*.

The poverty of the people as I have passed through the country has made *my heart ache*. I never saw greater appearance of *misery*; they live in great extremes, either *profusely* or *wretchedly*.　　i pp351–52

The party made excursions from the bishop's residence at Killala where they were staying.

Killala, 21 June 1732

Killala is a very pretty spot of ground; the house old, and indifferent enough, the sea so near us, that we can see it out of our window; the garden, which is laid out entirely for use, is pretty, – a great many shady walks and full-grown forest trees. The Bishop has added a field, and planted it in very good taste; there are abundance of green hills on one side of the garden, on the other a fine view of the Bay, and main ocean byond it, and several pleasant islands.

One day Miss Don, Miss Forth, Mr Crofton, Mr Lloyd, and your Penny [her own nickname], mounted their horses to take the air! We rode very pleasantly for a mile by a sweet river, were caught in a smart shower of rain, took shelter in a cabin as poor as that I described to you some time ago. The master of it, the *greatest bear* that ever walked erect on two legs, his wife little better and that man is absolutely worth two thousand pounds a year; "*muck is his darling*"; poor miserable wretch! but, however, he had hospitality to receive us as civilly as his sort of manners would allow, made a good fire, and his wife gave us tea; the sky cleared, we took our leave, and returned home wisely moralizing all the way and condemning the sordidness of the wretch we left behind us.

Last Sunday the Bishop gave us a very good sermon. Perhaps you think our cathedral a vulgar one, and that we have an organ and choir; no! we have no such popish doings – a good parish minister and *bawling* of psalms is our method of proceeding! The church is neat but you *would not dream* it was a cathedral!

Monday we made visits to some of the townspeople. Tuesday we had a very clever expedition, the Bishop and I in a chaise, Mrs Clayton, Phill, and Miss Forth on horseback, Mr Crofton, Mr Lloyd and another black coat [clergyman] made up the train. We went to a place about five miles off where the salmon fishery is [river Moy], the house put me in mind of Redgate,[on the Fowey river near Liskeard] in Cornwall,- the place Mama used to be so fond of. We saw the river drawn as we stood in the garden, and a whole net full caught of salmon and trout. It was very good sport, but what was best of all, those salmon were dressed for our dinner, and we regaled very plentifully; we might have eat *beef, pig, lamb*, or *goose*, but we stuck to fish and left the flesh for vulgar mouths. Phill and I changed places when we returned home; the evening favoured us; part of our way home was over a pleasant strand.

To-day we dined at one Mr Palmer's [Carrowmore House], a gentleman that lives a mile off, the only very agreeable neighbour we have; he is a very good sort of man, has a handsome fortune, his wife a civil, gentle, agreeable woman; they are very fond of one another, but both melancholy in their dispositions; they were married some time and had no children, at last she had one son, which is so great a darling and so much spoiled, that I believe she'll repent of her wishing so earnestly as she did for a son. He is a fine boy, has great vivacity (the more likely to prove her plague); we had a very fine dinner; she played once very well on the harpsichord, but has left it off, and I am in hopes she will lend us her harpsichord as she has no use for it herself; we have staid longer than we intended.   i pp354–56

The company stayed on still longer and whiled away their visit with expeditions and activities including shell gathering for the decoration of the grotto which gave great opportunity for Mary's creative talents. She does not seem to have taken much interest in the traditions of the local inhabitants.

Killala, 28 June 1732

Whilst I am writing this letter my ears are dinged with the Irish howl [the keening or Irish cry performed at funerals by parties of women, a traditional lament for the departed one] our window looks into the churchyard, and during the burial service there was such a *confusion of howls*, that 'tis enough to distract one.

The clouds interposed so much while we were at Dangan, that I could not pay my homage to the planetary world as I designed; but I forget myself, and I am talking like a mortal, though you must know that I am nothing less than Madam Venus, Mrs Clayton is Juno, Phill Minerva, Miss Forth the *Three Graces*, so named by Mr Wesley, who is Paris. Mr Lloyd Hermes, and Mr Crofton is the genius of the grotto that we are erecting. About half a mile from hence there is a very pretty green hill, one side of it covered with nut wood; on the summit of the hill there is a natural grotto, with seats in it that will hold four people. We go every morn at seven o'clock to that place to adorn it with shells – the Bishop has a large collection of very fine ones; Phill and I are the engineers, the men fetch and carry for us what we want, and think themselves highly honoured. I forgot to tell you that from the grotto we have an extensive view of the sea and several islands; and Killala is no small addition to the beauty of the prospect, for in the midst of it there is a pillar, not unlike a Roman obelisk, of great height. The town is surrounded by trees, and looks as if it was in the middle of a wood; this affair yields us great diversion, and I believe will make us very strong and healthy, if rising early, exercise and mirth have any virtue.   i pp360–61

Mary saw something of the grandeur of the western coast of Ireland and enjoyed an outdoor picnic that recalled ancient days of feasting.

Killala, 4 July 1732

Last Monday our family and Mr Palmer's met on a very agreeable expedition. We were in all twenty; we left home about eleven, and went four mile in coaches and chaises, then we all mounted our horses, and went to a place called Patrick Down [Downpatrick Head on the Mayo coastline], seven mile from Killala. The road is all the way by the sea-side, over vast cliffs, such as you have seen about Mr Basset's [nephew and heir to Mr Pendarves], in Cornwall. We had no prospect from the Downs where we stood, but the main ocean; about a mile from the cliffs, that are of an immense height, is a rock which formerly was joined, I believe, to the part where we stood, for it seemed to be the same height; grass grows upon it, and there is the remains of a wall; it is so perpendicular that no one could climb it. The day was just so windy as to make the waves roll most beautifully, and dash and foam about the rocks. I never saw anything finer of the kind; it raised a thousand great ideas; oh! how I wished for you there! it is impossible to describe the oddness of the place, the strange rocks and cavities where the sea had forced its way. For our feast there was prepared what here they call a "*swilled mouton*", that is, a sheep roasted whole in its skin, scorched like a hog. I never eat anything better; we sat on the grass, had rock for our table; and though there was great variety of good cheer, nothing was touched but the *mouton*. The day was very agreeable, and all the company in good humour.   i p365

Anne Donnellan.

Killala, 7 August 1732

I have been at an island inhabited by nothing but *bullocks, rabbits,* and *snails,* it is over against Killala [Bartragh Island]; we took a boat and away we went, the hottest day that ever was felt. When we came to the island every one took a way of his own, my amusement was running after butterflies and gathering weed nosegays, of which there are great plenty; Phil sat down on a bank by the seaside and sung to the fish, got up in haste when she thought it time to join her company, dropped her snuff-box in the sand, and did not recollect it till she was at home. The next day we were to dine at Mr Lloyd's sister's, who lives four or five miles off; we went by sea, passed the island; Phill said she'd go and look for her box, as odd an undertaking as "*seeking a needle*"; but she went and *found it.* So we proceeded merrily to the place appointed, walked a mile or two on a very pleasant strand, and gathered a fresh recruit of shells for our grotto; the whole day was very pleasant, and put me in mind of our jaunt to Rosteague; but the water was somewhat smoother. Mr Kit Donellan [held the living of Iniscarra in Cork] is come among us, and is a very good addition; he is a man of great worth, and must be valued by all that know him; his only fault is being too reserved, and not caring to preach – that last is unpardonable in him, because nobody does it better; his excuse is weakness of his lungs. I writ my mother word that we had company in the house with us; they stay till Wednesday, after that we shall have another supply; in short, we have almost as much company here as in Dublin, and that is *too much,* indeed we never are so well pleased as when we are by ourselves.

Tomorrow, madam, we are to have dainty doings; 'tis Killala fairday. There are to be the following games, viz two horse races, one race to be won by the *foremost* horse, another by the *last horse.* A prize for the best dancer, another for the best singer, a third for the neatest drest girl in the company. Tobacco to be grinned for by old women, a race run by men in sacks, and a prize for the best singing boy. Judge you if these will not afford us some good sport. I will let you know who are the visitors, and all the grand doings.   i pp368–69

Horseracing on the sands at Killala provided additional enjoyment.

Killala, 13 August 1732

This is Sunday morning. We had excellent sport at the fair; I gave you an account of the method that was to be observed, the games and the prizes. About eleven o'clock Mrs Clayton, well attended, in her coach drawn by six flouncing Flanders mares, went on the strand, three heats the first race. The second gave us much more sport; five horses put in, the last horse was to win, and every man rode his neighbour's horse without saddle, whip or spur. Such hollowing, kicking of legs, sprawling of arms, *could not* be seen *without laughing immoderately*; in the afternoon chairs were placed before the house, where we all took our places in great state, all attired in out best apparel, it being Mrs Clayton's birthday; then dancing, singing, grinning, accompanied with an excellent bagpipe,the whole concluded with a ball, bonfire, and illuminations; pray does *your Bishop* promote such entertainments at Gloster as ours does at Killala?   i p373

Despite all the magnificent scenery, Mary was not distracted from preoccupying thoughts.

Killala, 27 August 1732

Last Tuesday our family and the Palmers went to a place called Kilcummin, not very unlike Down Patrick, but nearer to us; the day was very fine, the sea in a great agitation; we had a magnificent entertainment, with a rock our table, and rocks for seats, where we had a full prospect of the sea in *all its glory*, and were shaded from the wind. We were exceedingly merry; no one of the company seemed to want anything to complete their pleasure, except myself. I fell into my usual reveries, which are now so well understood, that I am indulged in them. We returned home well satisfied with our entertainment.

Last Friday we were diverted in another way: it was Mr Lloyd's birthday, his father was bishop of this place, and Mr Lloyd was born in this house for which reasons it was thought proper to solemnize it. We all dressed ourselves out with all our gaiety and abundance of good tawdry fancy. After dinner a fiddler appeared, to dancing we went ding dong, in the midst of which I received your dear letter. Notice was given that a set of maskers desired admittance; so in they marched, three couple well adorned with leeks, and a He and She goat were led bridled and saddled with housings and pistols, and their horns tipped with leeks; the whole concluded with an entertainment of toasted cheese.　　　i pp378–79

More journeying began at the end of August and some of the accounts of visits come not from letters but from her sketch book and journal. She appears to have returned to Mayo after paying a visit to Dublin through the centre of Ireland.

En route from Dublin, [end of August] 1732

Dined at Lismullen [Tara, County Meath]; Mr Dillon's house made mighty neat; a vast deal of wood and wild gardens about it. Walked to see the ruins of the old Abby near them – a vast building enclosed with large trees, great subterraneous buildngs, with arches of cut stone, which make no other appearance above the earth than as little green hillock, like mole-hills. The arches seem to have been openings to little cells, rather than continued passages to any place; they are very low – whether it be that they are sunk into the ground, or always were so, I can't judge, but they are formed of very fine cut stone. The Abbey is in the prettiest spot about the house; 'tis surrounded with tall trees, and a little clear rivulet winds about it. The road from Lismullen to Naver [Navan] very pleasant; passed by Arsalah [Ardsallagh, County Meath] which lies upon the Boyn [Boyne]. The house seems a very antique edifice, it has fine gardens, but the trees and meadows that lie by the river are extremely beautiful; their domains reach all along the river, and half the way to Navan. Navan stands just where the Boyne and Blackwater meet, high over the river. I walked over the bridge by moonlight, along a walk of tall elms which leads to a ruined house they call the Black Castle, from a vulgar tradition of its being haunted; it lies over the Blackwater, has a vast number of trees about it, and seems to have been pretty. The "*spirit*" it was visited by was *extravagance*; it belonged to two young men, who in a few years ruined themselves, and let the seat go to destruction, and ever since they give out it is haunted, it is now another person's property, and going to be repaired.

The 25th, left Navan, and travelled through bad roads and a dull uninhabited country, till we came to Cabaragh, Mr Prat's house, an old castle modernized, and made very pretty; the master of it is a virtuoso, and discovers *whim* in all his improvements [she may have been referring to the delightful villa designed by Sir Edward Lovett Pearce which preceded the monumental nineteenth-century castle on an adjacent site]. The house stands on the side of a high hill; has some tall old trees about it; the gardens are small but neat; there are two little terrace walks, and down in a hollow is a little commodious lodge where Mr Prat lived whilst his house was repairing. But the thing that most pleased me, was a rivulet that tumbles down from rocks in a little glen, full of shrub-wood and trees; here a fine spring joins the river, of the sweetest water in the world.

The 26th, left Mr Prat's and travelled over the most mountainous country I ever was in; still as we had passed over one hill, another showed itself, Alps peeped over Alps, and "hills on hills" arose [the drumlin country of south Ulster]; the face of the country not pleasant till I came to Shercock, which is a handsome house, and stands over a fine lake, that has several woods and meadows on the sides of it. A vast deal of heath and ploughed land from that till I came within three miles of Coote Hill [County Cavan], then the scene changed most surprisingly, and the contrast is so strong that one imagines they are leaving a desert and coming into Paradise.

The town of Coote Hill is like a pretty English village, well situated and all the land about it cultivated and enclosed with cut hedges and tall trees in rows. From the town one drives nearly a mile on a fine gravelled road, a cut hedge on each side, and rows of old oak and ash trees to Mr Coote's house [Bellamont Forest, the exquisite Palladian villa built for Thomas Coote by Sir Edward Lovett Pearce]. Within two hundred yards of the house is a handsome gate-way, which is built in great taste, with a fine arch to drive through. This house lies on the top of a carpet hill, with large lakes on each side which extend four miles, and are surrounded by fine groves of well-grown forest trees. Below the house and between the lakes is a little copsewood which is cut into vistas and serpentine walks that have the softest sods imaginable, and here and there overgrown forest trees, in the midst of them there is jessamine, woodbine, and sweetbrier, that climb up the trees; and all sorts of flowers sprinkled in the woods; all these end in the view of a lake of four or five miles long. From the copse wood you go into a spacious moss-walk, by the lake side; on the other side towards a spacious kitchen-garden, there is a wood of scrub and timber trees mixed, of twelve hundred acres, with avenues cut for a coach to drive through, and up and down little openings into fine lawns, and views of the lake and town of Coote Hill. From this wood I rode and saw the demesnes in Mr Coote's hands, which are about thirty fields, finely enclosed with full hedge-rows, corn-meadows, pastures, and a deer-park, enclosed with a high stone wall well stocked with deer; it is a very convenient ground.   i pp374–77

The travels continued west towards Galway after returning to Killala and south to Nenagh, Tipperary where one of the Donnellans lived.

Nenagh, 27 October 1732

I writ to you from Mr Bingham's; we staid there Tuesday and Wednesday, and were very merry. Left that place on Thursday morning, and dined at another Mr Bingham's [at Newbrook, Claremorris] about eight miles from Castlebar, uncle of the Mr Bingham we left – a very good, agreeable sort of man, extremely beloved by all the gentlemen of the country; his wife – a plain, country lady, civil, hospitable and an immoderate lover of quadrille; their two eldest daughters are beauties – reserved, well-behaved, but not entertaining, so we passed that day *hum-drumish*.

The next morning we decamped, and travelled to Tuam [Galway]; nothing happened on the road remarkable, sometimes I rode, but generally went in the chaise with Phill, that being the way I like best. We got early into our inn, played at my lady's hole, supped and went early to bed.

The next day we arrived at Mrs Mahone's [Castlegar], staid there Sunday and Monday, were free and easy, lived as at Killala, everybody went their own way, we *danced and sung*, and were entertained in a very handsome friendly manner. We left them Tuesday morning; jogged on through bogs, and over plains, and about three miles from the place we were to rest, we passed a fine place called Aire's Court [Eyrecourt in Galway, a handsome seventeenth-century mansion, now alas, in ruins], a great many fine woods and improvements that looked very English.

We passed the finest river in Ireland – the Shannon, but it was so dark I saw but little of it; it parts Connaught and Munster. The town we lay at that night was Bannahir [Banagher], in the King's County [Offaly]. After very little rest in a bad inn, we rose at six and made the best of our way to the place where we are now lodged, which belongs to Mr Donellan. The country we passed through the last day was very pleasant; fine oak woods, great variety of hills, little winding rivers, and every pretty circumstance that can make prospect agreeable. I am summoned to breakfast, and after that we are to drive about Mr Donellan's grounds, to see his improvements. He is going to build, at present he is in a small house in the town, which is part of his estate. They have very fine children, are sensible and agreeable people, and live handsomely.　　　i pp385–86

At the time of Mary's visit some landowners were laying out or improving their demesnes. She and most of her friends were deeply interested in new ideas about managing the landscape.

Nenagh, 30 October 1732

Mr Donellan has only laid the plan of his improvements and raised fine nurseries for that purpose; he is going immediately to execute his designs, which when finished will be delightful. Nature has done everything for him he can desire – fine woods of oak, a sweet winding river, and charming lawns, that will afford him sufficient materials to exercise his genius on. He seems to have a very good taste, and if he could prevail on his countrymen to do as much by their estates as he intends doing, Ireland would soon be beautiful as England, and in some circumstances more so, for it is *better watered*.

We shall not go back to Mrs Wesley's [at Dangan, County Meath] till after we

George Berkeley, Bishop of Cloyne, the philosopher and enthusiastic garden improver.

have been at Dublin, which will be more convenient to us all, for our apparel wants to be recruited.

The weather has happily favoured us ever since our being here, by which means we have had an opportunity of seeing all Mr Donellan's estate, and knowing all his schemes. How much more laudable is his turn, than most country gentlemen's, who generally prefer a good *stable* and *kennell*, to the *best house* and *finest improvements* though the expense would be rather less.

We shall not go away till Monday; you must not expect to hear from [a piece missing here] the town of "Nenaghroon", that is, in English , *Sweet Nenagh*; at the bottom of the hill, which is covered with wood runs the river, by the side of which Mr Donellan can make a walk three miles long, of the finest turf that ever was seen. The river is so well disposed that he can make cascades, and do what he pleases with it; I almost envy him the pleasure his improvements will give him every hour. i pp386–87, 388

Fortunately, most of the country houses had large enough halls to provide space for activities apart from meals.

Dangan, Meath, 5 April 1733

All the company that I wrote you word were invited here are assembled; you are so well acquainted with their different characters that you may easily form to yourself how agreeably we live; liberty (*the great happiness of society*) reigns absolutely here – everyone does just as they please. We meet at breakfast about ten; chocolate, tea, coffee, toast and butter, and caudle [warm drink of gruel and wine or ale, sweetened and spiced] are devoured without mercy. The hall is so large that very often breakfast, battledore and shuttlecock, and the harpsichord go on at the *same time* without molesting one another. Mr Wesley (alias Paris) has provided everyone of us with a walking-staff whereon is fixed our Parnassus name. Mr Usher is *Vulcan*; young Nemmy Don, *Mars*; and Mr Kit Don (the Revd), is *Neptune*. Our staffs are white and when we take our walks, we make a most surprising appearance, somewhat like the sheriff's men at the assizes!

Yesterday we walked four miles before dinner, and danced two hours in the evening. We have very good music for that purpose; at nine we have prayers, and afterwards till supper is on the table the organ or harpsichord is engaged; Miss Wesleys are every day improving, they are engaging little creatures. Mr Wesley has three canals in his gardens; in one of them he has the model of the king's yacht, the Carolina. It was designed as a present for the Duke of Cumberland, but the person that had bespoke it died before it was quite finished, so Mr Wesley was lucky in meeting with it; 'tis worth fifty pounds – the prettiest thing I ever saw of the kind, and will hold two people, it has guns, colours with as much exactness as the original. In another of his canals he has a barge, which he calls the Pretty Betty, that will hold a dozen people: we are immediately going to try it; and in his third canal he has a yawl, named after Miss Fanny. In his garden there is a fir-grove, dedicated to Vesta, in the midst of which is her statue; at some distance from it is a mound covered with evergreens, on the which is placed a temple with the statue of Apollo. Neptune, Proserpine, Diana, all have due honours paid them, and Fame has been too good a friend to the master of all these improvements to be neglected; *her* Temple is near the house, at the end of a terrace, near which the Four Seasons take their stand, very well represented by Flora, Ceres, Bacchus and an old gentleman with a hood on his head, warming his hands over a fire. We shall stay here till this day se'night [week].
i pp405–406

Richard Wesley, born Colley, had inherited Dangan from a maternal cousin in 1728. He became the first Lord Mornington in 1746. The family adopted the Norman spelling of the name Wesley, which was Wellesley, after the death of the first earl of Mornington in 1781. There was a curious connection between these Wesleys and the Methodist Wesleys.

Mary had known John Wesley, founder of Methodism, and his brother Charles during her young days. These Wesleys were distant cousins of the Wesleys of Dangan, County Meath, and Charles was singled out as a possible heir. He, however, refused the chance to inherit an Irish estate and chose to follow his brother into holy orders. Thus Richard Colley inherited the Dangan estate and took the name Wesley. He became a close friend of Mary when she visited Ireland. His son, the first earl of Mornington, was her godson and was father to Arthur, 1st duke of Wellington. It is unlikely that there was much connection between the Methodist Wesleys in Ireland and their landed kin. John Wesley made twentyone preaching visits to Ireland between 1747 and 1789, but from the reminiscences of Mary Delany in old age we know there was no continuing contact between her and the fiery young preacher, because she disapproved of excessive religious fervour. Here she describes Richard Wesley of Dangan.

Dangan, Meath, 11 April 1733

The more I am acquainted with Mr Wesley, the higher my esteem rises for him. He has certainly more virtues and fewer faults than any man I know; he has a proper mixture of good and agreeable qualities, his wife, his children, his friends, his poor and rich neighbours, can testify the truth of what I say. He values his riches *only* as they are the means of making all about him happy; he has no ostentation, no taste merely for grandeur and magnificence. He improves his estate all the country round him as much as if he had a son to enjoy it (which there is no great probability of his having) [she was wrong!] and his estate goes from his daughters to a man that has always been his declared enemy.

Mrs Wesley has some very engaging qualities, she is generous and of a very easy temper, but I cannot say her merits are equal to her husband's. Their children are lovely creatures, their prettiness is the least part of their merit; Miss Wesley does everthing well that she undertakes; no child had ever more indulgencies, and yet she never does anything that can offend. She desired me to give her humble service to you and to assure you that she has "not forgot you, but loves you still" – these are her own words. All that I have writ here I believe I have said to you before, but when I name a man of so much worth as Mr Wesley, it is impossible not to give him part of that praise which he so well deserves. We shall stay here a week longer than we at first designed and I am glad of it, for we live very cheerfully. When the weather is fine we take the advantage of it, and walk, ride or go on the water; Mr Wesley has a very pretty boat on a fine canal that would *reconcile you* to the water, we carry our music on board, hoist our flag, and row away most harmoniously. The county town is called Trim.

We went one morning and breakfasted with a reverend clergyman who gave us very good coffee, and then we walked round the town, the chief part of which is a fine ruin of a castle that belonged to King John; his *butler, gentleman-usher*, and *standard-bearer* were the ancestors of the Duke of Ormond, Mr Usher and Mr Wesley. The situation of the castle is very fine, on a sloping green hill, with the river Boyne gliding at the foot of it; I never saw so pretty a ruin, nor so large a one. We have had some very good weather, and now the rain begins again. Two of our cavaliers have left us; Mr Usher, being high sheriff of Dublin this year, was obliged to go to town; and Mr Kit Don was called away by college business; they both said they would return to-day if possible; the wind and the rain will stop their design; but we can live without them. We dance, play little plays, and sometime cards and backgammon; Nemmy Donn, alias *Mars*, is my constant partner, and a very good one; Miss Fanny Wesley dances every night and *never is out*; she would surprise you.   i pp408–409

GENERAL JOURNEYINGS

After her marriage to Dean Delany in 1743 she returned to Ireland to live in
Delville, his home near Glasnevin, outside Dublin. When he was made dean of
Down in 1744, a pattern of visiting his northern parishes in the summer was
established. Besides these long expeditions, they enjoyed shorter trips round the
country. Whatever the length of journey, the paraphernalia of travel was much
more awkward than today and it was very expensive to maintain private transport
like horses and carriage as the Delanys did, and complicated to arrange for their
horses and carriage to be taken to England. There was also then the discomfort
and danger of a sea crossing.

Delville, 5 April 1746

We design bringing over with us a light four-wheeled chaise we have, besides
our coach, that when we have mind to make any little excursion, it may be ready.
ii p434

Delville, 6 June 1747

I am glad you have got the letter from Park Gate, with the verses; the race of
coachmen and postilions are a faithless generation; never more shall we bring coach
or horses over. They are a great expense, and the damage they receive by the voyage,
and the *great trouble* attending them at the *Custom house* is so teazing that I should
never wish to be so embarrassed again in a country where those conveniences *can be
had* for money.   ii p461

Many did not relish the prospect of travelling overseas.

Delville, 28 April 1753

Don't apprehend anything from the sea. It is a disagreeable element to deal with, but
it never hurts me any longer than whilst I am on board, and though I must confess,
and I fear you will find whenever you make me happy by coming here, that *a ship is
a most unpleasant thing*, yet the happiness it is to convey me to is a full amends for a
few hours distress, – and the passage is *seldom more* than *forty hours*, and often not
much more than half that time; so turn your thoughts as I will mine, from the
disagreeable part, and let us fix them on the joy of our meeting, which I trust in God
will be permitted soon after midsummer.   iii pp225–26

Delville, 15 June 1754

I bless God we are safe at home! We went on board the yacht yesterday at 6, sailed
half an hour after, and in thirteen hours after were at anchor in the Bay of Dublin – a
surprisingly quick passage, but a very rough. All on board excessively sick, and the
"*brown maid*" [Mary's goddaughter, Sally Chapone] more than anybody. D.D. pure
well, and now my giddy head will allow me to say no more.   iii p277

On some occasions the fear of the sea was justified.

Delville, 1758

Every passenger and all the cargo are said to be lost. Amongst them were Lord Drogheda and his third son, a clergyman; and a linen-draper of considerable repute in Dublin, a milliner who has left a necessitous family of six children, Mr Theophilus Cibber [actor], Mr Maddocks and Miss Wilkinson, the wire dancers, these are all I have heard named. It is impossible not to be shocked at such a calamity though a great consolation that none of one's particular acquaintance have suffered.   iii p527

At home in Ireland travel was more pleasant.

Delville, 20 June 1747

Yesterday we spent a very pleasant day in the country with Mr and Mrs Lawe at their bleach yard, 9 miles off, near the famous salmon leap of Leixlip. They have a pretty cabin there and gave us some fine trout caught out of their own brook just at their door, that were excellent and many other good things. I wished you there, it was so new a scene; and the men at work laying out the cloth on the grass full in our view was very pretty; the machine for rinsing the clothes is very curious. The happiness and good humour of the Master and Mistress and the industry going forward was an agreeable and rational entertainment. Mr Lawe drank your health and talks every time I see him of your civility and your charming children. As we returned home we called at Mr Conolly's house at Leixlip [before William Conolly, nephew to the speaker and heir to his fortune, moved to Castletown he lived at Leixlip Castle] and walked in his gardens; they are on the top of a hill that winds round the river Liffy, laid out into fine large grass walks well planted, and set with all sort of forest trees and flowering shrubs; openings here and there that show the river so far below you that it is almost horrible. A winding path and steps by degrees carry you down to a winding terrace by the river side above a mile long; every step there shows you some new wild beauty of wood, rocks and cascades.   ii pp469–70

JOURNEY TO CLOGHER

They visited Clogher to see the Claytons, because Robert Clayton had been translated from the see of Cork to Clogher in 1745.

Clogher, 2 August 1748

According to our design we set out from Clonfede [Clonfeckle] Dr Clarke's on Monday the 1st of August at eight o'clock; passed through very jumbling roads, narrow and winding but not dangerous; the country as we went along pleasant, but not so finely improved as what I have sent you an account of in my last letter. From Dr Clarke's to Callidon [Caledon in County Tyrone] where Lord Orrery lives, is ten miles, we sent our compliments but did not call on him, designing to have waited on him and his lady in our return; from thence to this place is 14 miles.

This house is large and makes a good *showish* figure; but great loss of room by ill-contrivance within doors. It is situated on the side of so steep a hill that part of the front next the street is under ground and from that to the garden you descend fifty stone steps which is intolerable and in hot weather such as we have had, a fatigue not to be endured. The garden is pretty; a fine large sloping green walk from the steps to a large bason [basin] of water, on which sail most gracefully four beautiful swans. Beyond the basin of water rises a very steep green hill covered with fir; in the side of it Mrs Clayton is going to make a grotto, the rest of the garden is irregularly planted; the Bishop is very busy, and I believe will make it very pretty.

The company in the house with them, besides ourselves, are – Miss Brown, Mr Burgh, a clergyman, a very agreeable gentleman-like man, Mr Brown, a nephew of the Bishop's and a Mr and Mrs Sandy, who always live here and take care of all their affairs in their absence. We came on Monday, dined, walked about, and chattered; on Tuesday, Mr and Mrs More and their two daughters dined here – they live about seven miles off; he is a great planter and improver, has a large estate, his house is bad, but the country about it and situation very fine.

Mary was able to study the local flora as well as sketch the local beauty spots.

On Wednesday, in the afternoon we went to Longford's Glinn [Glen], which is about two miles from hence. We went in the coach to the opening of the glen; it is a charming awful scene, but as you have the poem that describes it very exactly I shall not attempt a description of it: I have taken a sketch or two, but I am afraid I shall not be able to do justice to the original. I looked for mosses and herbs, but found no new sorts, part of the verdure is very fine. I gathered four sorts of fruit – raspberries, cranberries, strawberries, and nuts of which there are great plenty, the raspberries were particularly high-flavoured. I was resolved to send you *something* that grew in the glen, and have enclosed a piece of moss. The glen put me in mind of part of Matlock [Derbyshire], but more retired, and the water that runs through is a little bubbling brook instead of a river: the one looks as if frequented by human creatures, the other by nymphs and fawns. I returned home so thoroughly fatigued by scrambling amongst the rock and briars and by my great attention to every different view, that I could hardly hold out to supper.

I waked on Thursday well refreshed and in the evening it was proposed to eat a syllabub [drink of beer or wine topped with foaming fresh milk] about a mile off. For the frolic's sake, it being no coach road, we agreed to go, three ladies, on what is called here a truckle car (what they make use of for carrying goods), drawn by one horse and the wheels *not three foot high*; and one was prepared for that purpose, well-covered with straw, upon which with some difficulty we settled ourselves. As we were going through *the town* (which *entre nous* is not quite so considerable as *Welsbourn*), I found my legs, which hung over the side of the car, sliding nearer and nearer to the ground, and down I jumped; Mrs Clayton did the same, and behold our axle-tree was broken! The Dean and Miss Brown were in the chaise before us, and the Bishop on horseback. You may imagine this little adventure made some sport for us. No harm could happen to us, and we sneaked home on foot, not a little ashamed to be so exposed in the *midst of the city of Clogher*! The rest of the day past in laughing at one another, drinking tea and walking in the garden.

*Their stay in Clogher was broken by a visit to Lord Orrery who was planning
a new house and improvements to the grounds at Caledon. He was a friend of
Swift and an habitué of the Thursday evening dinners at Delville before Mary
married the dean. His second wife was Margaret, heiress of John Hamilton of
Caledon.*

Upon inquiry we found it would not be greatly out of our way to return back by my
Lord Orrery's so we chose to make him a visit and return back to this place, which we
did. We went on Friday, and got there by one. Lord Orrery is *more agreeable* than he
used to be; he has laid aside the ceremonious stiffness that was a great disadvantage
to him. He is very well-bred and entertaining; his lady (whose fortune is near 3000
pounds a year) is very plain in her person and manner, but to make amends for that
she is very sensible, unaffected, good-humoured and obliging. I spent the day very
pleasantly; it is a fine place by nature, and they are both fond of the country; *she*
delights in *farming* and he in *building and gardening* and he has very good taste.

They have a lodge about a mile from their house, where they spend most of their
time; it has all the advantages of water, wood and diversified grounds; and there the
new house is to be built. Nothing is completed yet but an *hermitage* which is about an
acre of ground, an island, planted with all the variety of trees, shrubs and flowers that
will grow in this country, abundance of little winding walks, differently embellished
with little seats and banks: in the midst is placed an hermit's cell, made of the roots of
trees, the floor is paved with pebbles, there is a couch made of matting and little
wooden stools, a table with a manuscript on it, a pair of spectacles, a leathern bottle:
and hung up in different parts, an hourglass, a weather glass and several mathematical
instruments, a shelf of books, another of wooden platters and bowls, another of
earthen ones, in short everything that you might imagine necessary for a recluse.
Four little gardens surround his house – an orchard, a flower-garden, a physick
garden and a kitchen garden with a kitchen to boil a teakettle or so: I never saw so
pretty *a whim* so *thoroughly well* executed.

We returned on Saturday, met the Bishop's family at Mr More's, halfway between
this and Callidon. Yesterday went to church twice – the Dean preached; walked in the
evening round Castle Hill, "*for royal Ergal's palace famed of old*": it is very high,
and a fine meadow around the sides of it, where we sat an hour on the haycocks,
refreshed by the fragrancy of the hay and the sweetness of the air, till the setting sun
warned us to bend our footsteps home. This is Mrs Clayton's birthday, and we are to
have a ball and monstrous fine doings; but I must prepare to do all the honour I can to
the day and am called away to dress. Tomorrow we go to Dr Madden's, fourteen
miles off in our way to Mr Preston's where we hope to be on Thursday next, and in
ten days after that at home: adieu.   ii pp489–92

Mrs Clayton's birthday brought great excitement.

Swainston [home of the Prestons], Meath, 13 August 1748

The celebration of Madam Clayton's birthday: there were eight couple of very clever
dancers, and Madame and I divided a man between us and made up the ninth couple
by turns; at eleven we went to supper – a sumptuous cold collation. At twelve the

fiddles struck up again, and every lad took his lass "*to trip it on the light fantastic toe*". D.D. and I took that opportunity of walking off to our own apartments, as we intended to set out early the next morning and soberly took our rest whilst the jovial company danced briskly away till past two o'clock: the Bishop always goes to bed at ten, but that night he sat up till eleven.

Here she describes the famous Samuel Madden (1686–1765), writer and philanthropist who held a living at Newtonbutler, near his family estate at Manor Waterhouse in Fermanagh. He was a friend of Swift and Dr Johnson, had helped found the Royal Dublin Society, and, through his generous contributions to students at Trinity, earned the nickname "Premium Madden".

The next morning we left Clogher at eight, where we had spent eight days very agreeably and went to Dr Madden's (fourteen miles from Clogher). *He is a very remarkable man*, and to give you a just portrait of him would take up more time than is allowed me at present. He has a very prating wife, who would pass for the grey mare, and *makes a boast of that* which a wise and reasonable woman *would not*. They have six daughters and five sons, all grown up men and women; fortunately for my head the *major part* were gone to a ball, for *they are* themselves a concert of *trumpets, French horns and bagpipes*. The place is pretty; a very fine wood of all sort of forest trees, planted by Doctor Madden just by the house, surrounded by a fine river. He has been a great planter and benefactor to his country on many accounts, and a great encourager of the premiums and charter-schools: we lay there one night. The country from Clogher to that place very pleasant; from thence to Virginia a very dreary country, but to make amends the finest roads I ever travelled. The next morning from Virginia we went to Kells; dreary enough still, where we dined. But we passed by a fine lake with several beautiful islands, twenty-five miles from Clogher. There my good Letitia [Bushe] met me in Mr Preston's coach, she looks well and sends you many kind wishes: we dined together at Kells, and came to this place by 7 in the afternoon. This place is the *quintessence of cleanliness and neatness*; but I cannot tell you more particulars at present but that I am well pleased to be here, and to be so near dear Delville where, please God, we shall go on Friday next.   ii pp494–95

Delville, 20 August 1748

I wrote you word of our progress as far as Mr Preston's of Swainstown, seventeen miles fom hence. Mr Preston's first wife was sister to my Mrs Hamilton; she left him three sons, now grown up pretty sensible young men, the eldest and youngest in the army, the second a clergyman just in orders – they were all at home. Mr Preston is an old prim beau, as affected as a fine lady: but a very honest man, obstinate in his opinions, but the pink of civility in his own house, which is as neat as a cabinet, and kept with an exactness which is really rather troublesome. The present Mrs Preston, who has been married to him about seven years, was daughter of the Bishop of Meath (Lumbard), is a most sensible, agreeable, conversable woman, plain in her person but in her manners genteel and friendly, an excellent good woman, and a great friend of Bushe's, whom I found there, and left in very good health. They are in a very pleasant

Swainstown House, Co. Meath.

neighbourhood and "live very elegantly" (*as Sally says*). Lord Mornington's (Dangan) is six miles from them, where I was to have gone last Wednesday, but a little disorder, occasioned by eating too many cherries, obliged me to come home.

Swainstown is in the county of Meath – a flat country and all corn, which though of benefit to those who have estates there, does not afford the traveller such *pleasant scenes* as lands better wooded and varied by hills and dales. The river Boyne runs through part of it and wherever it flows beauty attends its banks, which are indeed very fine. Mr Ludlow has a seat near it, and three miles from Mr Preston's called Ardsalla [Ardsallagh]. The house a good one, with some good pictures, the gardens fine, and laid out a great deal in the old taste, with high cut hedges and straight walks, but the part next the river is in a wilder way, planted with scattering trees, and pretty seats to take different views of the winding of the river. I was extremely delighted with one part of the garden which was designed by D.D. a place that was formerly a stone quarry, dug down so low that the rocks as you walk at the bottom are a considerable way above your head, and are so well crowned with trees of all kinds that they hover over you as you walk, and shade you entirely from the sun. Little plantations of trees and flowering shrubs in different forms adorn the walk as you pass winding along; nothing can be wilder or more romantic. I am afraid I do not give you a right idea of it.   ii pp497–499

Richard Wesley became the first baron Mornington in 1746. Even the weather could not cool Mary's enthusiasm for all his improvements to Dangan.

Delville, 15 August 1748

Last Monday we set out for Dangan, Lord Mornington's and were excessively pinched with the cold, for a colder day I never felt; but we were soon warmed by a kind welcome and good dinner. Lord Mornington is now the same good-humoured agreeable man he was seventeen years ago, when I made him my last visit, but his family much improved. You know Mrs Fortescue [eldest Wesley daughter whom both sisters, Mary and Anne, knew] – she was always a favourite of mine; her pretty husband was abroad which I was sorry for, as he would have been an agreeable addition to our society. Miss Wesley did the honours of the table, for her sister is confined to her chamber; she was so ill last year that they sent her to the Bath, she has not been returned above six weeks.

This is the first mention of the musical Garrett Wesley, afterwards second baron Mornington and then earl of Mornington.

My godson, Master Wesley, is a most extraordinary boy; he was thirteen last month, he is a very good scholar, and whatever study he undertakes he masters it most surprisingly. He began with the fiddle last year, he now plays everthing at sight; he understands fortification, building of ships and has more knowledge than I ever met with in one so young. He is a child among children, and as tractable and complying to his sisters, and all that should have any authority over him, as the little children can be to you.

The place is really magnificent: the old house that was burnt down is *rebuilding*. They live at present in the offices; the garden (or rather improvements, and parks, for it is too extensive to be called a garden) consists of six hundred Irish acres, which make between eight and nine hundred English. There is a gravel walk from the house to the great lake fifty-two feet broad, and six hundred yards long. The lake contains 26 acres, is of an irregular shape, with a fort built in all its forms; there are islands in the lake for wild fowl, and great quantities of them that embellish the water extremely. I never saw so pretty a thing.

There are several ships, one a complete man-of-war. My godson is governor of the fort, and lord high admiral; he hoisted all his colours for my reception, and was not a little mortified that I declined the compliment of being saluted from the fort and ship. The part of the lake that just fronts the house forms a very fine bason, and is surrounded by a natural terrace wooded, through which walks are cut, and variety of seats are placed, that you may rest and enjoy all the beauties of the place as they change to your eye. The ground as far as you can see every way is waving in hills and dales, and every remarkable point has either a tuft of trees, a statue, a seat, and obelisk, or a pillar. The weather was very stormy all the time we were there, but I took a small sketch or two, though I performed my operation like the witches – *in a whirlwind*: and I had so little opportunity of examining the whole disposition of the place, by reason of the bad weather, that I can give you but an imperfect notion of it.

How great a satisfaction is it to see so fine a place in the possession of a man so worthy of it! The maiden aunt, Mrs Sale, that has lived with her neices ever since their mother died is a quiet easy woman, who neither adds to nor checks any mirth. Mrs Fortescue [eldest Wesley daughter] has a beautiful boy about five years old, a jolly girl a year younger; she is very fond of them, but discreet in her management. We left them yesterday morning not without great solicitations that we would stay longer but D.D. was wanted at home by his workmen, and I don't care to stay long abroad; I found the little boy [Tommy Green, the dean's great nephew] very well at my return, and rejoiced at seeing me again.   ii pp500–503

VISIT TO WICKLOW

Other friends, further afield, had already established gardens. Mount Usher is still famous today for the beauty of its gardens and was where her friends the Ushers [Usshers] lived: Anne Donnellan's mother had been an Usher. The Moncks of Charleville were cousins through her uncle Stanley.

Delville, 22 April 1752

We propose making an excursion to Mount Usher, in the county of Wicklow, about twenty miles off, for a few days where I shall see groves of myrtle as common as nut-trees: *Powerscourt* and *Charleville* (Mr Monk's villa) is in that neighbourhood; I believe my brother knows both the place and person we are going to – Mr Kit Usher. iii p112

Mount Usher, 21 May 1752

Now you must follow me into the county of Wicklow. Mr Usher sent a chaise and a saddle horse for Mrs Donellan, her maid and Gran. D.D. and I travelled in our own chaise and the day being fair Don. rode part of the way. We set out from Delville about 8; passed through Dublin and a most pleasant country, till we come to Bray, (in the *neighbourhood* of which town *Bushe was born and bred*, the place called Cork). We did not stop till we came to Loghling's Town, eight miles from Delville, a very good inn, pleasantly situated; there we alighted to look about us, and bespeak our dinner for next Saturday. From thence we went to Kilcool [Kilcoole, on the coast], where we dined; I can't say much of the pleasantness of the country to that place, only a very fine view of the sea and good road; from Kilcool the scenes are more enlivened and extremely pretty – enclosures, fine meadows, shady lanes, one side skirted by mountains and hills of various shapes, diversified with cultured fields, bushes and rocks and some wood; on the other side a beautiful prospect of the sea, and the roads like gravel walks, the hedges enriched with golden furze and silver May. This country is particularly famous for arbutus (the strawberry tree) and myrtles, which grow in common ground and as flourishing as in Cornwall. Myrtles are so plentiful that the dishes are garnished with it, and next Xtmas the gentlemen in this neighbourhood are agreed to adorn Wicklow church with myrtle, bay and arbutus, instead of ivy and holly. I tell them it is well I am *not* to be *one* of their congregation – I should be tempted to commit sacrilege! The arbutus bears fruit and flowers (like the orange tree) at the same time, and is in its full glory about Xtmas; the berries are as large as the duke cherry and of a more glowing scarlet, the surface rough like a strawberry; I believe you have never seen it in perfection, which makes me so particular in my description of it. I can show you a draught [sketch] of one in perfection done by Mrs Forth Hamilton.

We arrived at our journey's end between five and six, called 24 miles, would measure 36 English. By the name I suppose you think this an exalted situation; *toute au contraire* it is as low as Bradley and hid with trees and hills. The house is a very good one, old fashioned, convenient and comfortable, the hall *very large*, in which is a billiard table and harpsichord, and a large desk filled with books; within it a large parlour where we dine; and within that a drawing room, but the spacious hall and the

Powerscourt Waterfall, Co. Wicklow, by Mary Delany, 1765.

amusements belonging to it make us give it the preference to all other rooms: the bedchambers are proportionally good to the rest of the house, and excellent easy beds; everything though plain perfectly clean, like the Master and Mistress of the place, who were bred up in Dublin and used to a great deal of company; but a large family – four daughters and three sons, (now men and women) and prudential reasons made them retire and settle down in this place about sixteen years ago, where they have lived a quiet philosophic life and brought up their children extremely well. The eldest daughter is married to a *worthy clergyman*, the second lives with her: they are now gone to the south of France for Mr Edgeworth's health and this morning Mrs Usher shewed me a letter from Mrs Edgeworth, written in a very fine hand and a very sensible, agreeable account of the place they are in; the eldest son is bred up a squire at home (their estate is but a moderate one) he is a modest dull sort of youth. The eldest of the two daughters at home seems to be *the housewife* of the family, the youngest plays very well on the harpsicord, and sings surprizingly, though she has hardly ever been taught; they are both very modest well-behaved young women, neither pert nor awkwardly bashful. Our entertainment is suited to the rest – excellent and good things, *well drest* in a *plain neat way*. And now, having given you an account of the country, the people and manners, I must give you rest till the weather permits me to say something of the environs. The chaise is ordered to carry us this morning to the Murrah, a strand two miles off, and whilst it is preparing I must thank you for your charming letter, ending the 14th of May.

The chaises came and we went to the Murrah. The weather was hazy and rainy which eclipsed greatly the beauty of the prospects. The Murrah is seven miles long by the seaside: I think it may more properly be called a terrace than a strand, as it is not even with the sea, but raised by a gentle slope, the turf as fine as any well-mown garden walk, between that and the sea, when the tide is out, is a strand covered with pebbles some of which are very beautiful, like the Scotch pebbles.

As we drove up the Murrah we had a view of the town of Wicklow, which lies close to the sea, and spreads on the side of the hill; a point of land makes a bay, and there is always some sort of shipping which enlivens the prospect. On the right there is a great variety of agreeable views of fields, gentlemen's houses, gentle hills, and towering mountains. One very remarkable circumstance belonging to the Murrah I forgot to mention which is that it is situated between the sea and the lake; the part we went over was about three miles, the lake continued all that way and runs into the sea at Wicklow Town. To make you comprehend it better than you can by this awkward description I send you a little scratch not worthy to be called a sketch.

We got home a little before dinner; the rain was so violent I could not gather any pebbles: so on Friday morning I got up at six, took one of the young ladies who drove me in a one-horse chair, her brother was our squire, and to the Murrah we went again. The day was clear, and I gathered several pretty pebbles and got home again by breakfast: as soon as breakfast was over we all set out except Mrs Donellan and Mrs Usher, in chaises and on horseback and went to the Devil's Glen, called two miles off, but will measure four.

The Glen is somewhat like Longford's and has all the horror but not the beauty. We went to the top and looked down into it; we could not go in our chaises above a mile, the rest of the way we walked and went on truckle-cars, part of the way was too steep and rugged for any carriage.

When we had satisfied our curiosity and looked till our heads grew giddy, we returned; but before we got home went to a place called Cronerow Rock belonging to Mr Eccles, a gentleman who lives in Glassnevin: the rock grows like a great wart on the top of a very great ascent, the whole hill is feathered with a fine young oak wood, and the rock is so mixed with woods in some parts that you can only see it through the trees. We climbed very nearly to the top of it with some difficulty and fear of stumbling among the loose pieces fallen from the rock; but I could have spent a whole day in picking up the fragments, some glittering like diamonds, others like fine marble – I never saw so beautiful a rock. I wish I had an enchanting wand and could by a stroke place it just beyond my brother Granville's fine cascade. There are several natural caves in it, and the wood, which continues from the utmost top of the rock quite down to the valley, by so good a taste as his might be made the finest thing I ever saw; but by this robbery could I effect it, I should indeed do great injury to one of the prettiest countries I ever saw in my life. When you are on the summit of the hill I have described, the prospect is charming and terminates with the Murrah and the sea beyond it. I have seen nothing in Ireland so beautiful but it is more owing to nature than art.

From this letter it is evident that Mary and her friends were in direct contact with some of the foremost landscape gardeners of the day, notably Charles Hamilton who designed an ornamental park at Painshill, Surrey and Philip Southcote who devised the ferme ornée *on his estate at Wooburn Lodge, Chertsey, Surrey which the Delanys emulated at Delville.*

I saw several places worth taking notice of, but if I did I should send you a book instead of a letter, so I return to good Mrs Usher's house, where after a very good dinner we went to Mr *Tighe's*, Rosanna [Rossannagh] by name whose garden is divided from Mr Usher's by a very pretty clear river: he came in his boat to *waft us over*! It is a very pretty place and house, neatly kept, and capable of great improvement, which he is setting about with all speed. He went to England for six weeks, saw PainsHill, Mr Charles Hamilton's and Wobourn Lodge, Mr Southcote's and now says his own place is hideous and will pull it to pieces! His ground lies finely, his trees very flourishing; a river bounds his garden, and the fields and country about him lie very advantageously to his view.

We left Mount Usher on Saturday morning stopped at Loghling's Town where we had bespoke our dinner and whilst it was getting ready walked about. Mr Danville has an estate and seat just by the inn, the house old and ruinous and ingeniously situated to avoid one of the sweetest prospects I ever saw. There is a natural terrace on the side of the hill where the house stands, of about a mile at least; the part I saw of it is a gradual descent from that to the highway, but at such a distance as not to incommode you either with noise or dust; part of the bank is quite green, and smooth like a slope in a garden, the rest covered with shrubby wood or fir-trees. Across the valley where the road runs, is a river over which is a bridge and a bank divided into fields with little cabins; hedges and trees rise on the other side, overtopped with mountains, whose deep purple made the verdure of the nearer prospects appear to great advantage. Mrs Don. who had never been at this place to consider it before, says if she can bring Mr Danville to any terms (he always lives in England) she will *build a nest* for herself *there*. iii pp120–126

Not all the places she visited secured her approval. Back in Kildare she sees the house which had been built by William Conolly which, under the improving hand of his great nephew's wife, Louisa, would become the most beautiful house in Ireland, Castletown.

Lucan, 28 June 1754

I have formerly given you an account of most of the places I have mentioned, except St Catherine's, which is downright ugly, enclosed in high walls and terraces, supported by walls one above another, as formal as a bad taste could make it, and yet it is capable of being one of the finest places I ever saw; from the house to a chapel there was a fine gothic gallery with bow windows which the present owner *pulled down* and has put up a palisade in the stead of it. 'Tis provoking to see such beauties *thrown away upon Vandals*.

From St Catherine's we went to Castleton [Castletown], and saw a huge house, now *empty and forlorn*, that used to be crowded with guests of all sorts when last I saw it [it remained empty till Tom Conolly, William's great nephew married Lady Louisa Lennox in 1758]. Selbridge [Celbridge] is greatly improved; but as it is only *nature* humoured and adorned, it is not so easily described as a place composed by rule and art. On our return home we called at St Woolston's another place on the banks of the river Liffey, purchased by the Bishop of Clogher [Robert Clayton], and a fine bold situation. The only improvement yet made is a sea-horse (*a very ugly monster*) who watches a cascade; and a river-god who pretends to preside over a gushing brook, but in reality has retired to a ditch for a different purpose. iii pp281–82

EXCURSIONS ROUND THE NORTH

On their periodic visits to the deanery of Down, the Delanys made similar expeditions. Here she describes a visit to Hillsborough, County Down.

Belvoir, Belfast, 1 October 1758

We left Mount Panther on Tuesday, the 26th, at nine o'clock; a train of two chaises and two cars with us, Mr Bayly and Mr Mathews, one of D.D.'s curates, on horseback and our sumpter-car [for luggage]. From Mount Panther to Ballanehinch [Ballynahinch] (7 miles) is the rudest country I ever saw – rough hills, mountains, and bogs, but some of them covered with furze and blossom, heath, and thyme.

We got to Hillsborough about half an hour after one, which is fifteen miles from Mount Panther, and the scene was then much mended with the view of a very fine cultivated country, little inferior to some parts of Gloucestershire. The house is not extraordinary, but prettily fitted up and furnished; the dining room, not long added to the house, is a fine room, 33 feet by 26 feet. Lord Hillsborough is very well bred, sensible, and entertaining and nothing could be more polite than he was to all his company [Wills Hill, 1st marquess of Downshire]. Sally and I being the only women, we had the principal share of his address; he is handsome and genteel, and his manner (with somewhat more of reserve) not unlike Mr Berkelely.

We were twelve in company; among the number *three deans* and three other clergymen; we sat down to dinner at half an hour after three; Lord Hillsborough was very merry and said a great many lively comical things. He is there only for a short time, and *incog* [incognito], consequently not well prepared for company, but everything was clever for all that. After the ladies had given their toasts they were desired to "*command the house*"; the hint was taken and they said they would upon that liberty "go and prepare the tea-table for the gentlemen". Sally and I took a little step out into the garden to look at the prospect, but the weather soon drove us back. Candles lighted, tea-table and gentlemen came together, I made the tea. Cribbage was proposed and I consented to be of the party, thinking it would be some relief to Lord Hillsborough; at ten we went to supper, at eleven to bed; met at nine the next morning at breakfast. The day cleared up; Lord Hillsborough, Mr Bayly, and I walked round the improvements, a gravel path two Irish miles long, the ground laid out in very good taste, some wood, some nurseries: shrubs and flowers diversify the scene; a pretty piece of water with an island in it, and all the views pleasant. D.D. and Sally saved themselves, as the ground was damp, for another walk, which was to a castle that Lord Hillsborough is building.

In time of war in Ireland he is obliged to keep a garrison there and has a demand on the Crown of three shillings and sixpence a day; the old castle is fallen to decay, but as it is a testimony of the antiquity of his family, he is determined to keep it up [the star shaped Hillsborough Fort in the park built 1650]. The castle consists of one very large room, with small ones in the turrets; the court behind it measures just an English acre, and is laid down in a bowling-green, and round it is a raised high terrace, at each corner of which is a square of about fifty feet, which are to make four gardens, one for roses only, the other for all sorts of flowers – these on each side the castle; the other two for evergreens and flowering shrubs. The walls are built with battlements, and the measure of what they contain (the bowling-green and terrace) is just an Irish acre. When this is finished he proceeds to the building his house, which is to be magnificent, and in a finer situation than the one he at present inhabits, and about a mile from it: the castle will stand between them. And what do you think this *magnificent man* means to do with his present dwelling, improvements, lake and island? nothing less than making them a present to the Bishopric of Down! This is what *he declares*, and if he lives to accomplish his good scheme he *will certainly do it* [it remained a good intention]. At present there is no house belonging to the bishopric. Harry Russel [formerly gardener at North End, Fulham, home of Mary's uncle Stanley] lives with him and is a great favourite; he comes once a year for a month or two, to set forward his works at Hillsborough, and I was glad to see him. But I find I have forgot to mention the entrance to the castle, which is to be a court of a suitable dimension, with square towers and spaces between laid out for a menagerie or rather for foreign birds. iii pp511–13

EXPEDITION TO THE GIANT'S CAUSEWAY

On the way to the Giant's Causeway she visited Belvoir near Belfast. She was staying with Arthur Hill, later Viscount Dungannon, whose daughter married her godson, Garret Wesley, Lord Mornington in 1759. The fine parklands remain.

Belvoir, 1 October 1758

At one o'clock we took our leave [from Hillsborough] with a promise of calling there on our return; Mr Bayly went home, and we came to this place about three o'clock and this is indeed a charming place; a very good house, though not quite finished, and everthing very elegant. Mr Hill is a sort of *an old beau*, who has lived much in the world; his fortune a very good one. He is an original, and entertains Sally and me excessively. A *fine gentleman* is the character he aims at, but in reality he is a very honest, hospitable, friendly, good man, with a *little pepper* in his composition, but puts me often in mind of Mr Achard; but he has the advantage of seeing his own peevishness, and making a joke of it himself. Nothing can be more obliging than his behaviour to us, as well as Mrs Hill's, who is a well-behaved, good-humoured woman; her eldest daughter, about sixteen – a fine woman altogether; rather a little clumsy, but fine complexion, teeth and nails, with a great deal of modesty and good-humour [her godson's eventual spouse?]. Two other daughters: the youngest of which is very plain indeed, about ten years old; the other not pretty, but lively and natural, and very civil. They are all the morning employed in their exercises; the afternoons they spend with us. They have a pretty civilized gentlewoman, who is their governess – I think such a one as you would like; but she is on the footing of a companion, which is a troublesome thing. I say nothing of the eldest son – he is a mere Cymon.

This place is much more finished than Hillsborough, and in a finer country, and much enriched with bleach yards, farmhouses and pretty dwellings. On Friday we went in a boat on the river [Lagan] which runs round the improvements almost, and several turnings of it can be seen from the house. The grounds are laid out in enclosures, which with the hedge rows and woods on the sides of some of the hills make the prospect very rich. The town of Belfast, Cave-Hill and the bridge of 22 arches over the river, in a very clear day can be seen from the windows.

But I must come back to Friday and the river, the banks of which are delightful and I had the curiosity and courage to go *through a lock!* though I was assured there was no danger in it, for Mr Hill and all their family go almost every day for pleasure. The Dean preached today at Mr Hill's church [Knockbreda]; we have now above three-

The Long Bridge, Belfast, by Mary Delany, 1755. This drawing is one of the earliest known views of Belfast.

score miles to the Giant's Causeway, but the weather promises well for us, and we have had so many invitations from the Dean's old friends that we might have a baiting place every ten miles. From hence we go on Tuesday next to a Doctor Leslie's which will be a long day's journey; but Mr Hill lends us his horses for twelve miles, and ours are to be sent there the night before. From Dr Leslie's we go to a son of his, and in the way dine at a Mr Bristowe's. From Mr Leslie's we go to Mr Boyd's at Ballycastle where the coal-works are, and from thence to a gentleman's house, whose name I have forgot, who lives within half a mile of the Causeway. This is our present scheme, and has led me to sheet the third. I think our progress puts me in mind of a nursery tale – *and we went, and we went, as far as our legs could carry us.* iii pp514–16

The carefully planned visit to the Giant's Causeway was so exciting that Mary put pen to paper immediately she returned, despite the lateness of the hour. There, the extraordinary shaped masses of cooled volcanic stone rising out of the sea and towering over the sea was a sight that had both inspired travellers and attracted scientific attention from the late seventeenth century on. The Delanys stayed with Archibald Stewart and his sister who lived at Ballylough House, close by the Causeway.

Bally Logh, 5 October 1758

It is too dark, I can hardly see. I know my dearest sister will want to know how we get out of the Giant's claws, and I must tell her we are just returned from seeing the most wonderful sight that, perhaps, is to be seen in the world, but have not time for description, only to tell you we are well after four hours' walking, wondering and puddling – no accident.   iii p516

During their tour they visited friends they had met in Dublin.

Hazlebrook, 8 October 1758

As I was saying, we left Mr Hill's on Tuesday morning, the 3rd instant; sent our own horses to Antrim (the county town) the night before. Breakfasted at Antrim, got to dinner at Dr Leslie's, at Galgorm, thirty miles from Belvoir; nothing at Antrim worth giving any account of, an ugly old town: Lady Massareen lives there in a *very old house*, the garden reckoned a fine one forty years ago – high hedges and long narrow walks. The country about the town very *pleasant*, and some miles from Belfast, by the sea-side between Antrim and Galgorm, we pass by the famous lake, called in this country Loch Neagh, much celebrated by Dr Barton for its quality of petrifying. It is twenty-six miles long and twelve over; on the edge of it stands Shanes Castle, belonging to the ancient family of the O'Neils; we did not stop to see it, as they said there was nothing extraordinary but its situation which we saw as we passed by. I can't say much for the country from thence; it is dreary enough, though every here and there a farm house in a tuft of trees mended the prospect, and the quantity of corn shewed it to be not quite a desolate country.

Galgorm, the house Dr Leslie lives in, is old and in the castle style, with battle-ments round the court, large dark rooms more venerable than pleasant [built in the late seventeenth century by Dr Colville who is reputed to have sold his soul to the devil]. Dr Leslie is an old man above seventy, sensible, goodnatured, and an inoffensive joker; his wife an excellent woman, with a remarkable good understanding, of a good family and who has seen much of the world. But, alas, poor woman, sentence is pronounced against her, that she has a confirmed cancer in her breast, but she dined and supped with us and was amazingly cheerful. An accident of wine and water going the wrong way started us all extremely and we thought for some moments the good old lady was dying; the tender attention of Dr Leslie to her charmed Sally extremely. They had a married daughter in the house ready to lie-in who did not appear, two unmarried that did, plain, modest, obliging women; we had much (*too much* I might add) of food.

Next morning we set out, and breakfasted where we now are, at Mr Bristowe's, a clergyman, a pupil of D.D's. His wife a niece of the Grattans, whom you have heard the Dean often mention; he is a merry good sort of hearty man, and she a very goodhumoured prattling woman, much reserved the first day, but now very easy and seemingly well pleased with her guest. She has two pretty girls, one of twelve, the other five, and two sons, one a man grown. They are happy and contented, have not much address or elegance in their manner, but are clean and *more tidy* in their house than any place we have been at since we left Belvoir, and very hospitable. They have lived some time in England, a good while at Bath, and are fond of English ways; from hence we went eight miles to Mr James Leslie, a son of Dr Leslie, married and settled in this neighbourhood [Leslie Hill just outside Ballymoney]. We went to them in an inconvenient time, their house unfinished and full of company, but they crammed us in, and it was better than any inn we could go to. Mr Leslie is extremely civil, and attended us to the Giant's Causeway and lent us his six good horses to save our own. We altered our first scheme, which was to have gone to Bally Castle [Ballycastle], where Mrs MacAulay's father [Mr Boyd] lives, and carries on the coal-works; but the weather proving uncertain, we thought it best not to delay our visit to one of the *world's wonders*, for such it may be called.

Hazlebrook, 8 October 1758

So on Thursday the 5th of October we set forward: we had seven miles to go to Dr Stuart's [at Ballylough], a fine worthy old man of eighty-one years of age, as cheerful, hearty and good-humoured as if but forty! his maiden sister, called "Madam Jane" not many years younger, a very amiable woman, decent in manners and dress. They received us like old acquaintance, and engaged us to sup and lodge with them at our return from the *Causeway*, which is less than an hour's drive from them. We got *there* about twelve o'clock: I am still in an amazement at the stupendous sight; the Dean, Sally, Smith and I went in the coach, all our men with us, and Mr Leslie, Mr Edmund Leslie (his younger brother, a pretty young clergyman) and Mr Mathews escorted us. We passed over a dull country, till a mile before we came to the place where we were to alight; then the sea opened to our view and some romantic rocks, but no appearance of the Giant's dominions till we had walked some way.

I am now quite at a loss to give you any idea of it; it is so different from anything I ever saw, and so far beyond all description. The prints [probably by Francois Vivares] you have represent some part of it very exactly, with the *sort of pillars* and the remarkable stones that compose them of different angles, but there is an infinite variety of rocks and grassy mountain *not at all* described in the prints, nor is it possible for a poet or a painter, with all their art, to do justice to the aweful grandeur of the whole scene.

When we got out of our coach, Mr Leslie and his brother took the charge of me and Miss Chapone, and Mr Mathews of the Dean. We walked along a path on the side of a hill that formed an amphitheatre, of a great height above us, and sloped down a vast way below us to the sea from the path we walked on. The grass very fine and green, and a variety of field-flowers of the season, though none of a peculiar kind from those in your own fields. At the bottom, the sea foaming and dashing among the rude rocks; on the side of the hill, sheep feeding undismayed at the roaring of the sea and terror of its waves, and shepherds tending their flocks. Our next scene was a second amphitheatre, diversified with amazing rocks, and the pillars and loose stones which are peculiar to this place, the entrance guarded on one side by a range of rocky mountain and on the other two pyramidal mountains of a singular form.

From that point we walked round the semicircle that forms the second amphitheatre on a precipice that was very formidable indeed, persuaded by our guides that the lower way was not practicable ; but D.D. was not so ambitious and kept the low way on the rocky strand, and had the advantage of us, as our path led us a great way about, and was so frightful that we could not look about us. However, we got safely to the part that is called "the Causeway", which forms a point into the sea, and begins the third amphitheatre; this contains the greatest quantity of the pillars, some so very exact and smooth that you would imagine they were all chiselled with the greatest care. After gazing, wondering, and I may say *adoring* the wondrous Hand that formed this amazing work, we began to find ourselves fatigued. Our gentlemen found out a well-sheltered place, where we sat very commodiously by a well (called the Giant's Well) of as fine sweet water as any at Calwich [her brother's seat in Derbyshire], and cold mutton and tongue, refreshed us extremely after three hours' walking, climbing, and stumbling among the rocks.

I took an imperfect sketch of the place, which if I can make anything of you shall have a copy. Mrs Drury, [Susanna Drury (fl.1733 –1778)] who took the draughts (of which you have the prints) lived three months near the place, and went almost every day. I can do nothing so exact and finished; in the last amphitheatre facing the entrance, about half-way up the side of the rocky mountain, the pillars are placed in such a form as to resemble an organ; you will see it in one of Mrs Drury's prints.

What is called the Causeway is a most wonderful composition of pillars, which in some part form a mosaic pavement, in others appear like the basement of pillars; but when you are on the strand below, then you see they are all pillars closely fitted to each other, though the angles vary; they chiefly consist of hexagons. The sun shone part of the time and shewed the place to great perfection, but we had a sprinkling shower or two that made us wrap up in my brother's good lambswool cloaks, and shelter ourselves under some of the rocks.

Whilst we were at our repast our attendants were differently grouped, at some distance on the left hand the servants, a little below us women and children that gathered sea-weed and shells for us, about twelve in number, with very little light drapery; on the right hand men that were our guides, of different ages, seated on the points of rocks, whose figures were *very droll*, and I believe we ourselves were no

The Giant's Causeway, by Mary Delany, 1762.

less so; eagerly devouring our morsel, and every now and then a violent exclamation of wonder at some new observation. We sat just facing a most aspiring pyramidal hill, and whilst we were there a shepherd drove his flock to the summit of it, and they looked like so many little white specks; the shepherd stood for some minutes on the highest point of the rock. I don't know how to give you a clear idea of this place, such as it appeared to me, and shall only make what I have said already confused should I say more.

We got back to Dr Stuart's between five and six, excessively weary ; a good supper and tolerable night's rest recovered us pretty well. I own I could not sleep well, what I had seen filled my mind so much; and as no pleasure can be unalloyed, D.D. had hurt his shin the day before we left Mount Panther, and this expedition had inflamed it so much that on Friday morning I was quite frightened and prevailed with him, instead of branching out our travels as we intended and seeing more wonders, to return to this place, where rest and Turner's cerate has quite taken away the inflammation, and I hope in a day or two it will be quite healed. We go today to Dr Leslie's and propose going to-morrow to Belvoir, and so home as fast as we can.

How uncertain are human resolutions! We have left Hazlebrook (Mr Bristowe's) *persuaded* to take Coleraine and Derry in our way home as places worth our seeing; are now at a brother's of Mr Mathews, near Coleraine; the weather too bad to permit us to see anything, and I fear I shall hardly have an opportunity of writing till at home, where now I long to be. The want of your letters, which my wandering has prevented my receiving, is very vexatious but I dare not have them sent across the country for fear I should lose them quite.   iii pp518–23

An unexpected addition to this tour was a visit to the magnificent strand at
Magilligan, County Londonderry, then they went on to stay with Archdeacon
Golden near Downhill.

Delville, 25 October 1758

My head has been in such a whirl of late, that I cannot recollect where about in my
travels I broke off. Did I not tell you we went from Mr Bristowe's at Hazlebrook to
Derry? did I tell you how fine the situation? how good a house? and how pleasant the
country about it? not unlike the hills about Bath, but the river *infinitely finer*, very broad,
clear, and winds beautifully. We spent Tuesday, Wednesday, and Thursday very
agreeably there; met with an Archdeacon Golden, commonly called "*a Methodist*"
(much injured) and in his appearance a jolly, open, cheerful countenance, very
sensible and learned, and most particulary agreeable in conversation, but warm in
religious disputes, where he thinks it *his duty* to uphold any orthodox point, and that
I suppose has gained him the title of "Methodist". His wife a mild, sickly, sensible,
civil woman; they were very earnest with us to return by their house as they were
going home; making many apologies for the lowliness of their cabin, but promised us
clean, well-aired beds. We took them at their word; the way called 22 miles, would
measure in England thirty! Twelve miles of it we had passed before to a miserable
town called Newtown [Limavady] where we dined on good provision kind Mrs
Barnard [Bishop of Derry's wife] put up for us.

We set out for the rest of the day's journey, the roads in general good, though
jumbling; had we been two hours sooner, we should have been greatly entertained
with the road. We passed by a small valley under Magilligan Hill, the richest and
most varied scene I ever beheld – corn-fields incredibly filled with stacks of corn,
pasture-grounds full of cattle, sheep grazing, haycocks in abundance; it wanted
nothing but *shepherds and shepherdesses* to make it quite an Arcadian scene. These
fields and meadows bounded by the sea, and that by a range of hills well cultivated to
the top. Can anything be finer? And I assure you I do not take any traveller's privilege
in my acount. And as we had passed through some very dreary country, it made this
pretty spot appear to more advantage.

Another very extraordinary scene came next of a very different kind, which is
Magilligan strand, sixteen miles in length, opposite to the sea; a range of rocky
mountains of a vast height, that look like the ruins of castles and cathedrals, parts of them
projecting with an amazing boldness. The whiteness of some of the rocks, with the
mixture of grass, moss and ivy, embellishes the scene; and the caverns and cliffs in the
rocks with spouts of water running down, and the swelling and dashing of the waves of
the sea, add a magnificence that is quite awful. The light was sufficient to show what I
have described, but not enough to see millions of pretty shells on the strand, and many
other prettinesses that we had not time to attend to, night came on so fast; and we had a
horrible precipice to go over, with torrents on each side tumbling among broken rocks,
which we in prudence chose to walk over rather than sit in the coach, and got safe, thank
God, to the Archdeacons's just as it was dark! He met us on the strand to guide us over
the dangerous road, which is not more than a quarter of a mile.

The cabin is a lowly one, but elegantly neat, and decorated in a pretty taste with
some very fine pieces of china; very good tea, very good supper, and *above all* very

good instructive conversation! Though we were all so much fatigued on coming in, particularly D.D., we all grew sprightly, and were sorry to part at *nearly twelve o'clock!* Next day we left them *with regret*, and wished for a view at a more advantageous time of the day of that charming strand; we passed over about two miles of it. We went back to Mr Bristowe's, rested there; easily and kindly entertained till Monday the 16th.

After such an extended tour the Delanys were glad to return to Delville.

Lay that night at Antrim; dined next day at Moira, Lord Rawdon's; his house pretty good, but his improvements *not* in the best taste; the country about him very English and pleasant: he is very good humoured and obliging in his house. Lady Rawdon (Lady Betty Hastings that was) extremely civil and agreeable, has a *pleasing manner*, though not a pleasing person, has good sense and delicate *sentiments*, and very *high ones of friendship*, which incline me mightily to her. They have a delightful library, with recesses where you may sit and read books of all kinds to amuse the fancy as well as improve the mind – telescopes, microscopes, and all the scientific apparatus; everybody chooses their employments – it is the land of liberty, yet of regularity; constant prayers. We met there a very learned and extraordinary man, who lives with Lord Rawdon a good deal; he answered Mr Kennicott about the Hebrew text, and is well known among the learned world; a young man, but in a very bad state of health – his name Commings. I am sure Mr Talbot knows him. From thence we went to Newry, from Newry to Drogheda, and on Friday arrived safely at our own dear Delville. How my heart overflows with thankfulness for the peace and plenty restored to these walls! The Dean is very happy in reviewing, correcting and amending his works here, and I hope the healthful employment and the tranquillity now enjoyed will add health and length of days! He has not, I thank God, any particular complaint but that of being soon weary.   iii pp523–26

JOURNEYS NEAR DELVILLE

This was one of her last long journeys in Ireland. The Delanys made several visits to England for periods of up to a year from this time on. As age overtook the dean, they confined their visiting to areas near to Delville.

Delville, 3 February 1759

Tuesday, 30th January, after church, Mrs [Henry] Hamilton and her daughter, Sally and I went with the six horses to take the air as far as the Hill of Howth, which is about *ten English miles*; it is all the way on the strand close to the sea, the view of which, with the ships in the harbour, the city of Dublin, little villages, hills, mountains and beautiful fields and scattered houses, make a most delightful appearance; we did not return home till near six, when we found our little fasting dinner ready for us.
iii p538

Delville, 22 June 1759

Tuesday, the coach and four and chariot and pair, containing Mrs Hamilton, Miss
M.H. [Mary Hamilton, a favourite daughter], D.D. and your humble servant, Miss
A.H. and Sally (Mr S.H [Sackville Hamilton] on horseback) set out after breakfast to
go to a strand called Malahide, 8 miles off, which is a very fine one, to pick shells;
mistook our road, and made 12 miles at least of it! proposed returning to dinner,
travelled through *great part of Fingal* [Meath], pretty country, with fine views of the
harbour and shipping, the ocean beyond, the Hill of Howth and Islands of Lambay,
Dawky [Dalkey], and Ireland's Eye, and many more prettinesses too numerous for
the present time of writing; but we got *not* to the main strand we wanted to see, which
was *beyond* Malahide, and *time* allowed us to go no farther, that intruding old gentle–
man, who is always ready to put a spoke in one's wheel!

Mr S. Ham [Sackville Hamilton, one of Mrs Henry Hamilton's sons], by virtue of
belonging to the custom-house, got us admittance into a very clean room in the
surveyors-house, where we got very good bread and butter, and cold mutton and
plum-cake (excessively hot and hungry) and were entertained by seeing the fishermen
drag the net in the sea and catch a parcel of very fine mullet, two of the best I bought
and a great many *purple and yellow wild oysters*. Miss M.H., Sally and Mr Hamilton
walked on a little point of land towards the fishing-boat; the sea was coming in so fast
that they could not return the same way so they got into the boat and rowed to land
with the fish! Wednesday being our wedding day we had all our family friends. I
painted in the morning, the same on Thursday, and enjoyed the garden wonderfully in
the evening. To-day I hope will be a garden day.   iii p556

*Here she visits Summerhill, one of the most dramatic Palladian houses in
Ireland, built by Edward Lovett Pearce in collaboration with Richard Cassels
in 1731 for Hercules Rowley from County Londonderry who inherited the
estate through his mother from his grandfather, Sir Hercules Langford.*

Mary to her niece Mary Dewes
Delville, 12 May 1764

We went to Mr Preston's (Swainston in Meath) last Monday, got there by three, had
the pleasure of finding Mrs Preston [Mary Hamilton married Rev Nathaniel Preston,
one of the sons of the "old prim beau", in 1763] as well as any one can be in her
condition, agreeable and kind. I had not the pleasure of finding Miss [Sally] Chapone
well at all, and I think not better for her excursion.

Tuesday, after dinner, Mrs P., Sally and I (the gentlemen were lazy) went to
Summer Hill, a place so called in that neighbourhood, belonging to a Mr Rolly. It is
called fine, and in some respects it is so, the situation good. The house large but not
pleasant, and there are a good many trees, a fine lawn before the house, and a pretty
wood behind the house with winding walks, rustic seats, ending in a very pretty
menagerie well stored with pheasants. It was late when we got home. Next day spent
in walking about Swainston, and contriving works, and hanging a room with Indian
paper, which Mrs Preston is eager about. The weather too bad all Thursday for going
abroad, so occupations at home went on, and yesterday we came away, and though

sorry to leave our agreeable friend, were not displeased to return to our own Delville that is now in the bloom of beauty. I think the jaunt has done D.D. good. I must go this morning to town to take leave of the Castle grandees, and in the afternoon am invited to a private music at Mr Bayley's.   iv p24–25

When Mary moved back to London in 1768 she spent much time with her friend Margaret, duchess of·Portland, staying often at Bulstrode where the friends pursued their interests in botany and art vigorously. She continued to travel, to visit her friends and family and to enjoy the landscape in England for the rest of her life.

Bleaching linen near Londonderry, by Mary Delany, 1758.

CHAPTER 5

DELVILLE

HOUSEHOLD MANAGEMENT

After her marriage to Patrick Delany, Mary came to be mistress at Delville where he had lived for many years and had entertained her in the company of Swift on her first visit to Ireland. It was to become a much loved home and great care, energy and money was spent on its constant improvement. The small estate of' Delville was situated near Glasnevin just outside Dublin, at that time considered to be rural but within easy reach of the city whenever business and pleasure called.

Lady Llanover stated that:

"In relation to Delville, Walsh said that it was on the other side of the Tolka [river], and laid out by Dr Delany, who in concert with his friend, Dr Helsham, a physician and also fellow of Trinity College, erected the house and laid out the grounds. It was called Hel-Del-Ville, formed from the initial syllables of the names of the proprietors, to intimate their joint property in the place, but the *first* was soon dropped, as having a *strange association*. It was laid out in a style then new in Ireland." (Footnote i pp397–98)

The house was pulled down in the 1950s. Mary Delany's shellwork ceilings were still in position. There is a Bon Secours hospital at Delville today.

Mary Delany was a clever and capable chatelaine of her household. It was an extended household and included relatives of various sorts, as well as visiting friends and servants. At Delville and in County Down she had Smith, the personal maid who had accompanied her from England. Before Mary married the dean, she had employed and trained up one of his nieces as well as taking on another niece to help her manage the household, a Miss Delany later to become Mrs Green and mother of little Tommy Green. The food and the medical remedies were produced by the women of the house, relying heavily on the produce of the garden and estate. The fabric of the house, curtains, hangings, sheets, and some of the clothes were all worked on by Mary and her household helpers. Some of her friends spent many months of the year with her. Letitia Bushe, Mrs Donnellan, and Mrs Francis Hamilton (also known as Mrs Forth Hamilton) were very much involved in the home making at Delville and this busy companionship is part of the life described by Mary in letters to her sister. These friends who contributed so much to Mary's life were given a second home at Delville and, like Letty or Mrs Donnellan, were single women or widowed like

Mrs Forth Hamilton whose husband died in 1746. Later, the Delany household included the family of Sally, her goddaughter, the Sandfords.

Delville, 28 June 1744

My impatience to see Delville and read my dear sister's letter shortened my visit there [to Mrs Barber, an old friend of theirs and Swift], and we arrived at our own pleasant dwelling by 11, – and never was seen a sweeter dwelling. I have traversed the house and gardens, and never saw a more delightful and agreeable place, but particulars must come by degrees, and I have now the joy of seeing the kind and generous owner of it perfectly well, and well pleased to put me in possession. ii p306

Once installed, Mary planned many alterations.

Dublin, 12 July 1744

Yesterday morning (for Tuesday I spent the whole day in settling shells and papers) my upholsterer came, and my new apartment will be very handsome. The drawing room hung with tapestry, on each side of the door a japan chest, the curtains and chairs crimson mohair, between the windows large glasses with gilt frames, and marble tables under them with gilt frames; the bedchamber within hung with crimson damask, bed chairs and curtains the same; *the closet* within it is most delightful. I have a most extensive and beautiful prospect of the harbour and town of Dublin and a range of mountains of various shapes. The bedchamber and closet are on the left hand of the drawing room; on the right is a very pretty square room with a large dressing room within it, which I hope will be my dearest sister's apartment when she makes me happy with her company.

I have described my house very awkwardly to you, but to be regular: it stands on a rising ground, and the court is large enough for a coach and six to drive round commodiously. The front of the house is simple but pretty – five windows in front, two stories high, with a portico at the hall door, to which you ascend by six steps, but so well sheltered by the roof of the portico that it is secured from rain. The hall is 26 feet by 22, and 12 feet and half high, the ceiling finished in compartments, with a Doric entablature in stucco round the room. On the right hand is the eating parlour, 26 feet long and 16 feet and half wide, with a projection in the middle, which opens thirteen foot and is eight foot deep, with three windows, and large enough for two side-boards, one window between the tables and one at each side, which lights the room very agreeably; it is a very charming room, cool in summer and warm in winter; the chimney is at one end and a window over against it; on the left hand of the hall is another large room, which at present is unfinished, but is designed for a chapel when we are rich enough to finish it as we ought to do.

At the end of the hall is a very neat stone stair-case, well finished with stucco, which leads to the apartment I have described above. Beyond the staircase, below, is a little hall; on the right hand is a small parlour, where we breakfast and sup, out of it our present bedchamber and a large light closet within it; it is but a small apartment but very pretty, and lies pleasantly to the gardens, and as we sit by the fire-side we can

View of Delville, by Letitia Bushe, 1754.

see the ships ride in the harbour. From the door of the little parlour are about ten steps that carry you to my English room, and another flight of the same stairs lead to the rooms over the little parlour, and bedchamber and the maids rooms, and serve for back stairs to the great apartment. I forgot to add that out of my English room you go into the library, which is *most plentifully filled*, and D.D. has filled up the vacancies of my shelves with the modern poets nicely bound.　　　ii pp308–310

Mary Delany felt that she must supervise the work closely.

Delville, 26 July 1744

I expected a great deal of business, but not so much as I find: I have workmen of all sorts in the house – upholsterers, joiners, glaziers, and carpenters – and am obliged to watch them all, or their work would be but ill-finished; and I have not been one day without company since I came. I have a young woman now in the house with me, Miss Delany, very lively and good-humoured, and very ready to assist me in anything I want to have done. I propose having her a good deal as I believe it may be some advantage to her, and at present I see nothing in her but what is very agreeable. ii p319

Delville, 23 September 1744

Our workmen were waiting at home for us. My English room is quite unfurnished again and under the painter's hands. I have had it painted a sort of olive, somewhat lighter than my brother's, for the sake of my pictures, and because the room is very light. I have had the frieze painted with festoons of flowers and shells alternate, and you can't imagine what a pretty effect it has; as soon as the room is dry, which will be about a fortnight hence, I shall be very busy in replacing my goods. We now live in our great parlour, which is a most comfortable room. Oh that I could bring you and our dearest mama to this dwelling with a wish! You should have a very snug apartment for your purpose, and I should have the happiness of attending you as usual, but this is chimerical and at present impossible.   ii p330

The household did not always run smoothly after an absence in the north.

Delville, 24 August 1745

I am come home to a hurry and have found many things to settle in my household that all housekeepers are sometimes troubled with – servants, accusations that must be cleared and are very teazing, though I don't *torment* my self with those affairs; but as our family is large and consequently expensive, it requires both *my care and attention.*

    Got home to Delville about 7 and was charmed to see it look so gay and spruce. Had the pleasure of finding Mrs Green [the dean's niece] here ready to receive me and *my pussy* Tiger knew me and caressed me mightily.   ii pp379–80

Delville, 4 January 1745–6

The Dean has had a bad cold, which he caught by reading damp books; during which time I was so gracious as to indulge him with my English room, which is very warm when the wind is easterly. We lived four days in it, our quarters are now enlarged.
ii p410

Returning to Delville was always a pleasure, especially after the tiring journey from England.

Delville, 26 May 1747

Saturday I spent at home, unpacking and beginning to settle. We had the pleasure of finding house and gardens in perfect beauty; and Mr Greene has added three beautiful young deer to my stock with a milk white face; my swan is well; Tiger [her cat] knew me, and I have a very fine thriving colt and calf.   ii p460

Delville, 6 June 1747

I thank God the Dean and I have been perfectly well since we came home, and have enjoyed the sweets and sunshine of Delville as much as some rainy days and a great deal of company would permit. Yesterday we spent the whole day (but an hour at dinner, and that was partly) in the garden, for our *kitchen grate was down* and a new one putting up, stoves making and a boiler placing, so that we could have nothing conveniently drest at home: we sent our mutton and chicken to Mr Barber's [an enamellist married to one of the dean's nieces, Biddy] house at the end of the garden and had it drest in his kitchen and eat in his dining room which looks into Carlingford garden. His wife and children are gone further into the country for a little while. Mr Barber came home when we had half dined, in a great hurry, to burn some of his enamels, little thinking to find his house full of company, which occasioned some mirth amongst us. As soon as we had dined we adjourned to the Beggar's Hut [a garden feature], and had coffee there. Just as it was over, Mrs Clayton called on me to go to Lady Orrery's [Lord Orrery's second wife, Margaret Hamilton, heiress of Caledon, county Tyrone], who lives about half a mile from hence; she was not at home; we returned to Delville and drank tea in the garden.

You are very kind in inquiring after Smith; she was very sick at sea, but well again as soon as she landed; she is much delighted with Delville and (as much as she has seen) with Ireland. *She* and *my housekeeper* take to one another extremely; and I hope I am now settled with honest quiet domestics. Fribble behaves himself very well and Thomas will make I believe, in time, a good butler.   ii pp461–62

After several years the improvments still continued with an extension to the library.

Delville, 6 October 1747

We are going to be very busy in settling the library. The Dean has made an addition at the end of it of a sort of closet to which you ascend by one step; it opens with an arch, five foot and a half wide; there is to be a window at the end which is east, and on the south side, opposite to the south window, there is to be looking glass representing a sash window, which will reflect the prospect and prevent the cold of the north: it is to be all stucco and adorned with pilasters, a table in the middle for writing and holding papers, and only convenient room left for going round it and for seats. The old part of the library is 32 feet long and about 11 wide; it holds a great many books, and when finished will be very pleasant; the prospect from the new window charming. How often shall I wish for you to help settle the books – an employment you always were fond of; here you would meet some that would amuse you very well. The addition is 12 feet square.   ii p474

The following year the dean turned his attention to the chapel at Delville which became an ongoing improvement. They also rearranged the servants' accommodation.

Delville, 20 August 1748

On Monday, the Dean begins about his chapel; he makes an addition for the communion table to stand in *clear of the aisle*, over which is to be a round gothic window. When that is complete, he has promised to build me a kitchen out of doors, and that which is now my kitchen to be turned into a room for my maids, that they have *no call upstairs* but when they are about their *business there*.   ii p500

Mary Delany paid regular visits to England to see her family and friends, especially her beloved sister and her children, and friends. Sometimes the visits were of long duration and subsequent returns to Delville meant much rearrangment.

Delville, 18 May 1750

I had an intention of writing to you last post but – impossible – shoals of impertinences made it impracticable. A year's absence makes it so necessary to have a thorough inspection into everything, and I am settling my family in a different way from what it was formerly, which obliges me to be Mrs Notable, and to do much more that I ever did in my life and I hope it will agree with me; and own that the bustle of it,(which once I should have thought better executed by a servant than myself) has been of service to me, as it has occupied every moment and left me the less leisure to think of *some moments*, the recollection of which are yet too tender to dwell upon. Smith takes to her new employment very cleverly, and when once I have *fixed her* in the *method* I like, I shall return to my *less necessary* but more pleasing employments of painting.   ii pp544–45

In her letters Mary advised her sister on interior decoration and her advice has the confident ring of experience. She was always endlessly busy on her domestic projects. Her artistic talents were given great scope in the decoration of Delville. Her interest in nature focussed particularly on plants, especially flowers, and shells. Mary's compositions of shells set in stucco were used on the walls and ceilings of several of the rooms. She was also an accomplished needlewoman and provided many of the coverings and drapes.

Delville, 30 June 1750

I think the mosaick pattern with cloth work round, will be prettier than the flower pattern for your window-curtains. Have you put up your shell-work over the chimney and painted it? and how does it look? I am afraid I shall not be able to get any more thread of the sort you used to have, but when I go to the North I will try. I don't know what to do about the pattern for Miss Mordaunt: I am ashamed not to have done it, it sounds so like a trifle, but I really *have not time* to do many things that are more necessary to be done: I will enclose you Mrs Hamilton's [Mrs Forth Hamilton] fine pattern, and desire when they have done with it to return it. I suppose when you turn your kitchen into a parlour, you will fit the wainscot of the best bedchamber there, and hang the bedchamber with paper. Whenever you put up paper, the best way is to have it pasted on the bare wall: when lined with canvass it always shrinks from the edges. I have stripped down old stuff beds and sent them to Mount Panther, and in their stead am putting up *blue and white linen* and blue and white paper hangings, this has taken up a good deal of attention as I am new sashing the room, new setting the grate, enlarging the room, and several alterations that require my overseeing and must be done before we leave Delville, that the rooms may be fit for use by the time we return. My work-room I am going to new-model, the wainscot wants new painting, is cracked

'A view of Dublin Harbour and Delville Garden from the bow window in Mrs Delany's closet', by Mary Delany, 3 August 1759.

and has started in some places; the paper I have chosen is pearl coloured caffoy paper: the pattern like damask: the pictures look extremely well on that colour, and the crimson damask window-curtain and chairs will suit very well with it.

Tuesday went to Dublin on business: first to a place called the *World's End*, where I spent an hour and half in choosing out a set of earthen-ware for the Duchess of Portland, such as yours, and a dozen baskets from Mrs Montagu as she desired: then bespoke the paper for hanging my rooms; bought the blue and white linen for my bed; and had just time to dress before dinner.   ii pp561–62, 563

Mary Delany seldom shows signs of irritation in her letters except when she feels that precious time has been wasted.

Delville, 13 February 1745/6

To-day we dine at Lord Grandison's, and a strange *gibble gabble* woman has plagued me all the morning; I never was more nearly provoked to be rude in all my life. I crammed her with chocolate and plum-cake, and then sent her packing, but she has robbed me of what is not in her power to restore, *a good hour of my time.* ii p424

Delville, 7 July 1750

It is not possible to secure a day without interruption. I thought myself secure of this, having refused some parties on purpose not to be hindered; when last night a note came to inform me that Lady Caroline and Mr Fox, and the family at Lucan would breakfast here as they were going in a few days to England. I could not put it off, so have set all my best china in order and prepared everything for their reception.

Yesterday was spent in tranquillity at home; and this day may prove so too, for nobody is yet come, and 'tis past 12 o'clock, and a cloudy rainy day; *n' importe*, only bread and butter is spread, and water boiling without mercy. On Monday next we are invited to the *Virtuoso Epicuroso*, Mr Bristowe; and you shall know to a pepper-corn what we have to dinner.

I have painters and carpenters now hammering and brushing away; and I have determined about my Minerva and shall paper it; my cabinet of shells to be removed to the library whilst the room is sprucing up, for fear of my glass doors; the removing it will be a difficult affair, for I don't mean to take down any shells but those that are near the edge of the shelves. Was anything more teazing! almost 3, and no company come, and I have sauntered away the greatest part of the morning looking for them through the telescope and preparing the breakfast things; there must have been some mistake. I have not entirely lost time though, had I been more settled, you would have had rather a better letter.   ii pp565, 567–68

The annual trip to the deanery of Down often complicated domestic arrangements at Delville.

Delville, 15 July 1750

I am now as busy as a *notable housewife* must be on such an occasion, and the more so as alterations are going on here, as well as preparations for the place we are going to. I have done up a little apartment, hung it with blue and white paper, and intend a bed of blue and white linen – all Irish manufacture; and hope some day to be so happy as to show it to you.   ii p569

Mary to her brother Bernard Granville
Delville, 15 July 1750

For some days past I have been sending all sorts of household goods and stores for Mount Panther [their northern residence], and propose leaving this on Tuesday next. D.D is finishing alterations in his garden and giving directions for what is to be done in his absence. I am *preserving, pickling*, and papering and giving directions to my maids: and I have just spruced up a little appartment for you, come when you please. ii p570

Mary to her brother Bernard Granville
Delville, 22 September 1750

I have been as busy within doors; have hung my dressing room (which was painted olive-colour before) with a dove-colour flock paper, my pictures, books, china placed as they were before. My room is greatly improved.   ii p593

For once Mary Delany's contemplation of her many activities and accomplishments caused her to consider whether her time might be better spent in helping others.

Delville, 6 October 1750

I am going to make a very comfortable closet: to have a dresser, and all manner of working tools, to keep all my stores for *painting, carving, gilding etc.* for my own room is now so clean and pretty that I cannot suffer it to be strewed with litter, only books and work, and the closet belonging to it to be given up to prints, drawings, and my collection of fossils, petrifactions, and minerals. I have not set them in order yet; a great work it will be, but when done very comfortable. There is to my working closet a pleasant window that over looks all the garden, it faces the east, is always dry and warm. In the middle of the closet a deep nitch with shelves, where I shall put whatever china I think too good for common use, but trifling and insignificant is my *store-room* to what yours is! Mine fits only an idle mind that wants amusement; yours serves either to supply your hospitable table, or gives cordial and healing medicines to the poor and the sick. Your mind is ever turned to help, relieve, and bless your neighbours and acquaintance; whilst mine, I fear (however I may sometimes flatter myself that I have contrary disposition) is *too much filled* with amusements of no real estimation; and when people commend any of my performances I feel a consciousness that my time might have been better employed.   ii pp600–601

Delville was a place which excited admiration and the Delanys, as was customary with proprietors of larger and more lavish estates, were sometimes required to open their garden gates and their home to the curious in addition to their friends. Mary was well able to exercise a little hauteur to keep the more enthusiastic at a distance.

Delville, 13 October 1750

I am very happy that I have no *dangling* neighbours. I may be thought too reserved in our village, but I choose rather to be censured for that, than expose myself to the interruption and tittle-tattle of a country neighbourhood: my acquaintance is large in Dublin, and I *never want company.*

   D.D., I thank God, is very well and busy. He has laid me in such a stock of billeting, and fire-fuel out of his own garden, that I shall not, I believe, want coals for the whole winter, except for the kitchen, housekeeper's room and hall. I have now eighteen head of deer; we killed two bucks this year, that proved as fine venison for fat and taste as could be eaten; I own it is disagreeable to me to have them killed but it is unavoidable, they increase so fast.   ii p602

Between all the household chores there was household entertainment, again much of it conjured up in the home.

Delville, 10 November 1750

On Monday we go to Morella's concert, and then Mrs Hamilton leaves us; business obliges her to go, or she flatters me that she should with pleasure stay longer with me. We work hard all the morning, and Bushe reads to us in the afternoon; I read till seven and then we play at *puss in the corner* with the children [the Dean's great nephews and nieces] or dance country dances to a very bad fiddle, till eight – prayer hour, harpsichord after that, and *after supper cribbage* or *commerce*.   ii pp615–16

Delville, 28 December 1750

I thank God I have been very well, but very busy, though the main and most material business of the week I was not able to pursue; for since Xtmas day it has been perpetual rain, and our horses are all ill of the epidemic disorder; the distemper was brought here about three weeks ago by horses from England, and rages everywhere, and several have died of it.

I have just seen the sun rise most gloriously; the reflection of it in the sea and the gilding of the ships and buildings was beautiful. Now the days lengthen I shall grow again an early riser, for I have not *this month* past been up before 8.

I don't think I half answered yours of the 7th. I wish you joy of your curtains being done, and hope you have got my thread by this time: I am sorry to be so little assistant to you in it, but D.D. employs me *every hour in the day* for his chapel. I make the flowers and other ornaments by candle-light, and by daylight, when I don't paint, put together the festoons that are for the ceiling, and after supper we play at commerce, one pool. Our everday reading is still Carte's History of the old Duke of Ormonde: he is one of the greatest heroes I ever read of, such courage, prudence, loyalty, humanity, and virtues of every kind make up his character, but the sufferings of King Charles the First, though there but in part related, *break one's heart*!

I have just taken a run along my portico walk into the greenhouse; and send you an orange-leaf and a yellow Indian jessamine of my own raising; I wish they may not lose their sweetness before they kiss your hands.   ii pp632–634,635

The Delville chapel improvements continued but she also had to take in hand more tedious tasks.

Delville, 5 January 1750/51

Family affairs are a necessary evil that must be attended to, and sometimes will break in malapropos. My household at present is in pretty good condition: but I have a great piece of work in hand at present, which is, dusting and airing all the books in the library: for though there is a constant fire there and the room very warm, books contract much moisture, and I have great pleasure in keeping the library in good order.   iii p2

Mary seems to have been constantly occupied; one is struck very forcibly by her energy.

Delville, 28 February 1750/51

I have done nothing but knot or run a calico gown, which I keep at hand for idle hours. Bushe leaves me the week after next to prepare for her journey to Mrs Bush, General Parker's daughter, where she is going to spend the summer – she must give pleasure wherever she goes.   iii p22

Delville, 8 March 1750/51

The Primate [Stone] and his sister, and who he pleases to bring, dine with us today and having company in the house does not leave me so much leisure for my domestic affairs as is necessary, so that what with breakfasts and *instructing* and *helping* Smith [her housekeeper], I have not half an hour to write.   iii p23

If she was not working in her own house she was employed in her friends' houses. This account of cutpaper working is interesting since it shows that Mary's skills in that craft must have been exercised in interior decoration as well as silhouette making before she began her famous botanical series in later life. Decorating interiors with prints and other cutpaper work was a fashionable occupation. Elizabeth Vesey at Lucan was another woman after Mrs Delany's heart.

Delville, 11 June 1751

The pleasantest party I make out of my own villa is to Lucan; Mrs F. Hamilton [a cousin of Mrs Vesey] is generally of our company. It is a delightful place, and its owners perfectly agreeable in their own house, always busy, and have some work or other to set one to do. The last time we were there, which was last Friday, Mrs Vesey had a whim to have Indian figures and flowers cut out and oiled, to be transparent, and pasted on her dressing-room window in imitation of painting on glass, and it has a very good effect; we go again next Friday to finish what we began last week. iii pp39–40

The topic of servants was a constant one since they were essential to the household. The marriage of a good kitchen maid was a cause of dismay but also some excitement.

Delville, 14 December 1751

Condole with me; Sally [her kitchen maid] is just on the brink of matrimony and has sent to speak with me; you shall know the particulars of our conversation. Why, it was very short; she is to be married this evening, had bespoke a supper in the neighbourhood; but that I can't allow. The Dean will marry her himself; they are to have their wedding-supper and lodging here, and I shall soon lose my pretty cook. Her lover is a mason, settles above two hundred pounds on her, lives at Clogher, an old widower, and she has known him fifteen years!   iii pp66–67

Delville, ND

Last Sunday Sarah Hipwell [Sally] was married at Glassinivin [Glasnevin] church, by the Dean of Down, to Robert Rames, mason; I gave all the maidens and men new white ribbon favours, and we all marched and made a gallant show through the garden, D.D., Mrs Don., and I at the head of the company, to the church, as soon as the bell began to ring, and the ceremony was over just before the congregation came, and I gave them for dinner as much beef, mutton, and pudding as they could devour. Fourteen people dined in Smith's room (besides the servants of the family,) and now the bride is packing up to go away today; I am really sorry to part with her. I have got a modest well-looking maid in her place, but what for a cook I know not.　　　iii p100

During the long intervals between seeing each other, the sisters continued to send each other advice, puzzles and presents despite the distance.

Delville, 11 January 1752

If your parlour is stuccoed (though I think I should rather hang it with stucco paper), you must have plugs of wood where you think to hang pictures to fix nails in, as they cannot be driven into stucco. What a medley of a letter is this! You may depend upon my being very ready to add to your furniture, as far as *my pencil* can go; though this year I have nothing for you, and I must see what size and shape you want before I undertake to work for you. I hope your good pies were well eaten and your fiddle well danced to? such a hospitable day is very pleasant, and the fatigue that attends it more satisfactory than that after any drum, or any such senseless sort, where *no one* reaps *any benefit* but the chandler.

I forgot what I said to you, about a secret between B. and D., and cannot for want of recollecting my own sentence make out yours [a reference to puns and conundrums and abbreviated references which were included in the sisters' letters to each other for amusement as well as propriety].　　　iii pp76–77

As her stalwart housekeeper Smith advanced in age, she required more help.

Delville 3 June 1752

Tuesday I went to Finglass; Mrs Forth, who has been ill, is much better. Wednesday staid at home to do business, and spent a sweet evening in my garden, with no company but D.D. *and the birds*. Thursday settled affairs for the North, have taken a workwoman into my house who is to have charge of all my household linen and to wash my laces as Smith is not now able to do all. Biddy Barber [Dean Delany's niece, Rupert Barber's wife] is in great trouble, has just lost a very fine boy of the measles. iii p127

Delville 13 June 1752

Before I answer your letter I must thank you (D.D. most gratefully joins with me) for the prettiest and most elegant japan pail, spoon, china cup, cover and saucer that ever I saw.

Photograph of Delville, c.1946.

D.D drank your health in whey at 7 this morning out of *his cup*, and baume tea at ten! My cream pail is now before me in my china case and makes a very considerable figure.   iii p131

Delville, 19 June 1752

Though my baggage was gone [to the north] and my house in some disorder I was glad to spend a few more days with Donnellan amongst my haymakers and roses. D.D was so busy at home with his books and haymakers he could not go [to a social engagement at Lucan].   iii p133

Delville, 14 November 1752

I think you are right not to paper your room till you meet with one to your mind; it can be easily done at any time; I believe I must draw hangings to your bed, but you cannot expect *any paper* will look so rich and so well as work.   iii pp172–73

Mary was responsible for some of the livery servants.

Delville, 26 January 1753

I hope you got a good coachman – I believe we have; Will Vaughan, the wild colt I brought from England has left us; he was a slovenly, sullen fellow, and proved very ungrateful: after having been nearly a year useless to us, and a great expense, as soon as he was well he gave us warning – no loss. I have got a pretty little boy I am training up, but there's *not much encouragement* for such undertakings; he has been well brought up, and I hope may prove more grateful, but he has never had the small-pox which will make me afraid of carrying him with us to England.   iii p199

When she visited her sister in England she sometimes brought indoor servants. This letter indicates the Dean's simple tastes in cooking.

Delville, 23 January 1753

I have got now but a very indifferent cook, not worth transporting, but am sure we shall have no reason to wish for any other than your own. D.D., you know, loves only roast, boiled and broiled and if all fails, the greatest feast to him is a fired [fried?] egg and bacon, but when we are so happy as to be under the hospitable roof of Welsbourn [her sister's home] we shall enjoy every delicacy the heart can wish.   iii p198

The Delanys were glad to leave Delville in the hands of friends when planning a long visit to England.

Delville, 24 February 1753

Mr Adderley, a most kind friend of D.D.'s has borrowed Delville for this summer, and we have most readily complied with his request; so when we set sail he takes possession: he is building a house in the neighbourhood, and does not care to remain in Dublin all the summer.   iii pp208–209

Delville, 5 May 1753

Domestic affairs call me away. My old cook has run away: I have just hired a new one that has a very good character, and must go and settle matters with her. I have had company every morning this week which interferes with my housewifery, for afternoons are not fit for business.

    Should our new cook prove a very good one, should you like to have us bring her? iii pp228–29

Improvements continued in spite of Mary's short illness and she enjoyed planning her garden and installing mirrors to add to the view from her bed.

Delville, 30 December 1758

I have had my new gardener (who I like mightily) with me to consult about the order of my flower-garden, which is under my dressing-room window, and between us I believe we shall make it very gay and pretty: it is a great amusement to me to see the people at work in it, digging and painting. I can't say my four days confinement upstairs was dull. My bed-chamber is very large, comfortable, with pleasant views and the bow closet! I have now completed it by two looking glasses that fill the side panels of the bow window, and reflect all the prospects. You would say indeed I am greedy of prospect were you to see it, *not to be contented without those reflectors*; the glasses reach within a foot of the cornice of the ceiling, and are fastened up with double knots of gilded rope. They were put up whilst I was above stairs, and a great amusement. Working and reading and a little cribbage go on.

I was truly mortified at not being able to partake of the solemn ceremony of the season [Christmas], and make my household glad; but the new year I trust will make me some amends, and renew my warmest gratitude for boundless mercies received, particularly that on the *6th of March*, 1758 [when the lawsuit with the Tenisons was decided in their favour].

Our gentle kind Sally [her god daughter Sally Chapone was living with them] has not been wanting in her affectionate diligence in nursing me and entertaining D.D. I have two most beautiful kittens, who play their part incomparably well in the business of amusement; have I not said enough of myself? Yes, surely!

D.D. is very busy laying the foundation of the addition he intends to his library, and all his labours of attending his workmen and giving directions agree perfectly well.   iii pp530–31

Delville, part of a letter, 1758

My closet is just hung with crimson paper, a small pattern that looks like velvet; as soon as dry I shall put up my pictures: and I am going to make a wreath to go round the circular window in the chapel, of oak branches, vines, and corn; the benches for the servants are fixed, the *chairs* for the upper part of the chapel are a whim of mine, but I am not sure till I see a pattern chair that I shall like it: it is to be in the shape and ornamented like a gothic arch. If it pleases me in the execution I'll send you a sketch. iii p527

Here she frankly admits the size of her housekeeping allowance.

Delville, 23 December 1758

The Dean has now settled my allowance for housekeeping here at six hundred a-year, which I receive quarterly, and out of that I pay everything but *the men's wages, the liveries, the stables, wine cellar and garden, furniture and all repairs.*   iii p530

Delville, 27 January 1759

I believe my allowance will answer very well here, as provisions are cheaper than in Warwickshire; but in half a year I shall be a judge and I am to have whatever addition I please.   iii p537

While they were away in the deanery of Down they often took the opportunity to get work done at Delville.

Delville, 7 July 1759

Monday, a pleasant day at Lucan. Tuesday, in the garden. Wednesday, after breakfast, to Ballydoyle strand, gathered good store of cockles, mussels, and scallops, the
prospects beautiful beyond description; after dinner much company. Thursday, parted
most unwillingly with our agreeable guests; but could not well press them to stay
longer, having much papering, *locking up etc* to do before our journey, which we
propose to begin on the 17th. Great part of the house is to be painted and whitewashed,
and everything that can be damaged must be put safe. We have got a new book to
entertain us in the North which is greatly commended – Robertson's History of
Scotland.   iii pp557–58

One of their projects was the building and decoration of the chapel at Delville.

Delville 26 January 1752

Monday and Tuesday we enjoyed ourselves at home. I bustle about as much as I can,
and am very busy making ornaments for the chapel, which I believe will be finished
this spring. I don't know how to describe in a letter what I am doing, but I assure you
I do everything I can to rouse and amuse my spirits; and if you and I, my dearest
sister, had not many years pursued that method, *what would have become of us?* and
I have and always shall think it one of the *prime blessings* I have received from
Providence that he has graciously enabled me to do so.   iii p82

*After 1754 the dean's income was augmented by £600 a year, and in 1758 the
Tenison lawsuit was resolved in their favour so they were able to spend more
money on improving Delville and finishing the chapel.*

Delville, 11 August 1759

I am as full of business as a bee, having various workmen to attend. We are making an
addition to our library. I am now painting what the Dean calls "*the Minerva*" and the
house is whitewashing and sprucing all over; the chapel I hope I shall get finished by
the time D.D. returns [he was in County Down]. I fear it will not be in my power to go
to him, as I don't care to leave the house with so many workmen; but I hope to send
him some good company, being in daily expectation of a visit from Mr *Sandford* [the
dean's chaplain and librarian].   iii p562

Mrs Delany took great pains to have the correct materials for her improvments.

Delville, 18 August 1759

I was so nice about my bow window that I *sent to England* for *good glass*, and have
had the sashes new made in the narrow way, which makes them much pleasanter;
indeed, the prospect they open to ought to have every advantage.

   Today we part with our agreeable Miss M[ary] Hamilton [one of Mrs Henry
Hamilton's children, later Mrs Preston], indeed with regret; but it is unreasonable to
ask to keep her longer as she is the joy of her family.

The chapel will now soon be finished; the glass is put into the ground window, and the painted glass round the rim, and *the star* of looking-glass diamond cut at the edges has a very good effect; the frame, which is made of brass, is gilt; and I shall next week *add a wreath* round it of vine and oak branches entwined, and ears of corn mixed with it.   iii p563

Delville, 15 September 1759

My chief works have been the ceiling of the chapel, which I have formerly described, done with cards *and shells* in imitation of stucco. In the chancel are four gothic arches, two on each side, made *also of shells* in imitation of stucco, the arches no deeper than the thickness of the shells, to take off the plain look the walls would have without them. The wreath round the window is composed of oak branches and vines made of cards; the *grapes, nuts, and large periwinkles*, the corn, *real wheat* painted, all to look like stucco. I am working coverings for the seats in chenille on a black ground, which gives it a gravity; but I don't think it so pretty a ground for *all colours* as any of the *browns*. My pattern a border of *oak-branches and all sorts of roses (except yellow)* which I work without any pattern, just as they come into my head. iii pp564–65

At night all sorts of amusements were considered fit entertainment but the most ingenious way of keeping up the temperature was in playing games.

Delville, 10 November 1759

Last night how do you think we warmed and amused ourselves? why I taught them *French fox*, and D.D. played as briskly as any of the company for nearly an hour. iii p574

FOOD AND OTHER PREPARATIONS

All the women in Mary's set took their housewifry seriously and swapped receipts or recipes not only for dishes but also for wine; brewing was one of their responsibilities, and preserving, as well as patterns for clothes and accessories.

Nenagh, 30 October 1732
[while on tour with the Claytons visiting the bishopric of Killalla]

Oh, I had almost forgot a request I promised to make, which was for the receipt for your white elder wine; we met with some yesterday that was not quite so good as ours; and Mrs Clayton wants the receipt mightily. I am always troubling you with some trumpery thing or other: I wish you could contrive to send me over a pattern of your gloves, that I may bring you over a few pair, when I am come to you; not that the gloves are better here than in England but they are cheaper.   i p389

The eighteenth century table was a generous spread by our standards: the menus read like a test of gourmet gluttony. The variety of dishes was not as heavy on the stomach as may first appear because they were not cooked in great quantities.

Undated fragment

How I could run on, but must not. I am called to range dishes on my table, which is a long one, and consequently easier to set out than a round or oval one. The table takes seven dishes in length. Here follows my bill of fare for to-day; is not this ridiculous? but if you *wander [wonder] still unseen*, it may serve as an amusement in your retirement.

First course
Turkey endove [endive]
Boyled neck of mutton

Greens
Soup
Plum pudding
Roast loin of veal
Venison pasty

Second course
Partridge
Sweet breads

Collared pig
Creamed apple tart
Crabs
Fricassee of eggs
Pigeons

No dessert to be had   ii pp331–32

Delville 20 June 1747

He [the primate, George Stone], and his sister Mrs Stone, and the Bishop of Derry [William Bernard] and Mrs Bernard (another sister of the Primate's) dine here to-day. *You love a bill of fare*, and here it is.

First Course
Fish
Beefsteaks. Soup. Rabbits and Onions.
Fillet Veal.

Second Course
Turkey Pout [pullet?]
Salmon Grilde [Grilled or Grilse, a young salmon] and Quaills.
Pick. Sal. [Pickled Salad]
Little Terrene Peas. Cream. Mushrooms. Terrene.

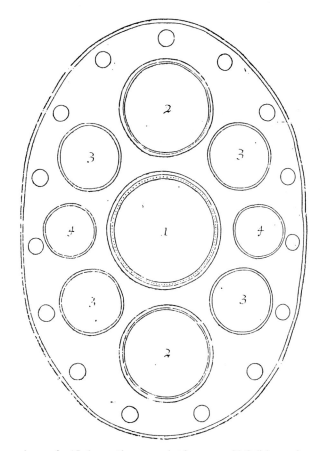

Table setting and menu for 15 place settings, served at 3 courses with 9 dishes each.

First course
1. Large joint of beef 'tremblante' garnished with small patés
2. Two soups (one partridge with vegetables in clear stock, one meat (lamb) stock)
3. 4 middle sized entrée dishes including pigeon pie, stuffed veal with parsley and cream, casserole with
    vin de bourgogne
4. 2 small entrée dishes including small chickens with eggs and sauce, and rare mutton

Second course
Large plate of Ham and baked tongue for the middle
2 plates of sugar for the end of the table
4 smaller roasts which include turkey, partridge and hare with accompanying side salads
2 salads for the sides of the table
2 plates of oranges and 2 sauces for the corners of the table
3 side dishes to serve with the roast which include Almond cake garnished with *croquantes*
Apple pie garnished with peaches *en sigovie*

Final course
4 medium dishes for the corners and 2 small dishes for the side
Mushrooms in cream
Foyes gras en ragout
Artichokes with parmesan

   Table setting from Le nouveau cuisinier royal et bourgeois *(Amsterdam, 1734).*

Apple Pye
Crab. Leveret [young hare]. Cheesecakes.

Dessert
Blamange. Raspberries and Cream. Almond Cream.
Cherries. Sweetmeats and Jelly. Currant and Gooseberries.
Dutch Cheese. Strawberries and cream. Orange Butter.

I have scratched it out very awkwardly, and hope the servants will place my dinner and dessert better on the table than I have on paper. I give as *little hot meat* as possible, but I think there could not be less, considering the grandees that are to be here : the invitation was to "*beef stakes*" which we are famous for.   ii p468

Undated menus on the back of an envelope in vol II of the Delany correspondence in Newport: these are in Anne Dewes' hand.

fricasey of chickens
minced venison   brawn
salver
sweetmeats
blackcaps [wild mushrooms]
roasted birds   white puddings

on the other side of the envelope

tongue   calves head
haunch of venison
fritters   veel
lamb   turkey   frye
a boyled pudding
duck or hare

Delville, 15 July 1750

Miss Hamilton [Mary Hamilton] is my confectioner today and is at this time making *orange-flower bread* of *my own orange flowers*, of which I am not a little proud: I am called to assist.   ii p571

Delville 8 November 1750

I have received an excellent Berkeley cheese, who am I indebted to for it? I owe Mrs Viney [family nanny to the Granville and now to the Dewes] for a Frogmill cheese I bespoke when last in Gloucester. I hope, *ague fits* are over now, and that you and the *Dew drops* [a nickname for her sister's family] are all in perfect health.
ii pp610–11

Delville, 12 January 1750/51

I have made a pipe of orange wine, and next week shall make rasin [raisin] wine by your receipt. This is an impertinent piece of news, is it not?   iii p6

Delville 2 September 1752

Yesterday, dined at Mrs Maxwell's at Finglass, and were most elegantly entertained, as she said, with her "own little dinner" – Mr Maxwell not being at home; I will give you our bill of fare:

Broyled Chicken, Bacon and Collyflower. Squad [Squab] Pigeons.

Stewed Carps. Epargne. Raised Venison Pie. Peas, Epargne, Mushrooms.

Chine of Mutton and hash under it. Turkey.

Dessert. Eight Baskets of Fruit.
Side table. Roast Beef, hot. Venison Pasty, cold.   iii p155

Lady Llanover quotes from Mary's letters written in July 1758

An amusing description follows of a dinner at Dr Clement's chambers in the college [Trinity College Dublin] where there was the largest turbot she had ever beheld at the top, roast veal at the bottom, pea-soup in the middle; "a whole pig that looked as if it had belonged to 'Martha of Calwich', it was so fat, and for a companion on the other side a shoulder of mutton both hashed and grilled: with a second course of grouse, partridges and lobsters and four other dishes", which unfortunately for the readers of the present century she had not time to particularize; the banquet was completed with raspberry cream and Chili strawberries.   iii p501

Some preserves had curative properties: the housekeepers were responsible for homemade remedies as well as eatables.

Delville 20 July, 1754

Don't you make a store of blackcurrant jelly? it is certainly a fine thing for a sore throat. iii p287

Delicacies were still procured from England via friends and relations. Mary Delany's mother had been very fond of chocolate, having been brought up in Spain, the country responsible for introducing it into Europe from her South American colonies.

Delville, 11 August, 1759

You talk of *candied orange flowers*; pray is it *clear* candy? if it is, I should be excessively glad of the receipt.   iii p562

Delville, 2 February 1760

I want six pounds of Mr Mawhood's best vanilla chocolate, such as he made for Sir Robert Brown, and should also be glad of four pounds of his best plain green tea at 16 or 18 shillings a pound.   iii pp583–84

PROVISIONS FROM THE FARM

Mary took a keen interest in the garden and small demesne surrounding Delville where they kept cattle for milk and deer, presumably for ornament as well as meat.

Delville, 26 July 1744

Today we are to dine with Mrs Ford. We have killed a second buck – I never saw finer venison; it would have grieved me to have any of my pretty herd killed, had they not been two mischievous old rogues that have almost killed the rest with their great unruly horns.   ii p318

Delville, 13 June 1747

And now I have a sad tale to tell you. My fine cow, who had just brought me a fine calf, died yesterday, just in the same manner as Fair Face; she was well at seven in the morning and grazing, and before eight, she was found fallen into a ditch, and died before night, very much swelled. The wise folks think it was some poisonous thing

View of cold bath field in Delville garden, by Mary Delany, 1748.

that she had eaten; we had her buried, skin and all, and her skin was cut cross and cross, that nobody might be tempted to dig her up. I hope it was nothing infectious, for thank God this country has hitherto escaped the sickness among the cattle. ii p465

Delville, February 1751

We killed a doe some time ago, as fine fat venison as ever was eaten, but I own, though D.D. laid a plot very cleverly to deceive me, when I discovered it was one of my own deer it took off my pleasure of eating it, but that's a folly I must try to break myself of, for they breed so very fast and thrive so prodigiously and our fields cannot well maintain above 15 or 16. I have a Nanny, a Mary, a Bell, and a Margaret that are to live as long as nature will let them. [Named after Ann Dewes, Mary Dewes, and Mary Dewes again, and the duchess of Portland, in that order].   iii pp15–16

GARDENING

Planning and working in the garden was Patrick Delany's great passion. Mary was very interested in flowers and had a serious botanical interest in them as well as a love of their beauty.

In the mid eighteenth century there was a great interest in estate management and improvement among landowners of all sizes of property. Many were interested in enhancing their estates with new planting and layout of the grounds. The new landscape or "landskip" movement and later, picturesque style, broke with the formality and stylised conventions of seventeenth century fashions in garden design and favoured the more natural look. Jonathan Swift was deeply interested in gardening and was in close touch with Alexander Pope, the influential poet and essayist. Swift's garden in the liberties of St Patrick's, Naboth's Vineyard, was acquired in 1721 and was the object of great interest and expense. Through Swift, Patrick Delany saw Pope's garden at Twickenham in 1726 and 1727. Pope was a friend of the architect William Kent, Lord Burlington's protegee, and encouraged Kent to develope his ideas on landscape. Delany was therefore in touch with and developing his ideas about garden layout at the same time as these great practitioners.

There were 11 acres of ground at the Delville property. There were paddocks for grazing the stock, besides the garden with all its features. Pope's three rules: Contrasts, the Management of Surprises, and the Concealment of Bounds were surely part of the Delville scheme of design. Patrick Delany was engaged in planting Delville at the time of his first marriage, and when Mary married him, she brought fresh impetus to his enthusiasm. The Delanys introduced as many fashionable features as would fit in their little kingdom, including the grotto made by Mary, the temple, "the beggar's hut", a bowling alley and an aviary or menagerie besides bridges over the river Tolka that watered their demesne. We know they kept deer and cattle, some of which were bred from her friend the duchess of Portland's Bulstrode breed. Many landowners were interested in livestock and new breeds in a scientific way which went hand in hand with the adornment of their property.

The Delanys invested much time and money in improving the Delville estate and were often called on to advise friends as they travelled about the country on duty and pleasure. They knew many of the famous gardens of the day through their English and Irish friends. Mary's immediate family were also keenly interested in gardening including her sister and brother Bernard. Her uncle Stanley employed a man called Russell in his garden at North End (Fulham, London), who became gardener to the marquis of Downshire at Hillsborough in County Down.

Dublin, 30 March 1732

I already delight in your garden; pray have plenty of roses, honeysuckles, jessamine and sweet briar, not forgetting the lily of the valley, which I would rather be than any flower that grows – 'tis retired, lives in shade, wraps up itself in its mantle, and gently reclines its head as if ashamed to be looked at, not conscious how much it deserves it. How pretty it is! Who would not be that flower?   i pp344–45

*Lily of the valley
by Mary Delany,
8 May 1776.*

On her visits to England, Mary collected plant seeds from the best sources for her garden in Delville.

Clarges Street, London, 30 March 1744

I have sent you by Mr Dewes some garden seed from the Oxford physic garden; you are to divide with my brother those that are for the natural ground and those for hot-beds are all your own, and some of the produce I bespeak for Delville, and hope you will sow them there with your own dear hands.   ii p286

Social life for the newly married Delanys took much of their time, although the garden was a focal interest. She paints an idyllic picture of it for her sister.

Delville, 19 July 1744

I shall be glad when I have time for sketches, but I believe that can hardly be this year; I have had twenty visitors already, and have returned but two. I wish I could give you an idea of our garden, but the describing it puzzles me extremely; the back part of the house is towards a bowling green that slopes gently off down to a little brook that runs through the garden; on the other side of the brook is a high bank with a hanging wood of ever-greens, at the top of which is a circular terrace that surrounds the greatest part of the garden, the wall of which is covered with fruit-trees, and on the other side of the walk a border for flowers, and the greatest quantity of roses and sweet briar that ever I saw; on the right hand of the bowling green towards the bottom is placed our hay-rick, which is at present making, and from our parlour-window and bedchamber I can see the men work at it, and have a full view of what I have described; and beyond that, pleasant meadows bounded by mountains of various shapes, with little villages, and country seats interspersed and embosomed high in tufted trees: to complete the prospect a full view of Dublin harbour which is always full of shipping, and looks at this instant beautiful beyond all description.

These are the views from the house *next* the gardens. On the left hand of the bowling-green is a terrace-walk that takes in a sort of a parterre, that will make the prettiest orangery in the world, for it is an oval of green, planted round in double rows of elm-trees and flowering shrubs with little grass walks between them, which will give a good shelter to exotics. The terrace I just mentioned is bounded at one end by a wall of good fruit, in which there is a door that leads to another very large handsome terrace-walk, with double rows of large elms, and the walk well gravelled, so that we may walk securely in any weather. On the left hand, the ground rises very consider-ably and is planted with all sorts of trees. About half way up the walk there is a path that goes up that bank to the remains of an old castle (as it were) from whence there is an unbounded prospect all over the country: under it is a cave that opens with an arch to the terrace-walk, that will make a very pretty grotto; and the plan I had laid for my brother at Calwich (this being of that shape, though not quite so large) I shall execute here. At the end of this terrace is a very pretty portico, prettily painted within and neatly finished without; you go up a high slope to it, which gives it a mighty good air as you come up the walk: from thence you go on the right hand to the green terrace I mentioned at first, which takes in the whole compass of this garden; in the middle, sloping from the terrace, every way, are the fields, or rather paddocks, where our deer and our cows are kept, and the rurality of it is wonderfully pretty. These fields are planted in a *wild way* with *forest trees and with bushes* that look so naturally you would not imagine it to be the work of art.

Besides this, there is a very good kitchen garden and two fruit gardens, which when proper repairs are made, and they are set in order, will afford us a sufficient quantity of everything we can want of that kind. There are several prettinesses I can't explain to you – little wild walks, private seats, and lovely prospects. One seat particularly I am very fond of, in a nut grove, and *"the beggar's hut"* which is a seat in a rock; on the top are bushes of all kinds that bend over; it is placed at the end of a cunning wild path thick set with trees and it overlooks the brook which entertains you with a purling rill. The little robins are as fond of this seat as we are; it just holds the Dean and myself, and I hope in God to have many a tête à tête there with my own dear sister; but I have had such a hurry of business within doors, and so many visitors, that I have not spent half so much time in this sweet garden as I want to do.
ii pp314–16

In order to entice her sister over to stay she had the idea of naming a feature, Pearly Bower, which referred to her nickname, the "Pearly Dews", for the Dewes family.

Delville, 9 March 1744/45

I thank God we are both at present in very good health, and the few warm days we have had, have given an air of cheerfulness and spring that revives all one's senses, Delville begins now to open its sweets, and yesterday and the morning before I spent two hours in my garden and paid my affectionate homage to the *"Pearly Bower"*. D.D. is restoring some winding walks that the encroaching weeds had almost smothered. The birds sing melodiously, and there is one chaffinge [chaffinch] and two robins that eat out of his hand; I wish they may not grow quite wild again before we return from the North; but cold and want will bring them to hand again – the great tamers of the human as well as the animal kind.   ii p342

Delville, 24 August 1745

Again I am returned to my dwelling. This place is now in perfect beauty, and the weather has been so fine that every hour of the day I could spare from business and meals has been spent in the garden, chiefly in *Pearly Dewes'* Bower where one of our tame robins welcomed us home, and flew to the Dean's hand for the bounty he used to bestow. But I have my hands so full of business at present that I much fear I shall not be able to make my letter so long so I wish to make it.   ii p378

Delville, 23 November 1745

I was going in all haste to have a new fruit wall built but it must now be deferred till spring. The lawn before our house, where our sheep are to feed, will be finished soon, and will be a great improvement to the view before that part of the house.   ii p400

Delville, 25 January 1745/46

Did I write you word we had got a new terene? [tureen or earthenware cooking dish] the Dean invented it, and drew the draught; it is very well executed, the chasing is mighty well done: it holds six quarts and has a very light look. My next work will be to make a nine-pin alley, which I have undertaken to do; we have a little odd nook of a garden, at the end of which is a very pretty summer-house, and in the corners of it are houses built up for blowing auriculas; it is upon the whole of a triangular form, long and narrow, much like this scratch.

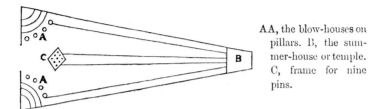

AA, the blow-houses on pillars. B, the summer-house or temple. C, frame for nine pins.

The walls to be covered with evergreens, and room enough for borders of flowers. It was originally designed for a nursery for flowers, but the walls are too close; it is very near the house, and will make a special nine-pin alley, which I think a *very merry exercise*. We had thoughts of having a bowling green before our house in the garden front; but the hill, which descends gradually to the brook, looks so natural and pretty as it is, that it would be a pity to make it level; and so we determine to keep it a lawn, and to have sheep.   ii pp416–417

Delville, 1 February 1745/46

We have lately had very sharp weather, frost and some snow; but the sun has shone between whiles, and the verdure of our fields gives a cheerfulness to our prospects in the midst of winter that I never saw in any other place. The spring appears in my flower-garden, but I am afraid the frosty mornings will nip the forward things. I am less concerned at any defect that may happen there this year, as I hope to spend the blooming season in England. D.D. and I talk every day of our intended journey; when he sees me in a sighing way, he then as a cordial *begins upon that subject*, and it never fails answering his kind intention.   ii p418

Delville, 22 March 1745/46

I have begun my morning walks. I was two hours almost in the garden this morning before breakfast. The sweetness of the air, the singing of the birds, and the charming prospect made it appear like an enchanted place after having been buried in snow and chilled with nipping frost for a fortnight together: we have had about a week of good weather.   ii p431

Delville, 29 March 1745/46

Our garden is now a wilderness of sweets. The violets, sweet briar, and primroses perfume the air, and the thrushes are full of melody and make our concert complete. It is the pleasantest music I have heard this year, and refreshes my spirits without the alloy of a tumultuous crowd, which attends all the other concerts. Two robins and one chaffinch fed off of D.D's hand as we walked together this morning. I have been planting sweets in my "Pearly Bower" – honeysuckles, sweet briar, roses and jessamine to climb up the trees that compose it, and for the carpet, violets, primroses, and cowslips. This year I shall not smell their fragrancy, nor see their bloom, but I shall see the dear person to whom the bower is dedicated I hope, and I think I shall not repine at the exchange.   ii p432

After a year in England Mary and the Dean returned to their home and garden. Each year brought new pleasures.

Delville, 13 June 1747

I have made my alley very spruce and sown in the border some of the flower seeds I brought with me from Welsbourne [her sister's home in Warwickshire].   ii p464–65

D.D. to Mary
Mount Panther, 15 August 1747
extract from unpublished manuscript, Newport Library Gwent

You have some little balance in the account of your trees of which I heartily give you joy and earnestly beg you may place and plant them where you think best, without loss of time; first soaking the roots for some hours in the warmest part of the Swift [the river running through their garden], then planting them carefully in pap [special compost?], which James Potter will very well do, under direction.

Poultry were part of the livestock kept at Delville.

Delville, 6 October 1747

The morning has been fair and tempted me to stay longer in my garden than I designed, and I received a present of two pair of beautiful shelldrakes, and have been settling them in their bounds – a pretty field called the *Star-Field*, joining to my garden, with a little pond in it. They have for companions a *colt* and a *barnacle*.
ii p473

Delville, 20 October 1747

This morning I was delighted with seeing the rising sun as I lay in my bed, rising above a tuft of trees that face my window. Our garden is still in high beauty, our elms as green as ever, and the evergreens are in perfection. We have a great number of holly trees in our evergreen grove, and they are now full of red berries, and look very rich – Why are you not here to see them?   ii p478

Delville, 20 August 1748

My orange trees come on finely; there is but one that has failed, and four of them bore prodigiously. All my plants and flowers have done very well, that is, all that came up before I went into the country, except the tuberoses and they promise but indifferently.

My flower garden which is now just under my eye, is a wilderness of flowers, the beds are overpowered with them, and though the enamelled look they have is rich and pretty, I believe it will be advisable to have the different sorts of flowers appear rather more distinct.   ii pp499, 500

Mary was ingenious when it came to transporting plants for her garden in Delville: her portable garden, alas, was mislaid.

Delville, 22 May 1750

I have found my house in pretty good order and the garden *is paradisaical*. Oh that my dearest sister could see it with as much ease as going to Stratford or Warwick and yet with *such* a passage as *we had* from Park Gate to Dublin, the voyage is not so formidable an affair as it appears to be; for we dined at Park Gate on Sunday at one, and the next day at Delville at 5!

After all the bother and rout I made about my *portable garden* it is lost; the box can nowhere be found. I gave it in charge my self to the captain of the ship that brought it over (it did not come with us) and he knows nothing of the matter. Our fruits and flowers have been much hurt by the easterly winds; it is now so cold that a fire is comfortable, though the sky is clear and the sun bright and *my prospects* in great perfection. Tiger is perfectly well, and our little robins as familiar as usual. ii pp546–47

Mary to her brother Bernard Granville
Delville, 17 June 1750

Did I write you word of my disappointment about my *travelling-garden?* Not a plant saved, all jumbled to pieces; so I shall no more attempt such difficulties, but must content myself with what I can raise from seed.   ii p557

Travelling to the north to visit the deanery of Down often meant that Mary missed the blooms in her Delville garden.

Delville, 8 June 1750

We have not yet fixed our time for the northern journey, nor can we, having everything to provide of furniture for the house we go to. Sometimes in the midst of my enjoyment of the garden it makes me sigh to think that my fruits and flowers, which I with care and pains have planted, will be gathered by others. Not that I am such a churl as to *grudge* my friends, or even my acquaintance, the produce of my garden, but I wish only to have the pleasure of bestowing them myself and of having some share of them; then, on the other hand, when I consider how much good D.D's presence must do in the North – and I hope *I may* in a small degree do some – I think of my journey cheerfully and set about preparing for it *manfully! That* expression

Beggar's hut in the Delville garden, by Mary Delany, 1745.

does *not suit the occasion*, for if *the men* were to go through all domestic bustle as we are obliged to do when we acquit ourselves properly, they would think themselves *somewhat obliged* by the trouble we *save them!*   ii pp551–52

Delville, 22 June 1750

My garden is at present in the high glow of beauty, my cherries ripening, roses, jessamine, and pinks in full bloom, and the hay partly spread and partly in cocks, complete the rural scene. We have discovered a new breakfasting place under the shade of nut-trees, impenetrable to the sun's rays in the midst of a grove of elms, where we shall breakfast this morning; I have ordered cherries, strawberries, and nosegays to be laid on our breakfast table, and have appointed a harper to be here to play to us during our repast, who is to be hid among the trees. Mrs Hamilton is to breakfast with us, and is to be cunningly led to this place *and surprised.*

Friday, spent the whole day without any interruption at home, worked, walked, talked till dinner, and sat quiet, listening to the harper, till 6; then picked roses – three baskets full. At 7, drank tea in the orangerie; then walked all over our meadows, fed our deer, saw two beautiful fawns and the two young favourite coach-horses eat their oats in the field; stood by whilst the cows were milking, till it grew so late that we thought it prudent to come home.   ii pp558–60

Delville, 15 July 1750

I never enjoyed Delville so much as I have done this year, there having hardly been a day that I could not live in the garden from morning till night.   vii pp570

Mary to her brother Bernard Granville
Delville, 22 September 1750

The weather is delightful at present. D.D. very busy, topping exuberant branches, transplanting, and giving air to his garden. The trees and shrubs are grown so thick we are obliged to thin them.   ii p593

Delville, 28 September 1750

Temperate and pleasant as May! I have just been gleaning my autumn fruits – *melon, figs*, beury pears, *grapes, filberts*, and *walnuts*. Walnuts indeed are but just come in with us. I loaded my basket and filled my hands with honeysuckles, jessamine, July flowers, and pippins. My letter begins like one of Millar's calendar months. I pleased myself whilst I was gathering Flora's and Pomona's gifts in thinking that my dear sister might be occupied in the same way. The garden was truly particularly pleasant to me this day, not having been in it since Monday last. D.D. has not been well, but, I thank God, is this day enjoying his plantations.   ii p594–95

Delville, 13 October 1750

It is well my good Dean has his garden to relax and relieve his spirits for now they are much turmoiled with his Tennison lawsuit; it is to come on next term; he prefers [profers?] his cross bill [a legal document] in a few days.   ii p603

Here Mary plans a green house which will also accomodate someone to care for her exotic fowl.

Mary to her brother Bernard Granville,
Delville, 19 January 1750/51

I am now considering about a green house, and believe I shall build one this spring; my orange trees thrive *so well* they deserve one. I propose having it 26 feet by 13, and 13 high, and a room under it with a chimney for my poultry woman) that will open into a little back garden, which I intend to make my menagerie. Will you tell me if the chimney will be any disadvantage to my orange-trees?   iii p7

Delville, February 1751

Freezing almost by the fireside, but the garden is pleasant, and the *violets and crocus's* very blooming. D.D. is raising his paddock wall. About a fortnight ago a man got over it with three dogs and set them at our deer, but luckily the gardener saw them before mischief was done; we now have sixteen deer.   iii p15

Mary to her brother Bernard Granville
Delville, 11 June 1751

We have just ordered the table to be laid to dine in the garden. I thank you for your kind hint about my orange-trees; when is the proper time for trimming them? I have lost one of the variegated sort; it died of an apoplexy – was in appearance healthy when I brought it out the 20th May with the rest of my trees, and in a day or two it dropped. I have not the heart to trim them now – they are so *thick budded* to blossom. I have laid aside my scheme this year for a green house, but am going to make up a menagerie, which is what I most immediately want. I have got fourteen young wild ducks, a cock and hen pheasant, and a black cock and hen with white toppings that are the prettiest things I ever saw; and four young beauty fawns, fallen within these four days: so my cares increase, and I have a great deal of business in a morning, walking about amongst my animals and seeing them properly attended.   iii p39

Delville, 19 June 1752

I have just inoculated two orange trees of my own raising and have planted 26 myrtles in my orangerie.   iii p133

In summer the Delanys rose early to take full advantage of the garden.

Delville, 29 May 1753

The weather is charming and Delville in the highest bloom of youth and beauty; I am in the garden every morning by 7 o'clock and great part of the day besides. iii p231

Delville, 22 June 1754

Our gardens are in high order and beauty: I have just agreed with a skilful gardener to take the care of all my fruits and flowers, without having anything to do with any other part of the garden, so I hope Flora and Pomona will both flourish. I have got a cook, housemaid, coachman and postilion to drive with four horses, and we talk of setting out next Tuesday se'night, but I believe our coach will hardly be ready to go so soon, but D.D. is impatient, though in the midst of his haymaking, to be on the spot where he thinks his duty most calls him.   iii p279

Delville, 13 July 1754

Our hay goes on marvellously well. Sally [her goddaughter] and I wandered over fields and garden and then settled in the orangerie.   iii pp285–86

This mock satirical poem is included in Lady Llanover's edition of the letters with a note that it was written by Sheridan (presumably Thomas) or Swift, in which case it must be Delville in the 1730s when they knew it.

> Would you that Delville I describe?
> Believe me sir I will not jibe;
> For who would be satirical upon a thing so very small?
>
> Yet in this narrow compass, we
> Observe a vast variety;
> Both walks, walls, meadows, and parterres,
> Windows, and doors, and rooms and stairs,
>
> And round this garden is a walk,
> No longer than a tailor's chalk;
> Thus I compare what space is in it,
> *A snail creeps round it in a minute.*
> One lettuce make a shift to squeeze
> Up through a tuft you call your trees;
> And, once a year, a single rose
> Peeps from the bud, but never blows;
>
> "In short, in all your boasted seat,
> There's nothing *but yourself that's great!*"   iii pp499–500

Over the years the garden and farm provided endless pleasure.

Delville, 10 March 1759

I have an additional beauty to-day to my prospect – *a fine lake* opposite to my window by the overflowing of a meadow! News just now brought me, – *my white cow* (of the Bulstrode breed) delivered of a calf.   iii p540

The Delville garden was small by comparison with many other Irish gardens, like that made by the Wesleys of Dangan, but the Delanys were able to include many features which involved a good deal of expense. Swift satirised Patrick's expensive hobby in "An Epistle upon an Epistle":

> But you forsooth, your all must squander,
> On that poor spot, call'd Del-Ville yonder:
> And when you've been at vast Expences
> In Whims, Parterres, Canals and Fences:
> Your Assets fail and Cash is wanting
> For farther buildings, farther Planting . . .
> Williams, *Poems of Swift,*   vol.ii p475.

Mary seemed to enter in to all the gardening schemes with the same reckless enthusiasm.

Delville, 7 July 1759

Since beginning this letter a whim came into my head of making a bridge from the walnut-path (which is bounded by a rill) to Elmy, proposed it to D.D., *approved*; am now finishing my letter near the spot, and the carpenter is *already* sawing and hewing with all his might to make room for my bridge; called to consultation!   iii p558

Delville, 11 August 1759

I am as full of business as a bee, having various workmen to attend. We have lowered the wall that encompassed the garden from twelve to five feet, which has a very good effect, and opens the view to very pretty fields of our own, where our deer and cows graze; they are rising grounds, with some clumps and scattered trees.   iii p562

After two and a half years absence in England while her sister was ill and then after her death in July, 1761, the Delanys returned to Delville where they took up their old interests of the garden and duties in the north. Mary also enjoyed botanising with her goddaughter, Sally Chapone.

Mary to her brother Bernard Granville
Delville, 20 June 1763

The Dean has been much revived by the enjoyment of his favourite Delville, which indeed looks very pretty and smells very sweet. Hay is making under my closet window in the lawn, and some improvements have been made that answer very well. I thank God, I am very well, but not quite as ready a walker, except on plain ground; however, I can creep round my garden, resting between whiles, and I gather strength every day.   iv p17

Mary to her niece Mary Dewes
[Hollymount? undated letter written after her sister Ann's death]

We found our cottage clean and the garden very sweet. I have brought a variety of works and Sally and I saunter abroad a good deal in the cool part of the day, bring home handfuls of wild plants and search for their names and virtues in Hill – but he is not half so intelligible as old Gerard.   iv pp19–20

As the Delanys grew older, their interest in the garden remained undiminished.

Mary to her niece, Mary Dewes
Delville, 12 March 1765

We have had the coldest winter I think I ever remember in Ireland and several of my finest myrtles cruelly nipt by it; and the spring in general very backward. I am going as soon as the frost will permit me to plant some more shrubs and happy should I be could my dear Mary accompany me through the windings and shade of my small

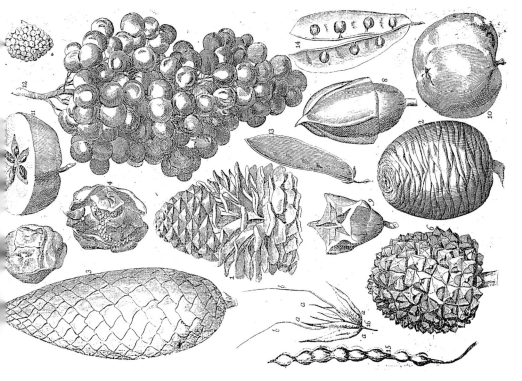

Illustration from Philip Miller's Gardener's dictionary *(Dublin, 1764).*

improvements, and partake of all my rural pleasures, such as I know she delights in.
iv p45

Mary to Viscountess Andover
Delville, 8 June 1765

I have lived much in my garden, and that prevents works at home. I am *afraid* to begin with painting; there is a time for all things, and when the sight grows dim, I think it is a warning to leave off *without* losing the small credit I may have gained! The warm weather has brought swarms to the garden, and I have seen more company within this fortnight than for four months past.

    Those that will come to me in *all* seasons are most welcome, and I have a few that *never fail me*; and fortunately they are the prime of my acquaintance.   iv p50

When she left Ireland, she developed her interest in flowers into another medium, that of paper collages, the famous cutpaper mosaics of botanical illustration, made in the 1770s (despite this last reference to fading sight).

FAMILY CONCERNS

Although she set up her own household in Ireland, she followed the doings of the Dewes household and children with great interest. Here she passes on to her sister the Dean's characteristically humane advice on education.

Hollymount, 17 August 1745

The Dean thinks you are in the wrong to teaze yourself about your little boy's not loving his book, and you should be cautious *not* to give him a *distaste* to it by *pressing him too much*, for he is young enough to be indulged another year.   ii p378

Delville, 30 November 1745

I am glad the fair little boy was so well before you were obliged to leave him. I think you have exerted the motherly authority very heroically, and I don't doubt but he will bless you in time for the *little smart* he has received from your hands. You have more merit in such a case than the generality of mothers can have, because you have more tenderness almost than any human creature.   ii p401

Luckily Mary was able to enjoy first hand the company of babies and infants because of the extended family of Delanys who lived with them.

Delville, 30 November 1745

Mrs Green [D.D's neice] had an extraordinary good time [referring to the birth of little Tommy]; she says that she expected to have felt a great deal more; I was surprised at that, for I always thought whatever apprehensions were, pain always far exceeded them. I pray God it may be so with you, on his mercy and goodness I rely, and that only can support my spirits at this time [her sister was expecting Mary Dewes].   ii p401

Delville, 18 January 1745/6

I am now under some distress for poor Mrs Green; her pretty little boy, [Tommy] I am afraid, is in a dangerous way. Dr Barber has attended him constantly and this morning desires the assistance of a man-midwife to consult with. Mrs Green is greatly afflicted, she is of a quiet, affectionate disposition and not apt to complain, which makes grief prey upon her more sharply; we had all grown very fond of the little boy; it is an exceedingly pretty child; but I hardly think he can recover [fortunately he did]. ii p413

Here she renames her little niece already named after her, and her remarks give an interesting insight into childrearing in her sister's household.

Delville, 28 February 1745/6

I have this moment received a letter from Mrs Viney [Granville family nurse], dated the 19th instant (which I think was your ninth day); she tells me you are better than you have ever been yet, and that my niece eats paps purely. It will save some trouble *if you can* bring her up by hand, and since she is naturally so stout *I believe it may perhaps be done.*   ii p425

Delville, 8 March 1745

I am very glad my niece Mary takes so well to her food: I don't see why it should not rear her up as it did me: I won't have her like me in everything that *is worthy* of your regard, but to endear her *equally to me*, I wish most heartily she may resemble my own dearest sister. You remember Madame de Sevigne: Mary must be *my Pauline*. ii p427

Delville, 29 March 1746

My little *"Pauline"* is (though unknown) a great favourite already, and you may command everything from me that can be of service to her, but you are so well furnished with materials to make her a complete valuable woman, that you will want no foreign aid; however, I hope we shall lay our wise heads together about her many and many an hour: in the meantime feed her and dance her well, for that is all can be attended to at present.   ii pp431–32

A sad development gave the Delanys more responsibility. The Dean's niece, Mrs Green, died, probably in the early part of 1748.

Delville 20 August 1748

All my domestics and neighbours rejoiced at our return; the sight of poor little Tommy Greene [then 3 years old] was a renewal of the concern we had felt for the loss of his valuable mother, and the little creature was so transported at my coming home, that it was moving to see the silent pleasure he had, for he could not speak, but hugged and stroked my arms, and would not stir one minute from me, as if directed to beseech my protection and make up in some measure his loss. His father (a most disconsolate man) is gone the circuit, and returns this week.   ii p499

She continued to follow the development of her niece and nephews with great interest and emphasised the learning of manners and graces early.

Delville, 15 July 1750

I hope you are now enjoying sweet breezes under Calwich trees, and my dear little Mary playing on the grass under your eye: she is too much a jewel to be trusted out of sight, and though the boys are as valuable, you must be a little weaned from them, as their different education must call them from you.   ii p569

Delville, 9 February 1750/51

About Mary: it is of much consequence to men and women to receive all instructions early, I am sure as many years *after* they are sixteen is not so advantageous to them as so *many months* before that age. Very young minds are susceptible of very strong impressions: they have then nothing of consequence to draw off their attention. As they grow older and mix with company, and in conversation, the *whole crowd* of youthful vanities breaks in upon their minds, and leaves but little room for instruction.   iii p14

Delville, 16 March 1750/51

I have consulted D.D. about Bunny [Bernard Dewes], as you desired, and though he is not, generally speaking, *for very young* children going to school, he thinks it best for Bunny to go as soon as his health is established; and that nothing will so effectually spur him on to learn as *emulation* (which he *cannot have at home*), nor get the better of any humoursomeness *(a strange word)* as in the discipline of a school; and he most heartily wishes and prays, that the excellent foundation you have laid in your children's early education may procure you all the happiness you deserve.

  If Pauline [Mary Dewes] proves handsome, which *indeed* I think she *bids fair for*, it is in vain to hope that she *can be kept ignorant of it*; all that the wisest friend can do for her is to teach her of how little value beauty is – how few years it lasts – how liable to be tarnished, and if it has its advantages, what a train of inconveniences also attend it; that it requires a double portion of discretion to guard it, and much more caution and restraint, than one that is not handsome.

  I do not wish to have our Pauline *blind* to her own perfections; but rather have her *so far* sensible of them, as never to do anything that can make the advantages providence has bestowed upon her a reproach, but an incitement to do honour to herself and her family. I wish you had an opportunity of having her learn to dance: I make it my request to you, if you have, that you will not lose it; her cousin Granville, who is one of the best dancers I ever saw, danced a minuet very prettily at five years of age; it is not only an advantage in giving a graceful air to the person, but it *gives strength* to the limbs, and is the *best sort of exercise she can use.* I hope you will have the boys learn when they go to Warwick; Garrick [the actor] is the genteelest dancer *I ever saw.*   iii pp24–27

Mary Dewes, from an enamel by Zincke.

In this letter Mary employs a striking image from nature to describe the family scene she is missing.

Delville, 23 January 1753

I hope you keep yourself very warm, and guard as much as possible against all chilling blasts. I *see* your children running like lapwings in the orchard, and then hovering round you with rosy cheeks and crimson noses, and their little hands blue and swelled with the cold.   iii p197

Delville, 7 April 1753

I don't doubt of my dear Mary's being perfectly well managed, but I shall be glad to have her learn to dance. It will help to strengthen her limbs, and make her grow, even though she may not be taught in the best manner. I hope you will give her every winter an opportunity of being taught either at the Bath or London, and of seeing variety of good company, which is of more use in forming a gracious manner from the age of seven to fourteen than seven years afterwards! Every impression taken in our tender years is more lasting than when the mind is more filled with a crowd of ideas.   iii p219

Delville, 5 May 1753

There is nothing I wish so much for Mary, *next* to right religious principles, as a *proper* knowledge of the polite world. It is *the only means* of keeping her safe from an immoderate love of its vanities and follies, and of giving her that sensible kind of reserve which great retirement converts either to awkward sheepishness, or occasions the *worst evil of the two – forward pertness*, but this must be matter of conversation, not of letters.   iii p227

The Delanys had leased a house in London which Mary urged her sister to use for bringing her niece forward in society, then 13 years old!

Delville, 16 December 1758

And now I must again entreat you to spend two or three months in Spring Gardens for the sake of Mary. You will do my house great service, and save me some trouble and some fibs, for I have been applied to often to lend or let my house, and my answer, "*it is engaged to you*," and the Duchess of Portland made me swear I would let nobody *but yourself* go into it!   iii p528

Delville, 23 December 1758

I have indeed set my heart much upon your going to town, and you have a draught on Gosling [bankers], etc., which I designed should pay for the Birmingham boxes, but that scheme is altered, and the toilette they were to stand on is banished from the bow closet, and I must take the liberty of begging you will lay that out for my Mary in the way you like best. Is she not tall enough for a *robe*? and would not a full pink colour satin become her? I am sorry I have sent for my sedan chair, as it might be of use to you; I want one here to carry me to church when it rains, and as I design having a new one when I go to London; I thought my old one would do very well here, and the carriage less expense than buying a new one.   iii pp530–31

Their bachelor brother took an interest in the musical education of Mary Dewes although Aunt Delany was more concerned about her gaining social confidence.

Delville, 27 January 1759

Mr Granville [Bernard, their brother] I suppose will lend you a clavichord; Mary has had *uncommon* advantages at home for the improvement of what is *most* material, and a foundation is laid, by her excellent and kind instructors, that will make her happy beyond this earthly tabernacle; but this is not all that is requisite, unless she is to turn hermit. There is a *grace* and a *manner* which cannot be attained without conversing with a variety of well-bred people, which when well chosen cannot efface what is certainly more necessary, but will give a polish, and by an agreeable recommendation render all the good part more useful and acceptable to those she converses with.   iii p537

The subject of marriage was inevitably discussed, although Mary shows a somewhat ambiguous approach to it.

Delville, 31 March 1759

I am quite of your mind about marrying; I should be very sorry to have Mary married before she was twenty, and yet if a very desirable match offers sooner, I don't know how it can be refused, if *she must* marry at all?   iii p544

Delville, 16 February 1760

Lady Cowper [her niece's other godmother] will like to be consulted about Mary's dress, and is a good judge. Dunoyer is now I believe the best dancing-master in London, his price is high, but he will give the Pauline a better air in a month than a less skilful dancing-master would in three.   iii pp584–85

She also gave encouragement in the more serious matter of religion.

Delville, 20 January 1760

I was pleased with your account of my nephew Dewes' desire of receiving the blessed Sacrament, and serious behaviour there. So good a foundation will enable him to support the trials *"that flesh is heir to."* If there *had been* any opportunity of his being confirmed before he received the Sacrament, I am sure it *would not* have been neglected; but I do not apprehend it so necessary now. Whatever is right I think we need not fear his doing, allowing for the errors of human nature, and I pray God bless him and make him a blessing to his excellent parents!   iii p581

*In the choice of a college for her nephew, Court Dewes the eldest, Mary was
inclined towards one where he would acquire social advantages as well as
learning.*

Delville, 13 October 1759

I have had much conversation of late about *Oxford*, and find all the men of learning
and sobriety think it more advantageous to enter a lad a *commoner* than a *gentleman
commoner*, and say it does not by any means shut them out from good company,
which if they are inclined to keep, they will always find the means of doing. Mr
Sandford is well acquainted with Balliol College and Mr G-n; he is a very learned
man as to books but *ignorant of the world*, and a stranger to all manner of politeness,
and not a conversable man. I am greatly inclined to wish you and Mr Dewes may
approve of Christ Church. There are many advantages in that college superior to the
rest, particularly his being admitted as a student is a very desirable thing, when a
vacancy happens, and I could make good interest with Dr Gregory, who is a very
worthy man.

As you have time to consider before you fix Master Dewes, it is not amiss for you
to hear different opinions, and I am sure you and Mr Dewes will not think me
meddling or impertinent in what I say.

The tutor at Christ Church that Mr Sandford mentioned is Mr Hollwell, about his
own age and standing. It is certainly a very great advantage to have the tutor and
pupils good friends, and a great difference in years makes that almost impracticable.
Mr Sandford says if my nephew is entered at any other college besides Christ Church,
he may be in two years time a fellow of New College by the favour of the Chancellor;
nothing is more desirable, and I believe I could be of service to him with Lord
Westmoreland.   iii pp569–70

*After her sister's death in 1761 she took her responsibilities as an aunt
seriously and wrote solemnly to her young niece.*

Mary to her niece Mary Dewes
1763

I make no doubt of your employing your time well, and like the provident ant, that
you will work in the spring and summer of your life for your support in the winter.
You cannot have too many *innocent* amusements, provided you do *not neglect* what
is essential to learn; and indeed an ingenious mind will always find most entertainment from those employments that improve it. All human creatures have a natural
inclination to knowledge, which is generally called curiosity, and if rightly directed it
will be the means of great improvement to yourself, and make you agreeable and
amiable to all your acquaintance. If it turns to mere frivolous curiosity it will lead you
astray, and instead of finding you are in the midst of roses and every desirable fruit
and flower, you will be entangled amongst briars and nettles, and all sorts of noxious
weeds.

Our business in this world, my dear, is preparing for another; and in order to make
that exchange a happy one we must act up to the name we have taken upon us of

Christianity. The rules are plain and easy, if indolence or luxury do not interfere and blind us. And a habit of doing our duty regularly is the best guard against the evils and temptations that beset us, and by accustoming ourselves to that regularity we shall find no manner of difficulty, but rather be uneasy at any omission. This is a long sermon, but you flatter me in saying you *like* to receive any advice from your friends, and are sensible that it can only proceed from true affection.   iv pp18–19

On Mary Dewes' nineteenth birthday, Aunt Delany wrote in a serious tone.

Mary to her niece Mary Dewes
Delville, 12 March 1765

My dear Mary, are *you* really a chess player? Why, it seems as extraordinary as if our Prime Minister was to dance a jig. Not that I question your ingenuity, which I am sure is equal to to the task, but it requires the sobriety of threescore rather than *nineteen*. Don't imagine I mean to ridicule your acquisition of this game, which I admire you for learning, and is an excellent school for keeping the thoughts steady, and therefore sometimes very useful.

I may say prayers for your enjoying many years of felicity; for bad as this world is, it has its felicities, especially when the hopes of future happiness is the chief point we aim at; indeed our *in*felicities are often of our own creating, by expectations that are *too high*, or by acting *too meanly*!

The first is not so desperate a case as the latter, as time will show the fallacy of unreasonable expectations; but *that of not acting up to our own dignity* is doing ourselves an *irreparable injury*. I am sure, my dear Mary, you know how to distinguish between a proper respect for ourselves, and pride.

You may shine at a ball, be as well dressed as anybody, and by a *proper* and *prudent* behaviour give and receive pleasure, without the least amputation of pride; and you may visit your poor neighbours, and with your own hands bestow every comfort, without the imputation of meanness, but quite the contrary when it is done with true Christian benevolence, but if your charity is bestowed with ostentation and arrogance, you then are *proud*, if you are *affected* and *impertinent* in your behaviour at a ball, you *then are mean*.

I congratulate you on the happy disposition, that leads you to *contentment*. Cherish it as the means of more certain happiness than any other inclination can give; *'tis the true cordial drop!*   iv pp43–44

At last, after 23 years living in Ireland, some of her immediate family visited her at Delville!

Mary to Viscountess Andover
Delville, 19 August 1766

I have been happy for ten days past in the company of my two eldest nephews [Court and Bernard]. Their father has kindly permitted them to make me a month's visit, and I rout about with them to every place within the compass of a day's journey; and the Dean has exerted himself so much for them that I hope we shall both pass the winter in better health for it. *Three years* has made a great progress in their lives, and I think improvement. Their good sense, *simplicity* of manners, and excellent principles make me so satisfied with them that I don't feel the least mortified they are not a *foot taller*, and have not the "*bon tons*" at present so much idolized, but they have, I trust, qualities that will make them valuable to their friends and useful in the world. Consider, my dear Lady Andover, *whose* children they are, and how long since I saw them, and forgive this long harangue, which in truth is more natural than polite. iv p69

Mary to her nephew Bernard Dewes
Delville, 16 October 1766

I am glad you had the satisfaction of finding your father and brother John well. As to my own health, I have reason to be very thankful it is so good. Friends in Granby Row and Summer Hill all pretty well. No end of kind inquiries about you and regrets for your absence. Mr Edward Hamilton still in Swainston, doing all his good nature dictates to amuse his sister [Mrs Preston, formerly a Hamilton], who is very reasonable, and complies with everything she is desired to do, but still sad at heart, and not as well in health as her friends wish her to be, tho' time, I hope, will befriend her; it is her first loss, and a very tender one. If my nephew John is unwilling to increase his number of friends and well-wishers I give him warning *not* to come to Ireland, for all your friends here are so disposed to a brother of yours that it will be impossible for him to escape the snare.   iv p86

The Dewes family continued to be a source of great interest and comfort to her; no doubt her return to London and England gave more opportunities for them all to enjoy her company.

CHAPTER 6

THE NORTH: LIFE IN COUNTY DOWN

Soon after their marriage in 1743 Mary exerted all her efforts and family connections to obtain a position for Patrick Delany which would combine status and income, or at least worthy remuneration of his talents. Although she cherished ambitions of a bishopric for him, after a few years she acknowledged that the comfortable existence they enjoyed at Delville was infinitely preferable to an episcopal palace in a remote diocese.

Patrick Delany took his responsibilities seriously when he was appointed dean of Down in 1744. This represented an increase in his income and a considerable increase in pastoral and administrative responsibility. The dean of Down at that time was in charge of the corps of the Dean, a grouping which consisted of the parishes of Downpatrick, Saul, Ballyculter, Ballee, Bright and Tyrella. He relinquished his Dublin and Kildare parish livings and the chancellorship of St Patrick's on his appointment to the deanery. He maintained some links with Trinity College where he had been a fellow and lecturer. In an age of clerical absenteeism, full of the abuse of pluralities, Patrick Delany was rather exemplary. He and (sometimes) Mary made annual summer visits to Down, despite the lack of a deanery house, where he devoted himself to his flock with zeal, rebuilding churches and the Downpatrick jail. The cathedral was in ruins and many of the local churches had suffered from neglect after the upheavals of the seventeenth century.

At first the Delanys stayed in a house called Mount Panther, then, for the next two years, closer to Downpatrick in a small house called Hollymount, eventually returning to Mount Panther. There was a close-knit society of gentry and clerical families in the area who provided hospitality and amusement for them there and whom they also saw in Dublin: the Annesleys, the Bayleys, the Fordes and the Prices to name but a few.

Mount Panther, Down, 10 September 1744

I wrote to you the Saturday I arrived here, which was this day se'night – with an account of our having been at Down Patrick. Last Monday we dined at Mr Forde's, three miles from hence, a very pleasant place and capable of being made a very fine one; there is more wood than is common in this country, and a fine lake of water with very pretty meadows. The house is situated on the side of a hill, and looks down on his woods and water. The house is not a very good one, but very well fill'd; for he has *ten children*, the youngest about 10 years old, – but that's a *moderate family* to some in *this country*.

In the afternoon came in two ladies who had been to see me at Dr Mathews's and missing me followed. One is a Mrs Annesly (a relation to the present disputants) [a

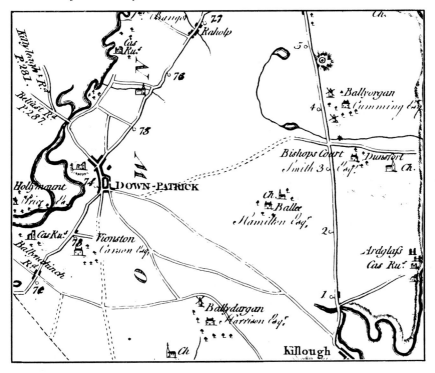

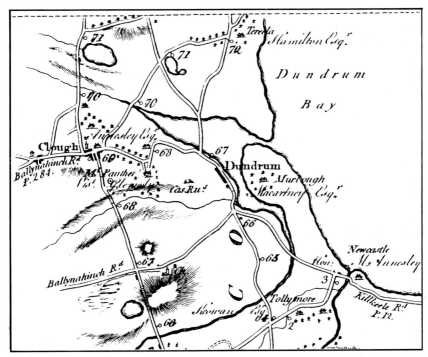

Maps by Taylor and Skinner, 1778.

lawsuit over the inheritance of titles] she is daughter to my Lord Tyrone, such another slatternly ignorant hoyden I never saw, and the worst of it she is very good humoured, but *will be familiar*: her husband is very like the Duke of Bedford and well enough. The other lady is a Mrs Baylis [Bayley], a handsome sprightly woman, well behaved, with a little dash of a fine lady. Her husband, a genteel agreeable man, brother to Sir Nicholas Baylis, that married the Paget, a clergyman well esteemed in the neighbourhood. On Tuesday the Fordes dined here; and on Wednesday Mr and Mrs Mathews of Newcastle, about six miles from hence. The whole family of the Fordes are religious, worthy people.

On Friday we dined at Newcastle at Mr Mathews's: it is situated at the foot of a range of mountains so high that they are at top seldom free from clouds, and the water has made a winding channel and falls down in a cascade; the main ocean bounds them on one side and is so near them that the spray of the sea wets them as they stand at the hall-door. On the other hand of them are hills, fine meadows, winding rivers, and a variety of pretty objects for so bare a country of trees, though on the side of the mountains there are scattering shrubby woods which make the view pleasant.

This country is famous for the goat's whey; and at the season for drinking it, which is summer, a great deal of company meet for that purpose, and there are little huts built up for their reception, and they have music and balls and cards, and happy are the family at Newcastle when that season comes, for there are thirteen sons and daughters, most of them never out of that part of the country. Mr Mathews is an attorney, has a very good fortune, is a good sort of man; his wife a sensible agreeable woman, and has brought up all her children extremely well – they are as decent and as healthy a family as ever I saw; and to make up the company at the head of them are placed both Mr and Mrs Mathews's mothers; old Mrs Mathews is eighty-seven years of age, and the most venerable fine figure I ever saw, and as apprehensive as a woman of five and twenty. A lady that went to see her this summer found her darning fine cambrick; her hearing is a little impaired. There was something so extraordinary in the appearance of the family, and the situation of the place, that I was extremely entertained with my visit. Mr Mathews waited for us at the door with his fishermen and as soon as we arrived had the net thrown into a river near his house and took a large draught of fine salmon trout; the sun shining on them made them quite beautiful.

Their neighbours were the Annesleys who lived in Clough before they built at Castlewellan, and the family of Edward Bayley, Treasurer of Down, who lived at Belville, a small house on the shore just over the road from Mount Panther.

On Saturday we dined at Mr Annesly's; it was a *mere rabble rout*.

Yesterday the Dean preached at Down [the parish church of the Holy Trinity], and we women went to Dr Mathews's church two miles off – a very pretty church and full congregation. We were invited and dined at Mr Baylis's [Bayley] but a small mile from hence. They live in what is called in this country "*a cabin*" – that is a house of one floor and thatched; it is situated very near the sea, with a pretty neat court before it; the outside promises very little, but the inside is quite elegant, as much as I saw of it, which was the hall, a large parlour, drawing room and bed-chamber. We were very handsomely entertained. There is a Mrs Murray, a cousin-german of Mrs Baylis, that is now with them, – a very sensible agreeable woman, and a great proficient in miniature painting; the likeness of her portraits, of which she showed me a great number, I was no judge of, I did not know the persons for whom they were drawn, but they are prettily pencilled, and some of her *landscapes* are really fine.

The weather is so excessively bad that I don't believe we shall be able to set out tomorrow for home as we designed, not that we have anything to apprehend from the roads, for I never travelled such fine roads as are all over this country, but I shall be afraid for the Dean's travelling in damp weather.

D.D. is very busy in making a plan for the Deanery House. He is very much shocked at the present jail at Down, and is determined to have it altered and to have one built with different apartments for men and women and a chapel; he gives a hundred pounds towards it and endows the chapel with twenty pounds a year for a clergyman to give them divine service, and to finishing and beautifying the church, which will be very handsome when done.   ii pp322–25

The next year they moved from Mount Panther, which they rented from Rev. Bernard Ward, to Hollymount, owned by the Prices, a family soon to be part of Mary's circle of friends. Bernard Ward, who had been tutored by Patrick Delany at Trinity College Dublin, leased Mount Panther from one of the Annesleys.

Delville, 20 May 1745

We shall lie the first night at Mr Hamilton's [husband of Mrs Forth Hamilton] at Dunleer, the second at Newry, and dine the third day at Mount Panther, at Dr Mathews's, where we were last autumn, and where we propose staying some days, till my domestics are settled.

The Dean and I travel in our chaise, which is easy and pleasant; Betty and Margaret, the cook and a housemaid in the coach and four, and Peg Hanages (who I am breeding up to be a housemaid) in a car we have had made for marketing and carrying luggage, when we travel. Our new coach will be ready when we come home, but now we hire one for the northern expedition.   ii p347

All that remains of the house at Hollymount are some buildings which were used for farm purposes when a later house was built. The surroundings are now a forest but some of the views are still reminiscent of the scene that would have greeted Mary's eyes.

Mary to her mother, Mrs Granville.
Hollymount, 8 June 1745

I gave my sister an account of our journey as far as Mount Panther, which is six miles from hence. We came here last Tuesday and brought all the family with us, and found the house in very good order, and a good dinner ready. The house is very indifferent, but the situation pleasant.   ii p358

Hollymount, Co. Down, by Mary Delany, 1745.

Hollymount, 11 June 1745

This is really a sweet place, the house *ordinary* but is well enough for a *summer house*. Two rooms below, that is a small parlour and drawing-room, and within the drawing-room a little room in which there is a bed, but the Dean makes it his closet. Above stairs four pretty good bedchambers and a great many conveniences for the servants. I have a closet to my bedchamber, the window of which looks upon a fine lake *inhabited by swans*, beyond it and on each side are pretty hills, some covered with wood and others with cattle. On the side of one of the hills is a gentleman's house with a pigeon-house belonging to it, that embellishes the prospect very much.

About half a mile off is a pretty wood which formerly was enriched with very fine oaks and several other forest trees (it covers a hill of about twenty acres); it is now only a thicket of the young shoots from *their venerable stocks*, but it is very thick, and has the finest carpeting of violets, primroses, and meadow sweet, with innumerable inferior shrubs and weeds, which make such a *mass of colouring* as is delightful. But thorny and dangerous are the paths, for with these sweets are interwoven *treacherous nettles* and *outrageous brambles*! but the Dean has undertaken to clear away those usurpers and has already made some progress: it is called Wood Island, though it is no more than a peninsula; the large lake that almost surrounds it is often covered with threescore couple of swans at a time.

On the other side of the lake are hills of various shapes, and on the side of one of them the town of Down. The ruins of the old cathedral are on an eminence just opposite to Wood Island, from whence I have taken a drawing D.D. is making a path round the wood large enough to drive a coach; in some places it is so thick as to make it gloomy in the brightest day; in other places a view of the lake opens, and most of the trees are embroidered with woodbine and the *"flaunting eglantine"*. Four extraordinary seats are already made, one in an oak the other three in ash-trees. This afternoon we proposed spending some hours there, but the rain drove us back again; on the beach of the lake are a great many pretty cockle shells, which will not be neglected when the weather will permit me to go to it.   ii pp360–61

Hollymount, 20 July 1745

This is Holly Mount, not Holy-mount, and does not belong to the Deanery, but is a *hired place* the Dean has taken till a Deanery-house is built.   ii p370

In spite of the lack of a deanery house, Dr Delany set about his clerical duties with vigour, apparently making up for years of neglect. The previous incumbent, Thomas Fletcher, was translated to the bishopric of Dromore.

Mary to her mother, Mrs Granville
Hollymount, 8 June 1745

The Dean has agreed for the building his new church, and is very busy visiting *all the families in his Deanery*, which will be a laborious work, but what he is determined to do. It is very strange, but the poor have been so neglected here, they say they *never saw a clergyman in their lives but when they went to church.*   ii p358

Hollymount, 11 June 1745

Never did any flock want more the presence and assistance of a shepherd than this Deanery, where there has been a *most shameful neglect* and I trust in God it will be a very happy thing for the poor people that D.D. is come amongst them. The church of Down is very large, but it is *not a quarter* filled with people; the curate has been so negligent as *never to visit any of the poor* of the parish, and a very diligent and watchful dissenting preacher has visited them on all occasions of sickness and distress, and by that means gained great numbers to the meeting. D.D. has already visited a great number; when he has been with all the *Protestants* he designs to go to the *Presbyterians*, and *then to the Papists*; they bless him and pray for him wherever he goes, and say he has done more good already than all his predecessors; the last Dean was here but *two days* in *six years!*   ii p359

To avoid travelling back to Hollymount on Sundays between services, the Delanys dined in Downpatrick (probably in the now Denvir's Hotel) and used this as an opportunity to play host to the people of the town.

Hollymount, 11 June 1745

This has been our chief entertainment abroad. At home, on Sunday last, it being the 9th of June (a day I have great reason to celebrate [her wedding day]), we had Dr Mathews's family and Mr Bayley's to dine here; they are the best of our neighbours, and I was not a little pleased to find that we have none nearer only some good plain sort of people at Down, that don't *set up for visitors*. As Down is three miles from hence, and we cannot go to prayers in the afternoon if we dine at home, the Dean designs to dine every Sunday at Down. There is a public-house kept by a clever man who was butler formerly to one of the Deans; he has a very good room in his house, and he is to provide a good dinner, and the Dean will fill his table every Sunday with all the townsmen and their wives *by turns*, which will oblige the people, and give us an opportunity of going to church in the afternoon without any fatigue.

Domestic life was busy as at Delville; for Mary this included sewing for the poor and for the dean this included clearing the grounds.

We rise about seven, have prayers and breakfast over by nine. In the mornings D.D. makes his visits, I draw; when it is fair and he walks out I go with him; we dine at two; in the afternoon when we can't walk out, reading and talking amuse us till supper, and after supper I make shirts and shifts for the poor naked wretches in the neighbourhood.   ii pp361–62

Hollymount, 21 June 1745

The Dean wheedled me away to *his wood* in the morning as soon as breakfast was over. I returned before twelve, in hopes of having time to write my letter; but just as I was preparing materials, Dr Mathews and his family came; so I chose to defer, that I might send a long letter. They were all the company *I expected*, but there were added to them by dinner-time, Mr Johnston, a very good sort of man (agent, that is, rent-gatherer, to the Dean); his wife and niece, both *fine ladies*! the sheriff of the county; and *three persons* of very different characters – Mr Hall, a crafty mercenary man, not at all esteemed or countenanced by the good people of this country; Mr Ward, a plain, honest curate; and Mr Cornabée, a Frenchman by birth, who has a living in this neighbourhood – a polite, lively, entertaining man, just come from the Queen of Hungary. He was chaplain some years abroad to Mr Robinson, the envoy, and much esteemed by him; he is a particular friend of Lady Colladon's, and has been recommended to the Dean by her; he is agreeable and well behaved, but as for any other merit he is too great a stranger to make any other judgment of him.

Downpatrick is anciently associated with St Patrick and it is stated in the Book of Armagh, written in 807 A.D., that he was buried there. A church has existed on the prehistoric hill fort which is the site of the cathedral church of the Holy Trinity since the thirteenth century at least. In Mary Delany's time it was in a picturesque state of ruin. It is now restored and St Patrick's grave is signposted!

Wednesday I went to Down with the Dean, and whilst he was visiting the poor, walked round the ruins of the cathedral, which has been a fine Gothic building; it is situated on an eminence just above the town, and commands an extensive view of mountains and lakes. I was called from my attention on this venerable ruin, by the bell that rung for prayers, after which we went home, and as soon as dinner was over we walked to Wood Island, where the Dean amused himself with his workmen, and I at my work under the shelter of a young oak in which D.D has made a very snug seat. When he had discharged his labourers we set forward for adventures; and as bold as Don Quixote, he undertook, armed with a stout cane instead of a lance, and I (with my shepherdess's crook followed intrepid, to penetrate the thickest part of the wood, where human foot *had not* trod, *I believe for ages.* After magnanimously combating brakes, briars, and fern of enormous size and thickness, we accomplished the arduous task, and were well rewarded during our toil by finding many pretty spots enamelled and perfumed with variety of sweet flowers, particularly the *woodbine and wild rose* which grow here in great abundance. We came home as weary and warm as we used to do frequently at Calwich, and enjoyed the refreshment of an easy seat, and the pleasure of talking over our toils.

Mary, herself such a sophisticate, laments the changes in rural life. She refers to the decline of syllabub, a drink made by milking a cow, or pouring milk from a height, onto ale or wine, not the whipped cream confection of today.

I am very sorry to find here and everywhere people *out of character*, and that *wine* and *tea* should enter where they have *no pretence to be,* and usurp the rural food of syllabub But the dairymaids wear large hoops and velvet hoods instead of the round *tight petticoat* and *straw hat*, and there is as much *foppery* introduced in the *food* as in the *dress, the pure simplicity of ye country is quite lost!* The Dean is much obliged to you for your caution of not over-fatiguing himself; but he served you as he is often served, – he hears you *preach* and *owns* your doctrine *good*, but does *not* practise: the truth is he cannot, for he finds there has been such a *total neglect of a parish minister's duty* here, that it has cut out a great deal of work for him; but as it is a work worthy of a good Xtian, I don't doubt but he will be enabled to go through it.

Yesterday, Mr Bayles [Bayley] and his lady and Mrs Murray (a lady painter) who live five miles off, dined with us. We dine with them tomorrow, and as soon as the weather is settled enough for an expedition, we are to meet at Arglass [Ardglass], about seven miles off, where there are fine ruins, to carry cold meat, and make a merry day of it; and I am to provide paper and pencil for taking views: I have taken two of Down and they are placed in the book, which will travel with me to England – *but when?* that the *Ld Lt* [lord lieutenant] in whose hand the gifts of episcopal livings were] *must determine.* I feel very oddly about it, and cannot tell *how to wish heartily* for this bishopric, and yet I do wish for it too, for if it does not come now it never will come.   ii pp362–66

Hollymount, 28 June 1745

Last Monday there was a fair at a town four miles from hence called Clogh, where Dr Mathews's family were to have met us, and we proposed it a day of mirth; but it proved so wet and cold we sat by the fire all day.

I have drawn a good deal since I came here, taken three views, and finished some I had sketched out. I have borrowed a fine picture of the old Duke of Ormond's, done by Sir Peter Lely, which I hope to copy; but we are going on a little progress next week. D.D. is to preach the visitation sermon for the Bishop of Down at Lisburn, twenty miles from hence. They say that part of the country is very pleasant, and the Dean will not go without me; so on Monday we set forward, and shall return on Saturday. We are to be at a clergyman's house (a nephew of Mrs Mathews's) Mr Geer [Gayer?] by name; he lives within two miles of Lisburn. Our best love and service salutes Welsbourne [the Dewes home].

We have got an Irish harper in the house, who plays a great variety of tunes very well; he plays to us at our meals, and to me whilst I am drawing.   ii pp367–68

They visited the dean's churches round about. During this time the dean organised the rebuilding of churches at Ballee and Bright. William Carson (mentioned below) was curate for Ballyculter, where the church was serviceable, unlike Ballee. Mary meanwhile had more urgent matters on her mind – the arrival of the new lord lieutenant – who was the famous Lord Chesterfield and married to Melusina de Schulenberg, probably an illegitimate daughter of George I.

Hollymount, 26 July 1745

To-morrow we go to a place called Ballyculter, where one of the Dean's curates [William Carson] lives; he is to preach on Sunday at that church, and in the evening we return again: it is about 8 miles off. I hope we shall get home to my dear Delville by the 20th of August. I had yesterday a letter from Lady Chesterfield who says "*I hope to see you soon in Ireland, which will be a great pleasure to us,*" and as they are to be in Dublin by the latter end of August, it would not look well in us to run away without waiting on them, and I would willingly give my Lord Chesterfield an opportunity of knowing D.D., which cannot be but by their spending a *quiet day* together at Delville, where we shall not entertain them as a royal pair, but in a private quiet way.

Yesterday we had seventeen people to dine with us and as this house is not bigger than Bradley, we were well stuffed.   ii p374

Hollymount, 17 August 1745

I had on Tuesday sixteen people here at dinner, on Wednesday ten, on Thursday twentytwo; and yesterday we dined abroad eight miles off, and have only this one day to pack up; and glad – *very glad* – shall I be to see again my pleasant dwelling at Delville.   ii p378

Delville, 24 August 1745

We left Hollymount on Sunday. After church at Down we went to Mr Forde's at Seaford, which was some miles on our road towards home; there we dined and lay that night. The next morning set out at seven, and lay at Newry. The next day bad; dined at a place Castle Bellingham, one of the prettiest places I have seen in Ireland, but the weather so bad I could not look about me at all. Lay that night at Dunleer at Mrs Hamilton's; Miss Mary Forth was gone to town.   ii pp379–80

The Delanys had an agreement which ensured that Mary should visit her family in England every third year where they had a growing family of Dewes to see and a wide circle of friends and relations. This meant they could not come north every year, and some years the dean made pastoral visits on his own; then there was a tender exchange of letters. The dean tried hard to find a suitable site for a deanery house.

D.D. to Mary
Mount Panther, 15 August 1747
extracts from unpublished manuscript, Newport Library, Gwent

We want but seventy yards of Mount-melick flag for the church of Bright which I wish to be sent thither immediately and to be landed at Killough and committed to the care of my curate Mr Hamilton; the rest I would have deposited in our future chapel at Delville, in the upper part of the room next the chimney. I have at length, I hope, found out proper ground for a glebe, on Mr Southwell's estate; it is a hill, about two miles from Down, on the road from hence thither. It hath not the advantages of situation, which the other, last mention'd to you hath but then it hath many others, to counterveil this want. 'Tis much better land, and at a much less distance from Down, and more central to all my parishes; and hath one very distinguished peculiarity, a source of sweet water on the very summit of the hill, twelve feet deep at this instant; so that wherever I build my house (for I can only build it on some side of the hill) I can with ease convey water to the highest part of it.

When she did go north, Mrs Delany's housekeeper Smith helped make the difficult transition between households easier.

Mount Panther, 21 July 1750

I know my dearest sister wishes to hear if I am safe at my journey's end: thank God we are! We arrived a little fatigued last night: but a good night's rest has refreshed us, and we are both very well. We had intended staying some days with Mrs Forde in our neighbourhood, not thinking we should find our habitation so fit for our reception as it is: but as there were so many things to settle, which could not very well be done without D.D. and my directing them, we thought it best to rest here. We shall dine to-day at Seaforde, and tomorrow at Downpatrick. You who have had the experience of such affairs, can figure to yourself my present bustle – trunks, hampers, unpacking, hay flying all over the house; everybody scrambling for their things, asking a thousand questions, as "Where is this to be put?" "What shall we do for such and such a thing?" However the hurry is pretty well over, the dust subsides, the clamours cease and I am hurried away to dress. I am really surprised at Smith's thorough cleverness in going through her work. She has got everthing almost in as much order as if she had been here a week.   ii pp571–72

Here Mary Delany's comments on family arrangements are surely based on her own experience as a dependent female.

Mount Panther, 28 July 1750

We asked our good friends the Fordes to dine with us on that day, but Mrs F. had a bad cold and could not come, and Mr Forde staid at home to take care of her, so they sent three of their daughters and one of their sons, a young cornet; very pretty young people, modest and sensible, especially my favourite, Cherry [Charity], who used to spend some time with me, but I am afraid her eldest brother's wedding will rob me of her this summer, He is going to be married to an agreeable young woman, Miss Knox [sister of the first Viscount Northland], with ten thousand pounds fortune; the wedding is to be next week, at the young lady's father's, and I hope they will all come together to Seaforde, which will make our neighbourhood very lively. Mr Forde, the father, has done very generously by his son, has settled £2100 a year on him; £1000 per ann. at present, and his house at Seaford furnished as it stands – which is a fine settlement for a man who has six sons and three daughters; but there is one *error* which most fathers run into, and that is in providing *too little* for daughters; young men have a thousand ways of improving a little fortune, by professions and employments, if they have good friends, but young gentlewomen have no way, the fortune settled on them is all they are to expect – they are incapable of making an addition.

And now to tell you a little of Mount Panther. To begin then: last Sunday dined at Downpatrick (after church). Mr and Mrs and Miss Leonargan, Mr Bereton, curate of Down, Mr Trotter, agent to Mr Southwell, dined with us; went to church again at 4 o'clock, went home at 5, *two hours on the road*, and visits to Lady Anne Annesley and Mrs Bayley and their husbands made half an hour: tired, supped, talked over the company of the day: went to bed before eleven; up next morn early; routed about the house, found many repairs wanting; sent for smith, carpenter, and cowper; catching showers; peeped now and then into the garden – *excellent gooseberries, currants, potatoes,* and all the garden stuff; *fine salmon, lobster, trout, crabs,* every day at the door. Monday evening went to Dundrum, a mile off, a pleasant nest of cabins by the sea-side, where may be had kitchen chairs, French white wine, vinegar, Hungary water, and capers; *mugs and pigs* [kitchen utensils], of which we bought some. The French white wine is five pence per bottle – we have not yet tasted it. Tuesday, busy all the morning with carpenters. We dined at our neighbour's, Mr Annesley; his father is dead, and has left him above £7000 a year;. Yesterday we went in the morning to Hollymount (5 miles off) to see the Prices, who are in great affliction, having buried a favourite daughter three weeks ago. Came back to dinner, and had for company Mr Sturgeon, Mr Mathews, Revd Mr Johnson, (D.D.'s agent) and his nephew. Today I propose writing abundance of letters and going again to Dundrum; tomorrow to preach and dine at Down and so ends *the round O of my journal.*
ii p574–77

The church at Ballee mentioned in this letter was restored under Dr Delany's auspices in c.1749. He also made a gift of communion silver.

Chalice, Ballee Church, inscribed: 'Given and most humbly Dedicated to the service of the Christian Communion in the Church of Ballee by D.D. Dean of Downe A.D. 1759'.

Mount Panther, [?August 1750]

I must go back to Sunday, on which day I went with the Dean to Ballee, one of his churches, where he preached and afterwards dined at Mr Johnston's, his agent and receiver: there we were stowed up in a very tiny house (but very neat) in a sultry day, with a table *crowded* with all sorts of good things; our coming home was very pleasant, great part of the way over a fine strand. The place I gave you an account of, where we went to gather shells is not within a walk, 'tis *two long miles* from hence [Tyrella]; next week hope to go again. You have never mentioned Carolan's tunes [the famous blind harper and composer, 1670–1738], since you said you had received them, have you tried them? I think some are *very pretty*: *Sir Toby Buck* and *Michll [Michael] O'Connor* are great favourites. We have the *same harper* in the house we had when at Hollymount; he plays very well, and knows a vast variety of tunes: and hot as the weather is the young folks meet here once or twice a week and make up at most three couple, always dance six *or* seven *dances*, and I love to see them mirthful, though I don't *find myself always* inclined to join with them.

The happiest mortal breathing *(if ever they think)* must sometimes feel an alloy to their most enliven'd pleasures. Thursday and yesterday I spent very calmly and agreeably. On Thursday, D.D. and Dr Mathews went to Downpatrick, Miss Ford (of whom I have given you a character I believe) read to me whilst I worked at my quilt till the gentlemen came home to dinner. In the evening when it grew cool we went to Clough to see Lady Anne Annesley in the chaise and walked home. Yesterday morning between six and seven we walked *(with our harper)* to *Mount Panther* [must have been another house, perhaps to the Bayleys] to serenade the ladies who were wakened with the music; but the heat was so intense, tho' I walked like an Indian queen with my umbrella over my head, that after taking the tour of the garden with D.D. we all came home in the chaise. All this was performed before our prayer hour, nine o'clock; after that and breakfast we took to our work and book and only allowed ourselves dining-time and an hour's composure after it, and finished the day as we had begun it, at Mount Panther.   ii pp580–82

Mount Panther, 24 August 1750

Last Monday we began again our public days, and shall have two more. We propose leaving this place on Tuesday the 11th Sept. Yesterday we dined at Mr Bayley's; they enquired much after you and your pretty son that they are acquainted with; their daughter is a fine girl, she has begun on the spinnet, and promises to have a good hand. Tomorrow we dine at Mr Price's; and Sunday the Dean preaches at one of his new churches (Bright) and we dine with his curate, Mr Hamilton; and on Monday is our public day. The last we were fifteen in company.   ii p585

Perhaps the expense of rebuilding the ruined church at Bright caused the friction with a neighbour mentioned here. The work began in 1745 and Dr Delany provided communion silver here as at Ballee.

Mount Panther, 1 September 1750

Last Sunday we set out at nine from hence, and arrived at Bright church (6 miles off) at a little after eleven. It is placed on an eminence that commands a very extensive view of the sea, the harbour of Killough, full of shipping, mountains, hills, and valleys, diversified with cattle, corn, and bog, the solemnity of which last *(like a faded leaf in work)* makes the rest more lively; nothing was wanting to make the prospect excessively beautiful but trees. The church is that which hath raised so much *rancour and malice* in a certain neighbour of ours and which you have had explained in the letter before – (the discourse on tithes) it is not quite finished within, but when it is, will be a pretty, decent church.

D.D. preached and with as much spirit as ever I heard him. We were to dine at his curate's, Mr Hamilton's, half a mile from the church nearer home. D.D. was excessively fatigued (and I hope it was nothing else) with preaching, and could not eat a morsel, was sick and faint, and continued so all the way home, hot and feverish, and had a very bad night; but I thank God, he is very well again now, and at this moment watching his workmen, who are putting up new palisades before the house. Wednesday, being much better, he insisted on my going to a fine strand about two miles off, where there are a great many very pretty shells, though none curious: accordingly I went to satisfy him and, had I been then really easy on his account, should have been very agreeably amused.

Mrs Delany was such good company that the opportunity to spend time with her was not to be lightly dismissed. Sophia Leonargan was the daughter of Vere Essex Leonargan, vicar of Saintfield and Kilmood.

I don't know whether I told you that Miss Leonargan is with me and has been about a fortnight; she is a clergyman's daughter, who is a very sensible entertaining man, an old friend of D.D.'s. Mrs Leonargan is a sensible good woman – they have both kept very good company and seen a good deal of the world. This young woman is their only child; and the greatest advantage she has ever had has been conversing with her parents. In her appearance she is plain, but not vulgar; her manner, from shyness and reserve, a little awkward: she is about 27 years of age, and has, on acquaintance, very good sense, pretty sentiments, loves reading, has read a great deal, reads French into English as fluently as I read English, is humble and obliging, and very smart and comical when she thinks she may be so without giving offence, and a most tender and dutiful child. I knew her a little when I was in the North before, but she improves very much on better acquaintance, and it is an agreeable circumstances to me to have a young woman in my neighbourhood (for she lives at Down) who is always pleased to spend some time with me when convenient, and that I need not treat with much ceremony; I have sent her this morning to Down market for me.

Mary was quite willing to help with her neighbour's needlework projects. Was Mrs Bayley "the friend in the north who is working a fright of a carpet"?

Yesterday morning I went to Belville [house below Mount Panther near the shore] to work a corner of Mrs Bayley's carpet; they would fain have kept me to dinner and have sent for the Dean, but I feared his being out in the evening and *made an excuse,* and how do you think he served me? why, walked away in *the evening* and made them a visit, while I sat quietly at my work.

Tomorrow we go to church at Downpatrick, it being the 1st Sunday in the month, but the Dean will not venture to preach; next week will be a hurry. Monday, our last public day; Tuesday, I go to Down to the assembly, and lie at Mr Leonargan's; as it would be a mortal offence if I did not make my appearance once there; and that day the new married couple, young Mr Forde and his bride come home so on Wednesday I must make my compliments there. Thursday, spend at Belville, Friday, Fordes dine here; Saturday, pack up and settle household matter; Sunday, preach, and dine at Ballee, another new church, 6 miles off; Monday, finish packing; Tuesday, we shall hoist sail for fair Delville.   ii pp587–89

Mount Panther, 16 September 1750

I was at Down assembly, and it put me much in mind of the Gloucester ones that we used to have *before Whitfield's was the fashion;* I paid my compliment and hope it

Belville, Co. Down, by Mary Delany, 13 September 1758.

obliged. I am now in a hurry – I prepared you in my last for a short letter this. Yesterday we went to Seaford to pay our compliments to the young married couple, who came home last Tuesday; the bride is a handsome, well-behaved young woman. Today we dine at Mr Annesley's, a mile off, to morrow the Dean preaches at one of his new churches called Ballee, and we dine at his agent's who lives close to the church. Monday packing and company dines here into the bargain, which *is a little troublesome*. I can get some good thread for you – let me know what you would have – 7s the pound.   ii pp590–91

The following year they picked up the thread of their social life again, at Mount Panther. Their neighbours the Annesleys (afterwards Viscount and Lady Glenawly) were building a mansion in Castlewellan.

Mary to her brother, Bernard Granville
Mount Panther, 13 July 1751

We set out as we proposed on Tuesday morning, had fine temperate weather for our journey, and got home without any accident or adventure on Thursday to dinner. Within four miles of Mount Panther we met Mrs Annesley and Lady Anne Annesley on horseback, going to dine under a tent on cold meat about a mile from that place, where they are going to build. They say it is a fine situation, has much of the majestic about it – as mountains, wild rocks, woods, and an extensive view of the main ocean;

but much must be done to it to give it the comfort and agreeableness requisite for a dwelling; they have walled in, and planted with oak, three hundred and fifty acres of ground, for a park. Near them is a large bleach-yard, and Mr Annesley is going to *build a town*. They would fain have had us go to dine with them, and I had a great mind to do it, but we were at a loss what to do with our cattle and men, so resisted and came prudently home. We dined with them yesterday, they live at Cloghe [Clough] about half a mile off, that is near an English mile. I cannot say they are *very agreeable*, but as they are *very civil* to us, and singular in their manner, their acquaintance is entertaining. Mr Bayley, a clergyman, who is our nearest neighbour, a brother of Sir Nicholas, and his lady are very agreeable, good neighbours, and so are Mr Forde's family (about three miles off) in a very friendly way. I don't know whether I introduced you to this company before, but if I did this is to rub up your memory, so that when I mention my engagements you may not be quite a stranger to them.   iii pp42–43

In 1752 the journey north was combined with sightseeing in Drogheda.

Mount Panther, 25 June 1752

We breakfasted at the Man-of-War, 12 miles from Dublin. Dined at Drogheda: did not get there till almost five – fainting with heat. Thought it most prudent for ourselves and cattle to stay all night; sallied forth at seven to see the church, which is on a high hill; it is not quite finished, but will be very handsome; then descended and went quite through the town, which is large, and went up to what are called "Ball's walks". You wind up a very high, steep hill (which otherwise would be unsurmountable) planted with trees – some in walks, others in groves, so that part of it looks like a thick wood; on the top is a long level walk, with old trees on each side of it, and at the end a pretty clean house and spruce garden full of flowers, which belongs to Mr Ball, who is so obliging to the town as to permit that fine walk to be a public one, and that is *the mall* of Drogheda. The view from it is surprizingly beautiful. At the foot of this fine hill winds the river Boyne, one of the finest rivers in Ireland, and which yields the best salmon in great plenty. The town lies on the side of a hill on the opposite side, disposed with little neat gardens, old walls covered with ivy, a ruined castle, and variety of objects, that it makes a better and more pleasing show than I can describe; and the river, which winds and widens with a handsome bridge over one part of it, and shipping beyond that, complete the scene. On the one hand you see the obelisk erected in memory of the famous battle of the Boyne; on the other several gentlemen's seats on the banks of the river. Unluckily it happened to be the Eve of St John – a great Roman Catholic holiday, and at our return to our inn we were forced to pass by several monstrous fires *(actually made of bones)* and firing of guns and squibs, and by the time we got to our inn, the whole air was impregnated with the vile stench.   iii pp134–35

Here the Delanys seem weary of social life; the race course at Downpatrick which is still a lively scene for race meetings was much less attractive than all their home improvements.

Mount Panther, 10 July 1752

All this neighbourhood are now in an uproar of diversions. They began last Wednesday and are to last till Saturday, each day a horse-race, assembly and ball; we did not find ourselves inclined to enter the list. I have more pain than pleasure in seeing any horse-race and yesterday a poor man was thrown down and trampled to death, such a sight would have embittered whatever diversion the race had given. The balls are too late for sober people, and too far off; Downpatrick is six long miles from hence. We have had three fair sunshining days very quietly to ourselves. D.D. is busy planting; when I *am weary* of dangling after him I come in to my *home occupations* and when *he is weary* he comes and *reads to me* while I work. He is now reading the Life of Constantine the Great. What a glorious man he was! Last Tuesday, we had 14 people to dine with us. We have not yet been able to begin our public days; last Monday the Dean was obliged to attend a vestry and to bury one of his curates at Downpatrick, I spent the day with our agreeable neighbour Bayley. We propose making no invitations on *any other days*, and then invite only one family and let chance comers fill the table: we do this to divide our company more equally, otherwise some days we might be alone and overpowered on others.   iii pp136–37

In 1752 the dean was greatly annoyed by an adverse judgement in a lawsuit over his first wife's estate. He had married a Mrs Tenison, a wealthy widow, in 1732. She died in 1741 and in her will she appears to have made conditions affecting her legacy to him which gave her relations cause to contest any money he enjoyed from her estate. The threatened loss of income, not to mention the publicity of the case, was disconcerting to the Delanys and threatened their comfortable style of living. At one point they contemplated moving to County Down so as to economise and to avoid unpleasant chatter. Mary Delany was prepared to make the best of any change of fortune.

Mount Panther, 20 July 1752

I hope the Lord Chancellor's decree will be more favourable than our adversaries [the Tenison family] would have it, and should he do the worst I trust we shall do very well, and that a little management for a year or two will establish us again: if we find we cannot live so retired here as we wish we will come to you: this winter we now propose spending here. I believe we must go to Delville for a fortnight or three weeks to provide some winter-entertainments – books, work and my harpsichord. This is really a pretty place, though *it is not a Delville*, and the most disagreeable circumstance will be the distance I shall be from my good and kind friends in the neighbourhood of Delville. Donnellan has been very affectionate and kind to me, and would have come to me here upon this disagreeable change in our affairs but I have prevented her.   iii p139

Delville, 14 August 1752

I feel little or no distress at the thoughts of giving up many expenses, which, though like ornaments to a building, were agreeable embellishments, are not at all *necessary*, either to the strength or convenience of the building.

Anemone appenina, *26 March 1776.*

Don't be uneasy about our going to the North; we have really a very pretty convenient house there, shall keep good fires and provide ourselves with books and work, and I shall send down my harpsicord and hope to have Mrs Bushe with me, who has in the kindest manner offered me her company. Nor shall I want for neighbours there, and the satisfaction of doing what I think is right will make me amends for leaving Delville, and being removed further from Dublin will be another very good reason for spending the winter at Mount Panther. You'll say, suppose the decree should be in our favour, why then retire? Why, prudence I think requires it; for we have been at great expenses without any farther demand, and it is *not so easy* to live with frugality at Delville as at Mount-Panther, where every thing bears but *half price*. In time D.D. hopes to send Mr Dewes a fuller and more satisfactory account of the state of his affairs; he has also perfected a new and short *will*, wherein he has left me everything he had in the world to dispose of, and now he is much relieved. iii p147

Lucan, 26 August 1752

From hence it is impossible for me to write a long letter; company kept us late last night, and now breakfast waits for me. To-morrow I return home and my next letter shall be longer. We propose going towards Mount Panther on Tuesday night, and shall return, please God, the latter end of October. D.D. does not choose I should pass the whole winter there, and indeed I hope there will be no occasion for it.   iii p152

Mount Panther, 30 September 1752

We have been come about half an hour, and find our house very clean, cheerful and well aired, and had two very sleek, *comely cats to bid us welcome!* We set out last Wednesday morning from Delville at 8 o'clock breakfasted on the road at eleven, on poached eggs, and got to Dunleer, to Dr Forster's, at 4 to dinner, where we were very kindly and agreeably received, and staid there all Thursday. Dr Forster's eldest brother, who lives in that neighbourhood, is one of the Dean's council, a very sensible, clever, friendly man. He came on Thursday morning to the Dean, and they had much discourse about our affairs.   iii p160

Mount Panther, 7 October 1752

We are both much better for our journey and I am, thank God! quite well; the weather has been good, and we are in a very sociable, agreeable neighbourhood; Mr Bayley has had his house full, and we have met almost every day at his house or this.

A love affair is going on there in which *I am called to council*, there are difficulties, but I hope they will be overcome as the young parties like one another. The tale has too many circumstances (as you are a stranger to the whole) for a letter; but when we meet they may serve for conversation, if we can find a leisure moment for its introduction, for after an absence of three years how much shall we have to say to each other!

This week's journal runs thus; on Sunday at Down church, dined at Belville; Monday, dined there again with Mr Price's family and some Fordes. Tuesday, they all dined with me. Wednesday morning, walked to Clogh to see Lady Anne Annesley,

The five castles of Ardglass, Co. Down, by Mary Delany, July 1745.

spent the rest of the day quietly at home. Thursday, the Bayleys, Prices, and Fordes drank tea, played at cribbage and commerce, prayed and supped with us.

I have heard from Lady Sarah Cowper [her niece Mary's god-mother], and find she has had ill-health : I will not answer her letter till the decree is given. I send Mary the enclosed moth and view *(B.[Bushe] fecit)* and the caricatures by a worse hand to begin her collection. I think it not necessary that my brother Granville should be troubled with the papers about our affairs; but I should be glad Mrs Chapone could see them, from whom I have received an affectionate and good letter.
iii pp161, 162

Mount Panther, 14 October 1752

I have not found the North colder than it was at Delville. Just before I went last to Delville I stuck a slip of myrtle I took out of a ladies breast into a pot of earth, and it is *now in blossom* – I wish you had it in your garden. We had such a storm on Monday night that I thought the windows of the house would have been blown into the room; I thank God, it did us no harm, but blew down two large ash-trees, and Mr Annesley had a new farm-house blown down to the ground.

I am glad my sweet little Mary learns so fast: oh, that I could share with you the pleasure of instructing such an intelligent little creature! Last Sunday, D.D. went to Ballyculter [one of the Dean's parishes], 19 miles off; I spent the day at Mr Bayley's, and he called on me at six, when he came home to our snug tête-à-tête ; he was much fatigued and had a great pain in his shoulder which lasted two or three days, but he is now very well. Monday and Tuesday, walked in the sun in the morning; drawing, reading, prating made the time pass very well; after supper a game at cards – a new game of D.D.'s inventing called *double commerce*: if you have a mind to have it, I will send you a receipt for it, if in return you will send me the *veritable receipt* of the *Irish plum* cake. Tomorrow, pray and preach at Ballee.   iii pp163–64

While the Delanys settled contentedly into life at Mount Panther, not all the news was good.

Mount Panther, 20 October 1752

Yours and Mr Dewes' kind letters of the 7th I picked up on the road yesterday morning, in our way to Downpatrick, where we went on a double score – pleasure and duty: I think I might have placed *duty* first. Mr Mathews, one of the Dean's curates, *gave a breakfast* to all the fine ladies that were at Down assembly the *night before!* and though I made not one of that number, I was glad to meet all my agreeable neighbours together, and to take leave of them at once. We got to Down by ten, and as soon as breakfast was over *we all* went to prayers; the church was just opposite to where we were. After that, the Dean went to pray by poor Mrs Lonargan [wife of his collegue Vere Essex Leonargan], who is in the lowest state that it is possible for a human creature (that is alive and sensible) to be in, she seemed much comforted and pleased with the D.D.'s prayers: I saw her afterwards; a most melancholy spectacle she would be, were she not a very good woman, but her present weak condition may be considered only as a necessary preparation for joys not to be found in this world [she died in December 1752]. She has an excellent daughter, who attends her with the utmost duty and affection – the young woman who used to be with me here sometimes.

The bishop to be enthroned by proxy was Robert Downes.

To-day, Mr Annesley's and Mr Bayley's family dine here; last night Mr Frank Price (nephew to Mrs Conway, our acquaintance) who is to be married to Miss Forde, gave a ball at Downpatrick. This morning D.D. set out at eight for Down in order to enthrone our new Bishop's (Down) proxy; and though it is not post day, as I was quiet and alone I chose to write to you for fear to-morrow might bring interruptions. iii pp164–66

Between 1752 and 1758 the Delanys spent over 4 years in England. The law suit against the Tenisons was protracted and distressing to them both but was finally cleared up in 1758 when the dean felt his character had been vindicated as well as the case settled. By this time, Sally Chapone, Mary's goddaughter and child of her old friend Mrs Chapone, was living with her.

Mrs Delany points out that the building works carried out by improving estate owners benefited local people by providing employment.

Mount Panther, 8 August 1758

Mr and Lady Annesley [born Lady Anne Beresford], their son, daughter, and two or three friends live in *ten houses* laid into one [Castlewellan], situated on the summit of a high mountain, and surrounded by several very high and very melancholy ones [the Mournes], *I think*, but if he goes on with his wonderful improvements he may make them beautiful; for the land surrounding his present dwelling (which is part of a town he is building) was the last time of my being in this country a mere bog, and as unpromising as any land I ever beheld, and now hay is making, corn is growing, trees planted and cattle feeding; and above an hundred and twenty labourers constantly employed, and fifteen hundred pounds a-year expended on the improvements. It really is a noble undertaking, and if you saw *how dismal their situation is at present* for the sake of carrying on these works, it increases their merit! The poor have reason to bless *them,* and I hope *they* are actuated by a better motive than that of only enriching themselves and their family.

On Saturday we dined at Mr Bayly's; Miss Bayly had gone on a party of pleasure. They have with them a Miss Newcomb, a relation of Mr Bayly's, a good, quiet, sickly young woman, who has a sad father, is to have ten thousand pounds to her fortune, and they have out of good-nature taken her from her unhappy home.

Mary Delany notes the arrival of a talented music teacher, Cecilia Young, who was married to Dr Thomas Arne, (1710–78), a composer and one of two brothers prominent in eighteenth century Dublin music.

I was surprised there at meeting Mrs Arne, (Miss Young that was); they have her in the house to teach Miss Bayly to sing; she was recommended to Mr Bayly by Mrs Berkeley as an object of compassion. She looks indeed much humbled, and I hope is as deserving as they think her to be; great allowances are to be made for the temptations those poor people fall under. She has been severely 'used by a bad husband and suffered to starve, if she had not met with charitable people. She behaves herself very well, and though her voice has lost its bloom as well as her face, she sings well, and was well taught by Geminiani and Handel, and had she not been idle should have been a charming singer. Mr Bayly plays on the violin, his curate on the German flute; Mrs Arne and Miss Bayly sing, and a girl of nine years old accompanies them on the harpsichord most surprisingly – she is a niece of Mrs Arne's; the race of the Youngs are *born* songsters and musicians. It is very agreeable to have such an entertainment in our power to go to whenever we please. Mr Bayly's house [Belville] is not half a mile off, and a very pleasant walk.

Sunday we went to Downpatrick; D.D. preached as well as ever I heard him. We had a dinner as usual for as many as filled a table for twelve people. Our dinner was boiled leg of mutton, a sirloin of roast beef, six boiled chickens, bacon and greens; apple-pies, a dish of potatoes – all set on at once; time between church and church does not allow for two courses; after tea we came home, and talking over our company was refreshing to us. We brought a *young cat* home with us, *but she was so cross* we sent her home again this morning, and I, alas! am catless! Our church and congregation at Down very decent and there were a great many at the Sacrament.

Monday evening came Mr Sturgeon [possibly William Sturgeon, curate of Ballyculter]: his puritanical figure and singular manner entertained Sally. We gave her another surprizing appearance – a priest called the "Bishop of Down", the quintessence of an Irish brogueneer; he had lived twenty-four years in Spain, and speaks hardly any language, talked much of the Queen of Spain and Farinelli [the famous Neapolitan singer], and said the Spanish women were very handsome "*like that young lady*", pointing to Miss Chapone.

As mistress of the household, she was in charge of medication for her employees.

I have been acting as surgeon, as poor John [employee] cut a terrible gash in the fleshy part of the inside of his hand. I washed it well with arquebuzade and put on the black plaster [seaweed or sphagnum moss?] and in a few hours it was easy, and I hope will be soon well; it bled very much, and frightened our poor Welshman to a great degree; and the consternation of the house was as great as if his head had been cut off.

The receipt for tooth-ache is "*Little trefoil leaves, primrose leaves and yarrow pounded, made into a little pellet and put to the tooth or tied up in muslin and held between the teeth.*"   iii pp501–504

The Delanys were able to entertain more liberally at Mount Panther than in the smaller Hollymount.

Mount Panther, 21 August 1758

Tuesday, our public day, expected the large family of the Annesleys: they sent an excuse, and instead of 20 sat down ten; *not the worse*, so much the more *overplus* for the poor! Wednesday very busy making candlesticks to illuminate my ball-room and other preparations. On Thursday before six o'clock were assembled our company.

Two Mr Fordes, Mrs Forde, two Miss Fordes, Miss Knox, Lady Anne Annesley, Miss Annesley, Mr Charles Annesley, Mr Mark Annesley, Miss Jenny Bayly, Mrs Price, Miss Price, Miss Brett, *Mr Cole* (five thousand a-year and just come from abroad) a pretty, well-behaved young man. Mr Bayly, Mrs Bayly, Miss Bayly, Miss Newcomb, Mr Savage, nephew to Mrs Bayly, Mr Ned Bayly, nephew to Mr Bayly, two Mr Hamiltons, two Mr Montgomerys, Mr Marley, D.D., *M.D., and Brunette* [Sally Chapone]! in *all* 29! Miss Bayly was queen of the ball, and began it with Mr Cole; Mr Bayly danced with Sally, of which she was not a little proud, but one partner was not sufficient for her, so she danced part of the night with Mr Montgomery; there were ten couple of clever dancers. Remember my room is 32 feet long: at the upper end sat the fiddlers, and at the lower end next the little parlour the lookers-on.

Tea from seven to ten: it was made in the hall, and Smith presided. When any of the dancers had a mind to rest themselves they sat in the little parlour, and tea was brought to them. They began *at six* and *ended at ten*: then went to a cold supper in the drawing room made of 7 dishes down the middle of different cold meats, and plates of all sorts of fruit and sweet things that could be had here, in the middle jellies; in all 21 dishes and plates. The table held twenty people; the rest had a table of their own in the little parlour, but all the dancers were together, and I at the head to take care of them; everybody seemed pleased, which gave pleasure to D.D. and myself.

This evening Miss Bayly gives a ball to the same company that were here. I have been trotting about the garden with the Dean, contriving new works and weighing grains of ipecacuanha and rhubarb for poor patients.   iii pp504–505

Not all the local clergy found favour. Here Rowley Hall, rector of Killyleagh, is frowned on, but her curiosity got the better of her when an invitation was received.

Mount Panther, 28 August 1758

On Wednesday we dined at Killalee [Killyleagh], 12 measured Irish miles from hence, at Mr Hall's, a clergyman of a very singular character, not very worthy; but we wanted to see the place, which we had heard much commended: Mr Bayly's family were of the party which made it more agreeable.

The situation is on the side of a hill with a most extensive view of the sea. In one place they tell you is *Portaferry*, in another *Lady Anne Ward's Temple* [in the grounds of Castleward], in another *Strangford*, but it requires such very clear eyes and weather to distinguish these objects, that I confess they gave me no more pleasure than only reading of them that they were there would do. The wind was high, we walked up a high hill to a castle, our *negligees* [loose dresses] fluttered like the streamers of a ship, and when we came to the castle where we were to see wonders of prospect, no admittance, the gates locked and we staggered back again with much difficulty, facing the wind, but we had a good dinner and good company. Mr Bayly went in the coach with us; the scene was new, the road excellent, and part of it very pleasant, – so on the whole it was an agreeable day, but we were most heartily tired.

Sally and I grumble a little at the weather, which prevents our going about among the *herbs and flowers* to find out some that may be rare to you. There grows a little pale purple aster, with a yellow thrum (very like the *asterattims*) in all the borders near the lakes and sea; it grows in great clusters, and in some places near two feet high, and we have great plenty of thrift grows wild between this and Belville. As to the common plants they seem much the same as in the high ways, rather more luxuriant; the tawdry rag-weed in vast abundance, but mollified by the bloom and hue of the scabius and rest harrow. *Matfellon* and *figwort* flourish here remarkably, and the purple vetch and eyebright soften the golden furs [furze] and glowing heath. A poetical pen might have done their beauties justice.   iii pp505–507

A long walk did not deter Mary and her goddaughter Sally from examining the flora and scenery of the Down coast with the Mourne mountains as an impressive backdrop.

Mount Panther, 2 September 1758

According to the country phrase, yesterday Sally and I "fetched a charming walk" – at least six miles! We set out at a quarter after ten with bags and baskets to store our curiousities in. John, like a pedlar, with our cloaks buckled to his back by a belt – or rather a pilgrim, with his hat slouched and a long staff in his hand. Fitz Simmons, our harper, who knows all the paths and walks of this place, with our store-basket. We left the Dean with his workmen, about *ten such invalids* as are fitter for an hospital than a spade; but with good clothing and gentle work they *come on finely*, and gather strength!

If I were to tell you where we walked, you would not know whereabouts we were;

Moira castle, 1799, by Gabriel Béranger (1729-1817).

Rhododendron maximum, *by Mary Delany, 25 June 1778.*

The ruins of Dundrum Castle, Co. Down, by Mary Delany, 1758.

the [Norman] castle of Dundrum is a ruin on a very steep rude shapen hill, a vast extent of the sea, on which were several vessels, chiefly fishing – boats; and the vast mountains of Moran [Mourne], which are so near us that we can perceive the rivers which run down the side of them. The highest mountain, they say, is a mile and half perpendicular, and on the top of it is a well of fine water; there is a ridge of these mountains – they are indeed tremendous, but make a fine back-ground to our picture. In our way to Dundrum, which was the point we aimed at, we walked over a hill covered with bushes, intermixed with rocks, the verdure fine and soft as velvet; sheep, goats, and cows with little ragged shepherds attending them.

We examined every blade of grass for new plants, but found only a purple flower, four-leaved like a star; it shuts up in the middle of the day, it is of a violet colour. I wanted to know what species it is of? but fear before it reached you, it will be too much withered for you to find out its family? I will watch for the seed and save it. A little yellow and white flower we found, like linaria [flax], but grows thinner.

Thursday spent the day at Castle Wellan, Mr Annesley's, and walked two or three miles before dinner, saw all his farming affairs, which are indeed very fine. Three large courts; round the first, which is arched round a kind of piazza, are houses for all his carriages, and over them his granaries; the next court are stables and cow-houses and over them haylofts; the third court two such barns as I never saw, *floored with oak*, and finished in the most convenient manner for all the purposes of winnowing and in that court are the stands for hay and corn. I am sure Mr Dewes would be pleased with the whole apparatus; it is so neat, strong, and clever.   iii pp508–509

The assembly rooms in Downpatrick were the scene of much gaiety. Company from the surrounding countryside as far away as Hillsborough gathered to enjoy themselves.

Mount Panther, 9 September 1758

We cannot possibly pretend to vie with you in splendid appearance, *nobility*, and *jewels*, nor can I say much for the beauty and elegance of *our room* at Downpatrick on Thursday last, where I carried our Sally, but I had much more diverting company than you can boast of, I am sure, with all your lords and ladies! though we had *one earl as well as you* – Lord Hillsborough, a very sensible agreeable man, with whom I had a great deal of conversation about *poor Northend* [formerly home of her aunt and uncle Stanley]. I am glad to hear Harry Russell is a great favourite [the gardener at North End now worked for Lord Hillsborough]. We went to *the assembly at seven*. Three sets of dancers, not more than ten in a set; they *draw* for partners (except the strangers) and then *choose first*; Sally chose Mr Cole, Mrs Price's nephew – a vast estate, and a very good sort of a young man; he seems (and I hope is) much enamoured with Miss Bayly. After four dances they sat down, and Sally was chosen in the second set by a strange man indeed, but to her credit – I can't say comfort – he fell to Miss Bayly's lot afterwards. Such a figure, such a *no-dancer*, a *mopstick* with a brown, *dirty mophead!* and his sense (if he had any) seemed as *stupid* as his figure and his heels, all but in the choice of his partners.

How magnificent the Wests! I wish I had some of her fine things here to make my neighbours stare; but as for pine-apples I can almost vie with them, having had *ten* sent me from Dublin since I came here, as fine ones as ever I tasted, by Lord Charlemont's orders. Mr Adderley is going to be married to Miss Ward, daughter to the landlord of Mount Panther – no great fortune; her father a clergyman, a very worthy man. She is, they say, a pretty kind of girl, and well brought up, which is the *best fortune*.

What is become of your tortoiseshell? I have no less than three kittens that divert us very much.   iii pp509–10, 511

Once or twice the dean went on his own to attend to his duties in Down. In 1759 Mrs Delany's goddaughter Sally Chapone, "the nut brown maid", was very ill and she sent her housekeeper Smith, and a manservant to look after her husband. They exchanged fond letters frequently.

Dean Delany to Mary
Mount Panther, 20 August 1759
extracts from unpublished manuscript in Newport Library, Gwent.

You remember, my dearest life, Indiana says upon some occasion, "all the rest of my life is but waiting till he comes". I can truely say so of your letters. I feast upon them for a post present, and a post to come.

The judges dined with me yesterday, and were very easy and agreeable; but J. Crawford went away much sooner than I expected and left me much vexed, that I lost the opportunity of drinking [to] his fair niece, and doing her merits that justice which I fear he doth not. This was not my only misfortune: I forgot my spectacles, and with great difficulty hammered out my sermon; and was (I hope sufficiently) mortified but I thank God I find myself less and less fatigued, every time I preach and I sometime fancy I walk with more activity.

I am sorry you have lost your very agreeable companion, and I my correspondent [probably one of the Mrs Hamiltons], but I thank God mine is a much less loss: your letters fully supply the place of all others. Their elasticity (like that of the air) expand and leaves no emptiness about them.

My dearest life, you reckon wrong; you should only count by months, whilst there is any part of another month to come and then you may begin to count by weeks. The last week of the next month will, I hope, bring me to you, care of my greatest happiness; but I desire I may not be expected to a day.

Next summer they were back at Mount Panther together. Here she comments on the cheerful disposition of her Irish neighbours.

Mount Panther, 14 June 1760

Sunday set out *"all in our coach and six"*, at nine o'clock and got to Down a quarter before eleven. D.D. preached with a great deal of spirit. Dined afterwards as usual at the *public house*, which is indeed *very clean*, and they dress our dinners tolerably well; seven dishes on at a time and *no second course*.

Monday, walked to Belville [Bayleys' house] in the evening and round our own domain, which Mr Sandford is delighted with, and it is really very pleasant.

Thursday we went to see Mrs F. Price (Miss Cherry Forde that was); she was at a place five miles off called *"the Goat's Whey"* where people have lodgings that are in a course of drinking the whey. She was there with her son, a sweet boy between five and six years old; but there is no hope of his recovery and she with her care and attendance on him is worn to a skeleton. Her husband is nephew to Mrs Conway, your old acquaintance, who I hope will remember them in her will. I expected a pretty situation, as there are very pretty ones in its neighbourhood; but it is in a dreary wild spot – no tree, no hedge, no bush, all dull and dismal, and the cabins such as have never come in your way to see, and yet this place is often full of very good company, and has its balls and gaieties! I think the *Irish spirit* very nearly allied to *the French*; it makes them happy and they bear with many inconveniences which would discompose the more serious temper of the English.

Saul, just outside Downpatrick, was an ancient ecclesiastical foundation and associated with St Patrick.

To-day we dine at Seaford, Mr Ford's, three miles off; to-morrow go to Saul Church, and dine afterwards at Mr Ward's, who lives in that parish near the church.

We have brought down Madame Beaumont's maps, and are much amused with them. D.D. is reading her Magazine, and much pleased with it; he is *as busy* here as at Delville. It does him a great deal of good; for as his spirit and body are *greatly enfeebled*, if he has not something that rouses him to activity he would lead too sedentary a life , and that I am sure would soon destroy him. I cannot say but I am now easily alarmed about him, but I endeavour to suppress my fears, though it is a hard task where such a friend is in question.

We had a wonderful little man begging here yesterday, not more than *three feet* high; he looked about forty; a sensible look, could only speak Irish and was very much deformed.

To whom was I obliged for Mr Handel's life? Mrs Don.[Donnellan's] hand was on it, and you sent it. I like it very much, though I don't *give up* a point or two, which we shall talk over, and I have not time to write about it. iii pp594–95

Mrs Delany was kept busy visiting and entertaining, sometimes giving impromptu dinner parties, and still found time for diversion through studying a globe of the world.

Mount Panther, 21 June, 1760

Sunday we went to Saul church, where D.D. preached, and we dined with Mr Robert Ward (the gentleman Mr Sandford made a visit to last winter), two miles beyond Saul, where we were kindly entertained by a melancholy pair, who are still lamenting the loss of an only son who died three years ago. The place (a most charming situation, with every advantage from nature but *none from art*) hardly habitable from the great neglect of its owners, whose dejection of spirits is seen by the little attention paid to their habitation.

On Thursday, at two o'clock I was preparing to dress for the day, when who should arrive but my Lord Annesley and Mr Harrison in a post chaise, and Lady Annesley, Miss Annesley, and Mrs Harrison, in a coach. To dinner they came, but as I had no expectation of anybody, I was not prepared for grandees, and gave them only our dinner, which would have done very well had not Mrs Overall's zeal to *make it better* made us wait for a dish of peas till the rest of the dinner was overdone! When our company was gone we *took a lesson* of geography till the prayerbell rung; but though we take a lesson every favourable opportunity, we have not gone above half way round the globe. As far as we have gone the parts connect very well, and no damage hath been done by the carriage, though we should make bungling work of it were it not for the adroitness of Mr Sandford [the Delanys' protegee and later husband of Sally Chapone]. We have hitherto only made *a play-thing of the world*, and when any of us hit off the right situation of any of the divisions it is matter of brag and merriment! In time I hope to make a better use of it. It is no uncommon thing now for

Saul Abbey, Co. Down, by Mary Delany, 1745.

an old woman to be more engaged with the *follies* of the world, than to consider how to make a good and right use of our *knowledge of it!*

Tomorrow we go to Ballyculter church, fourteen miles off, and dine at Castle Ward, a mile further off.   iii pp596–97

Here she visits Castleward around the time the present house was being built. The Wards had owned this estate since the sixteenth century; there is a seventeenth century castle and the earlier mansion, where she was entertained, was in between the stables close to Strangford Lough and the Temple built by Lady Anne Ward.

Mount Panther, 12 July 1760

We went to Castle Ward on Wednesday, and staid till yesterday noon. It is *altogether* one of the finest places I ever saw. Sunday last Mr Sandford gave us an excellent sermon at Down, where the Dean administered the Sacrament; we dined there, went to prayers after dinner, drank tea with Mrs Mathews, one of the curate's wives, and came home by nine. Monday, spent the day at Castle Wellan, where Mr Sandford saw Lord Annesley's wonderful works and designs. The young lady is to be married this day – Tuesday; about fourteen in company.

The spa at Ballynahinch was credited with the cure of the little boy so ill with wasting disease, son of her favourite Cherry Price, one of her neighbour Mathew Forde's daughters.

Master Price is much better with drinking the Ballynahinch waters, – a chalybeate in this neighbourhood.   iii pp597–98

Mount Panther, 18 July 1760

Tuesday morning, had no crowd, only fourteen to dinner; good sort of people, who let us *make up tippets and knots* for the wedding visit, which we made on Wednesday. Miss Annesley was married to Mr Gore on Monday night. We went to Castle Wellan to dinner, it being too far for an afternoon's visit. Lord Sudley, Mr Gore's father, was there, an old acquaintance of Mrs Chapone's (Sir Arthur Gore he *was then*). The day passed off tolerably well; at first formal, – after dinner forms were over and *noise succeeded*; the bride looked very pretty and very easy, not much embarrassed by the company. Lady Anne Ward and Miss Magill were there, and many gentlemen, – the whole of the company two or three and twenty. We invited them to dine here yesterday or to-day, but they pleaded the necessity of staying at home to receive the compliments of the neighbourhood.

Don't fix any time in your mind for our leaving Delville. D.D. says it will not be in his power till the last week in August, which indeed will soon be here. I hope I shall find you at Calwich. We shall take our chariot and four mares, the coachman and postilion with us.   iii p599

Her sister's health had given cause for concern and these worries mounted in 1760. The Delanys travelled to England and were with her at the time of her death in Bath. Acquaintances thought that Mary's energies had begun to flag and attributed this to the loss of her beloved sister although she had the interest of her niece's education to console her.

A letter to her brother Bernard three years later shows no lack of variety of pursuits and a critical comment on the builders of the new Castleward. This was commenced circa 1760 and is a compromise between the tastes of Bernard Ward and his wife Anne. He favoured classical Palladianism which was adopted for the main west elevation and she Strawberry Gothic which was the style for the east elevation facing Strangford Lough.

Mary to her brother Bernard Granville
Mount Panther, 29 August 1763

Our weather has been so excessive bad that we have not had two days together without rain. It has broken into all our little schemes of pleasure, and made us prisoners to *a very bad house*. We have amused ourselves with work and books, and are now not sorry to leave it, and propose setting out to-morrow morning and hope to be at Delville by dinner on Thursday. Miss Chapone has, I think, found great benefit from sea-bathing and riding. Mr Sandford has been very well till to-day – that he has an attack of his old disorder, but Delville will set us all to rights.

I was much disappointed when I was at Castleward at the weather's being so bad, for it is so fine a situation that I wished much to take some views. Mr Ward is building a fine house, but the scene about it is so uncommonly fine it is a pity it should not be judiciously laid out. *He* wants taste and *Lady Anne Ward* is so whimsical that I doubt her judgment. If they do not do *too much* they *can't* spoil the place, for it hath every advantage from Nature that can be desired.   iv pp20–21

Mary continued to worry about the dean's health which had not been good for several years and their visits to Down were interrupted in 1765.

Mary to Viscountess Andover
Delville, 8 June 1765

The Dean has been so much out of order with his old complaint, and of consequence my spirits so much affected, that I have avoided writing to my dear Lady Andover till I was a more reasonable creature: I thank God he is rather better; he has given up his house in the Deanery [of Down], being unable to bear so long a journey without great inconvenience. The same painful reason puts a stop to an English journey this year – I *dare look no further!*   iv p48

Mary to Viscountess Andover
Delville, 3 June 1766

My spirits have been much sunk by the Dean's having been a good deal out of order, and finding himself too weak to undertake an English journey this year. He is very pressing to me to go without him for a few months, but that is impossible: I should be miserable to leave him.   iv p60

The Delanys went to England in 1767 and the dean died in 1768; his purpose in making the long uncomfortable journey was not so much to seek a cure at Bath but to leave his Mary near her family and friends. Mary did not return to Ireland but the Sandfords, her goddaughter and her husband, arranged everything relating to their properties. So the dean of Down died, leaving the improvements of the jail in Downpatrick and churches rebuilt, but not a deanery house in Down.

CHAPTER 7

THE ARTS

Cultivation of the arts was approved as an occupation, interest and pastime for gentlewomen in the eighteenth century, and the comparative leisure of women with domestic staff allowed practice of all branches of the arts. Mary Delany's family and her early education had encouraged her interest and skills in a number of ways: her mother had been a craftswoman skilled in spinning, sewing and needlework, so necessary for practical and decorative purposes within the home. Her sister and she were both interested in shellwork collages. In a musical family, Mary was a proficient harpsichord player, and she sang sweetly. She was interested in the theatre also. She had taken drawing lessons from a number of masters, possibly William Hogarth and the Goupys. In sum, Mary had many accomplishments in the arts, and other crafts. Today, she is best remembered for her Flora, a series of cutpaper collages illustrating botanical specimens, a development of her skills in cutpaper silhouettes.

NEEDLEWORK

Needlework was a matter of necessity as well as of artistic expression in eighteenth century life. Mary Delany was exceptionally talented at this most practical and decorative of the arts. She was occupied with it on all occasions when her hands were free from other activities in the house and garden, and whenever the dean or a friend could read to her. The "work", a term that was used to describe applied arts, very often needlework or sewing, usually took place in a sociable atmosphere.

Delville, 13 June 1747

Yesterday morning I for the first day since I came worked four hours at *my quilt*, and Mr Greene read to us. Bushe [Letty, her great friend] painted, and Mrs Greene [the Dean's neice, formerly Miss Delany] made a night-gown for the little boy [Tommy]. One day next week we are to go a house-warming to her.   ii pp465–66

Materials were not always easy to obtain and she, her sister and friends helped each other. She often got good thread while in the north of Ireland. Knotting thread was used for making decorative fringes to pillows, cushions and other soft furnishings.

Dean Delany to Mary
Mount Panther, 15 August 1747
extract from unpublished manuscript, Newport Library, Gwent.

Did I tell you that Mrs Dun has left nine pound of knotting thread here for you, at a crown a poun[d]; and do you want more.

Very often, Mrs Delany listened to historical works while working on embroidery.

Mount Panther, August, 1750?

I have finished a rose, a tulip, and auricula – with their leaves, since my coming here, and a dab of knot stitch that I began three years ago. I have read (or rather heard read) The Man of Honour, Roderick Random [Tobias Smollet's account of an abortive attack on Cartagena in 1741], and the sieges of Drogheda and Derry.   ii p582

Lady Llanover states that she owns a set of covers for chairs made of linen of the most brilliant dark blue, which are probably the covers referred to in the letter below. Some blue covers with white embroidery attributed to Mrs Delany came up for sale in Christies' auction house in February 1988. Lady Llanover describes the covers thus "They are bordered with a beautiful pattern by Mrs Delany, of oak leaves cut out in white linen and tacked down with different sorts of white knotting, which also forms the veining and stalks." She remarks that "Mrs Delany and her sister were in the habit of using their knotting shuttles (as was the custom of the time) for relaxation" , she says " it is almost incredible the quantity of knotting in various patterns and colours which was left by Mrs Delany, and which still exist, being the remains of the produce of tea-table leisure hours, although such a large supply was required for the works which she completed in this peculiar style. Her favourite colour for the wall of a room or for furniture, was blue in various shades, but either dark and bright or sky blues."   ii p607

Delville, 27 October 1750

I am glad your works go on so well, and am sorry I have no knotting of the sort you want done. I cannot promise too much for you till I have finished a plain fringe I am knotting to trim a new blue and white linen bed I have just put up; as soon as that is finished I will do some sugar-plum for you; but I fear you will want it before I can do any quantity: let me know, and mine may lie by till yours is done, and send me the sized knotting you want; I have a good knotting friend also that I can employ for you. ii pp606–607

Delville, 17 November 1750

I have sent you by Mr Dubourg [leader of the lord lieutenant's musicians], who sailed yesterday, all the knotting and knotting thread I have – it is not a pound, that sort of thread is *not to be bought in London* and must be bespoke in the country, so that the soonest I could get to send would be a month. The double knotting I have sent will be too fine for you, I fear. Are the curtains done in the mosaic pattern with the cloth border?

Can you get Lady Anne Coventry's recipe for the rose pattern cross stitch? Many thanks for that of the raisin wine.   ii pp617, 618

Delville, 22 February 1752

I am glad you are going to work covers to your chairs; I think you must alter your pattern, for as they will have more wearing and washing than the bed or curtains, I fear your cloth work will not be firm enough. The border will be too broad for the chairs, something of the same kind of border to the bed with the mosaic pattern in the middle, and instead of cloth, fill up part of it with stitches in thread; but don't you want your coverlid first?   iii p93

Delville, 27 March 1752

I am glad my sweet Pauline [a nickname for her niece Mary] finds out our likeness; I hope she will love us both the better for it. Did I send you any old linen for your bedwork? I forget; do you want more, if I did? I will try if I can make out a *border* for your chairs to my mind and send it you.   iii p106

Delville, 25 November 1752

Mrs [Letty] Bushe has been with me ever since Sunday; her agreeableness and good humour enlivens our fireside. We have just read the Belle-Assemblee, and the Lady's Travels into Spain; my candlelight work is finishing a carpet in double-cross-stitch, on very coarse canvass, to go round my bed.   iii p176

As a patron of Irish poplin, she took an interest in the Drumcondra factory. Lady Llanover writes that "she has part of a curtain which belonged to her mother, which has a beautiful design of boys on the branches of an oak-tree looking into a bird's nest. It is a very fine chintz, printed in brilliant colours on a white ground, and the shades appear like an etching through the colours; she was informed that the design was by a celebrated artist, and that it was engraved "on copper plates" iii p180. Copper plate printing on cotton was first invented in this factory in Drumcondra, but, the English parliament saw this development as a threat to their own industry, passing restrictive laws about export of cotton printed fabrics from Ireland. There were various ploys to get round this like printing on a mixture of cotton and linen or printing on linen.

Delville, 9 December 1752

Just here Bushe made me go with her to Drumcondra, half a mile off, to see a new manufactory that is set up there of printed linens done by *copper-plates*; they are excessive pretty, but I will not describe them as I hope to bring you a small sample next summer.   iii p180

*Coverlet embroidered c.1750 in the household of a contemporary of Mrs Delany, Lady Helena
McDonnell (1750–1783) the sister of the 5th Earl of Antrim.*

As well as material and ideas, Mary sometimes sent samples of work to her sister.

Delville, 24 March 1759

I have *just finished* running with mosaic ground in crimson silk, chintz covers for the couches and stools in the closet and Miss Hamilton has made a very pretty fringe for them. I send you a bit enclosed: it is made up with two knotting needles; if you do not know it already you will soon find it out. On Tuesday I worked at your chenille chair. iii p542

Mount Panther, 12 July 1760

I am heartily glad you have at last consented to X stitch ground, as it gives me *hopes* of seeing your set of chairs finished; and it is *provoking* to have the ground take up so much more time than the flowers. Had I known your resolution sooner, I should have *grounded* the two chairs I have, which are the mixed pattern of *roses, tulips, and poppy*; but I have not grounded any part of the anemony [anemone] pattern, one back and one seat of which I have almost finished, but I will now at my *leisure moments* go on with the ground. I did not see Mrs Grey's *worked picture*, which Mr Spencer has, but have seen some of her work, which has a surprizing effect.   iii p598

Early eighteenth century Irish child's linen embroidered coverlet.

After her sister Anne's death she advised her niece on patterns and techniques.

Mary to her niece Mary Dewes
Delville, 16 November 1763

My dearest Mary, I have broken my word, which is what I would never willingly do. I promised to send enclosed in your stuff the pattern of the X stitch, but before I could work it out I had an opportunity of sending the stuff, which I would not lose. iv pp21

Here she is instructing Mary Dewes on the embellishment for her dressing table.

Delville, 23 April 1767

I think your fancy about taking a gimp round the flowers on the toilet would be pretty, but too much work, nor would it I believe quite answer; I should think your best way would be to put the flowers between two fine catguts, and tack them slightly round the edges, to keep them in their place, with very fine thread or silk, and if with a brush pencil you put a little starch (which is better than gum) on the back of the flowers and leaves when you place them on the catgut that is to be the ground, it would give a stiffness that would be an advantage to the whole: it must be done in a frame, and were you to do it in flounces as mine was done, you would, I think, be better able to manage it; three flounces would be enough, and they should hang a little full; your largest flowers must be at the bottom. I am sure you will do better than I can direct you, this is only in complaisance with your request and so with love and best wishes from all here, I end my long recipe for a toilet! We are tolerably well.   iv p105

DRESSMAKING AND FASHION

Mary Delany was a great patron of Irish cloth during her residence in Ireland. The ladies of that period were competent patternmakers, designers of clothes, as well as dressmakers and the two sisters Mary and Anne often swapped patterns or made up clothes for each other. Her court dress, which survives to this day, is a masterpiece of her own working and the beautiful floral design is reminiscent of those patterns for rich woven silks designed by her contemporary Anna Maria Garthwaite for the Spitalfields silk manufacturers. It is interesting to note that Mary used an (unusual) black silk ground for the embroidery of her dress which was so effective for showing her design and which may have led to her preference for a matt black ground in her later masterpiece of the paper Flora.

She had a discerning eye for fashion and remarks on all the new styles, although she herself disliked and would not wear extravagant and ostentatious fashions, like huge hoops and later on, very high elaborate coiffeur.

Part of her preparation for travelling to Ireland was shopping for clothes; she and Phil (her great friend Philomel Donnellan) were determined to make an impression in the provincial circles outside London.

North End, London, 13 July 1731

I pick up by degrees the things I shall want for my Irish expedition; I have bought a gown and petticoat, 'tis a very fine blue satin, sprigged all over with white, and the petticoat facings and endings bordered in the manner of a trimming wove in the silk; this suit of clothes cost me sixteen pound; and yesterday I bought a pink-coloured damask for seven shillings a yard, the prettiest colour I ever saw for a nightgown. i p284

Dublin, 4 December 1731

Phill [Mrs Donnellan] says you are too good a creature for remembering her so kindly; she is even with you, and has her white satin hood in great esteem for your sake. She wore her green satin that is embroidered with gold and silver on the birthday, and I had a blue and white satin that I bought in England, and a new laced head [head dress].   i p326

There were trade restrictions governing the free export of Irish cloth to England because the authorities wished to protect the English industry. Irish poplin, the "brown stuff" was obviously less rich than the usual material used by Mary in her dresses, but even at an early date she took it up, either to encourage local industry or out of a fashionable desire for simplicity.

Dublin, 17 January 1731/32

Mrs Donellan and I have each of us made a brown stuff manteau and petticoat, and have worn them twice at the assemblies; pretty things they have produced; 'tis said now that people are convinced *"fine feathers do not make fine birds."* We *"adorn our clothes;"* other people are *"adorned by their clothes."* We gave sixteen pence a yard! I wish I could convey a suit to you, but they are *prohibited*; however I will, when I return, try if I can cheat for you.   i p334

Dressing the hair, and wearing of wigs was an appurtenance of fashion that demanded quite some consideration from persons of taste! Head dresses of powdered or pomaded hair drawn up over a cushion or stuffing were often worn for public occasions.

Killalla, 4 February 1732/3

You said not one word to me about Bunny's [her brother Bernard] wearing his own hair. I had a letter yesterday from Lady Carteret; she writes me word that he "looks *very well* with his new-adorned pate." Tell me what you think? I *fancy* a wig became him better; what provoked him to cut *so bold a stroke?*   i p364

When Mary returned to Ireland as Patrick Delany's wife in 1744, Lord Chesterfield was appointed lord lieutenant of Ireland. He was married to Melusina de Schulenberg, probably an illegitimate daughter of George I, and is famous for his letters to his illegitimate son, Philip Stanhope. Chesterfield is supposed to have looked forward to his appointment in Ireland and certainly it proved to be a successful period in his career.

The Delanys met them at the Castle frequently and entertained them at Delville. Mary continued her support of Irish cloth.

Delville, 24 August 1745

The yachts are to go this day for my Lord Lieut, so in a few days I suppose we shall have them. I design to make my first visit in an *Irish stuff manteau and petticoat*, and a head the Dean has given me of Irish work, the prettiest I ever saw of the kind; he has made me also a present of a repeating-watch and a diamond ring; the diamond is a brilliant, but such gems are only valuable when they are testimonials of a kind and affectionate heart; as such to me they are inestimable.   ii p380

Delville, 23 November 1745

On the Princess of Wales's birthday there appeared at court a great number of Irish stuffs. Lady Chesterfield [Melusina de Schulenberg, Lord Lieutenant's wife] was dressed in one, and I had the *secret satisfaction* of knowing myself to have been the cause, but *dare not say so here*; but I say, "I am glad to find my Lady Chesterfield's example has had so good an influence." The poor weavers are starving, all trade has met with a great check this year.   ii p400

Delville, 21 December 1745

The great folks at the castle continue to show great favour, but we pay them little attendance, no more than not to be remarked as backward. Everybody is to appear on the Prince of Wales's birthday in Irish stuffs, as they did on the Princess's: I have not yet bought mine.   ii p408

Delville, 18 January 1745/6

Next Monday we are all prepared to appear at the castle in Irish stuffs; I have bought a *sprigged* one. Some are made very costly, which *I think foolish*, for when they mix much silk they are not so useful, some are so silly, they tell me, as to have them sprigged with silver; by the by, I hear we are like to be disappointed; for Lady Chesterfield has been much out of order with St Anthony's fire [erysipelas], and yesterday was not well enough to see company.   ii p414

Delville, 25 January 1745/6

Our great lady [Lady Chesterfield] has been so ill as not to see company a great while; she did not appear on the birthday [of the Prince of Wales], so there was no morning drawing-room, but a ball at night, and my Lord Chesterfield did the honours. It was prodigiously crowded, and all the ladies were dressed in Irish stuff, and never looked

Poppy, papaver rhaes, *by Mary Delany, October 1779.*

Dublin Linen Hall, 1783 by William Hincks.

finer or more genteel: except five or six who wore silk, and they were not distinguished to their honour. The men were not so public-spirited as the ladies – most of them were in their foreign finery.   ii p415

The Delanys were prepared to break the embargo on Irish textile exports to send presents to their family in England.

Delville, 4 January 1745/6

Since the *very cold weather* we have taken to our old sports of hunting the fox and puss in a corner, which warms us better than a great fire. I have sent you a grey stuff such as is the present mode, and the Dean has taken the liberty to send my mother a brown one. They go with a cargo of goods, and a merchant has undertaken to send them all safely.   ii p410

Mount Panther, 10 July 1752

Mrs Donnellan says she shall go as soon as she can to England. Lord Holderness has quitted her house; she cannot undertake to carry the Irish stuff, it being prohibited; so I will send it when I return home to Delville some other way, and the gloves also, if she don't take them.   iii p138

Mourning dress was worn according to a strict code and was mark of respect adopted towards members of the royal family as well as members of the extended family in the Granville circle.

Delville, 20 October 1747

I think black bombazeen will do very well in a sack [formal dress which fell loosely from the shoulders]. I have one in a manteau and petticoat which I wear when in full dress, at home a dark grey poplin, and abroad, undrest, a dark grey unwatered tabby: I shall make no more dark things; after three months black silk is worn with a hood, and black glazed gloves, for three months more; your mourning must be the same for Mr Dewes of Mapleborough.   ii pp478–79

Delville, 6 April 1751

I have bought for my mourning a dark grey Irish poplin sack: I have an unwatered tabby nightgown and two black and white washing gowns, so I shall make shift with them till the second mourning, it is only for three months.   iii p34

Here she expresses her scorn of ostentatious fashion, particularly the wide panniered skirts or hoops of the later eighteenth century.

Mount Panther, August 1750

I am glad you *detest* the tubs of hoops, I keep within bounds, endeavouring to avoid all particulars of being *too much in* or out of fashion; youth and liveliness never prompted me to break through that rule, not considering I had graces enough of my own to carry off any extravagance, and now my years and station tie me down to that which has ever been my choice.   ii p580

As well as commenting on fashion, Mary often made clothes for her nephews and niece, and we know she ran up shifts for the poor when she was in County Down with the dean.

Delville, 13 June 1752

I am afraid poor Nanny Viney's [the Granville family nurse] constitution is too bad to mend. What a melancholy prospect, if her piety did not support her! I have sent my niece Mary, by Mrs D[onnellan] a strong piece of Irish cloth for *frocks*, and have got coats for the boys, but no opportunity yet of sending them, as they must go privately; you must forgive my *home-spun tokens* to the dear children. I had hopes of fitting their coats on this year, but since that hope is blasted, you must not chide me for this little indulgence. On Tuesday, please God, we set out for Mount Panther. I shall not be able to write, I fear, till I get there, and my letters will take an unmeasurable round. iii p132

The family of Thomas Bateson of Belvoir near Belfast, 1762; attributed to Strickland Lowry.

One of the last flower collages made by Mary Delany; Hollyhock alcaea rosa, *1782.*

Delville, 17 March 1753

Pray send me cut in paper the pattern of a bib that exactly fits Mary's [Dewes] coat, and the length of her petticoat from the hips and from the peak of her stays; it is to *try an experiment* in a coarse sort of work which, if it succeeds, you shall see; if not, forget I mentioned it.   iii p214

She maintained her interest in fashion, especially where it concerned her niece. Here negligee refers to a loose dress.

Delville, 2 February 1760

I can't but think that Pauline would become a *negligee* very well; for constant wear young people, (as you say) are better in a dress where their carriage may be more observed; but I don't by any means approve of gowns that button before. Anything that drags the shoulders forward at the growing-time is a great disadvantage; but if she like the appearance of it, a stomacher may be made to *pin on*, and that will look as well as if it really buttoned. The *vanity* and *impertinence* of dress is always to be avoided, but a *decent* compliance with the fashion is less affected than any remarkable negligence of it.   iii p582/3

Mrs Delany was considered by many to be the model of taste, and her ingenuity and skills often made up for a lack of fortune in that most expensive art of dressing well.

SHELLCRAFT

Using shells to make decorations in the home in arrangements set in plaster work, was a favourite pastime of Mrs Delany and a hobby which was popular in the mid eighteenth century. It was particularly suited to Mary's range of interests because it combined nature, the collecting and selecting of particular shells, with art, her own special flair for composition.

Her greatest pleasure was in adorning a grotto which was an ornament in the Delville garden. She had previously decorated a grotto at Killala for Bishop Clayton.

Killalla, 13 August 1732

Last week we were hard at work gathering a fresh recruit of shells to finish the grotto. i p372

Killalla, 6 September 1732

Do you not wish yourself extended on the beach *gathering shells*, listening to Phill [Miss Donnellan] while she sings at her work, or joining in the conversation, always attended with cheerfulness? Perhaps you had rather rise by seven and walk to the

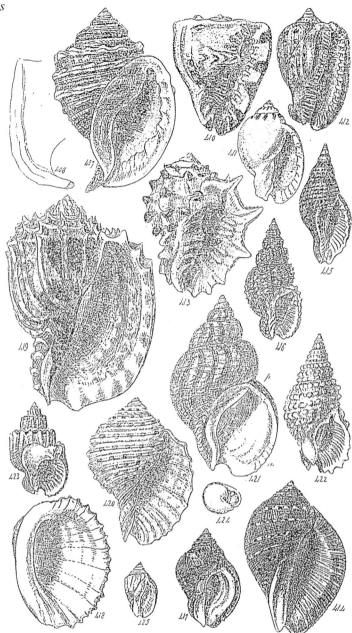

Nineteenth century engraving of popular shells, including a harp shell.

grotto with your bag of shells, and a humble servant by your side, helping you up the hill and saying pretty things to you as you walk? though maybe you choose to be at work in the grotto shewing the elegancy of your fancy, praising your companions' works, and desiring approbation for what you have finished? if this is too fatiguing, 'tis likely you would prefer working or reading till dinner, after that eating nuts and walking to gather mushrooms.

Mrs Delany in old age, by John Opie with a frame by Horace Walpole.

˜Yesterday at five o'clock in the afternoon we took boat and went to a shore about a mile off to gather shells, where we found a vast variety of beauties. We were very merry at our work, but much merrier in our return home, for five of us, viz., Phill, Mrs Don, Mr Lloyd, and a young clergyman (who is here very often, one Mr Langton), and Penelope [her own pet name was Penny from Pendarves as she was then hence Penelope] all mounted a cart, and home we drove as jocund as ever five people were. I laughed immoderately at the new carriage, and wished for you there, more than ever I did when flaunting in a coach and six. The rest of the company were conveyed home in a chaise, being too proud for carting.   i pp382–83

When she returned to Ireland as wife of the dean, much energy and skill went into the making of shellwork decorations for objects like the lustre described here, and bookcase ends.

Delville, 3 October 1745

I expect a visit this morning from Lady Chesterfield [the lord lieutenant's wife]; she said she would come the first fine day. My shell lustre [light holder, chandelier] I wrote you word I was about, was finished ten days ago and everybody liked it. 'Twas a *new whim* and shows the shells to great advantage. I had fixed it up in my portico which is dedicated to the Duchess of Portland; but the damp weather made the cement give and I have been obliged to bring it into the house, and it now hangs in my work-room and shows to more advantage. My present work is finishing some drawings for my book, and as soon as Lady Chesterfield has made her visit I shall set about painting again, but I don't care for interruptions when I am at that employment; my first work will be to give my mother's picture one more painting over – I don't like it yet.   ii pp391–92

Here she shows how much of her creativity was fostered by the interest and encouragement of Patrick Delany.

Delville, 22 October 1745

To drive from my thoughts unavailing fears, and divert my mind from thinking too much of my disappointment this year in not going to England, I employ every hour as much as possible. I have been sorting my mosses and ores, and am going to new arrange my shells, and to *cover* two large vases for my garden: my painting has lain dormant some time, having been in expectation of their excellencies [the Chesterfields] every morning; and I did not care to be found in a litter; and Shakespear and the harpsichord fill up the evenings. These are *my drams*, and such as refresh without intoxicating; but I believe my spirits would flag even with these amusements, did they not give so much pleasure to D.D; his approving of my works, and encouraging me to go on, keep up my relish to them, and make them more delightful to me than assemblies, plays, or even an opera would be without he shared them with me. *Eager* as I am in all my pursuits I am *easily checked*, and the least disapprobation or snap, from the person I wish to oblige, in thought, word, or deed, would soon give me a distaste to what was delightful to me before! I hope this does not proceed from pride, but from a disposition in my heart that will not suffer me to enjoy any pleasure that I cannot communicate.   ii p395

Shells were used for craft work but also kept as specimens, carefully recorded and displayed.

Delville, 11 July 1747

We are very busy in settling all my drawers of shells, sorting and cleaning them. I have a new cabinet with whole glass doors and glass on the side and shelves within, of whimsical shapes, to hold all my *beauties*. One large drawer underneath for the register drawer, and my little chest of drawers I have placed in my closet within my bedchamber, from whence I send you this letter.   ii p471

Shellwork was subject to damp and while the Delanys were absent in England, her creations suffered.

Delville, 22 May 1750

The greatest damage I have sustained in my absence is my shell lustres falling to pieces and most of my crayon pictures *mildewed*; I have got the harp-shell, and will send the prints of the gems by the first opportunity.   ii p546,547

Delville, 8 June 1750

Covered with dust and wearied with the toils of cleaning and new arranging my cabinet of shells, throwing out rubbish, adding my new acquisitions, all which has been the work of yesterday and this morning to the present hour of one (and which could not have been accomplished without the good assistance of my Mrs Hamilton and Bushe, who have toiled like horses) to refresh my body and mind I am retired to write to the sister of my heart, to thank her for her last charming letter, and to assure her that I continue in as good health as her own heart can wish me.   ii p551

Mary to her brother Bernard Granville
Delville, 17 June 1750

I have been very busy in cleaning my new shells, and arranging them in my cabinet, and adding those I brought with me, and now they make a *dazzling show*. I have got a good cargo of grotto shells for you, and will send them to Chester; let me know how they shall be sent from thence to Calwich.   ii p557

Often these shells changed hands for large sums of money.

Delville, 22 June 1750

The 15 guinea shell was the tender-shell'd nautilus; Lady Anne [Coventry] *has one* of the kind.   ii p558

Delville, 7 July 1750

I am glad Lady A. Coventry [in the duchess of Portland's circle and a fine craftswoman herself] liked the shell work I have sent you by Mrs Mountenay, (a lady that lives with Miss Frankland), the twelve tea napkins you desired, a little box of odd shells that I think you have not (amongst them the harp shell and two small *whole scollops*), and three old smocks for *cut out work*. I desired the parcel to be left with Mr Clerke in Jermyn Street, where you may send your commands for them.   ii p566

The sorting of shells must have taken considerable time, and friends were brought in to help.

Mary to her brother, Bernard Granville
Delville, 15 July 1750

I must first tell you that I have sent to Mr Luke Gavin, merchant at Chester, a barrel of shells, a mixture of all sorts, let them be separated as you unpack them all. ii p571

Delville, 28 September 1750

To regale and *compose me* the Hamiltons have promised to breakfast with me tomorrow and assist me in sorting shells, for now I am all *whip and spur* to get my lustre revived. I have stripped it of every shell and scraped it to the bone. I have now more choice of shells than when I made it, and hope the second edition will be more correct than the first.   ii p595

Delville, 13 October 1750

I have all this week worked most industriously at my lustre; two mornings more will finish the work. Mrs Hamilton ["her" Mrs Henry Hamilton] (of Usher's Quay) has began an imitation of carving with shells and pasteboard, to be fixed on the ceiling to hide the pulley, and for the line to come through that holds the lustre, it cannot be finished in a day, and I shall endeavour to prevail on her to spend some time with me here. Bushe is still detained in Dublin on business: my house has not been ready till now for company. I stripped it of many necessaries when I went to the north, and have but just recruited.   ii pp602–603

Delville, 20 October 1750

I have worked like a dragon this week at my lustre, and completed it on Thursday. I am now glad the old one was destroyed – this I think prettier, D.D. calls it *the Phoenix*: it was a vast work, every shell dried and sorted, and nobody assisted me, but Mrs Hamilton one morning made some of the flowers. Today Mrs F. Hamilton [Dorothea Forth, and sometimes called Mrs Forth Hamilton] and her son and daughter come to me to stay some time, and she is to earn her bread here, for she has undertaken an imitation of carving for the ceiling where the pulley is to be fastened. ii pp604–605

Delville, 27 October 1750

My lustre is finished, and Mrs Hamilton very diligent in making the ornament which is to hide the pulley; as soon as that is done it is to be put up, and then I shall take painting in hand.   ii p608

With all this hard work of providing decorations for her own home, she was very ready to admire the work of professional craftsmen in providing decorative accessories although the cost was unthinkable, nearly half a year's housekeeping allowance was quoted on the articles described.

Delville, 8 November 1750

Mrs F. Hamilton and Bushe are now with me I fetched her yesterday; Mrs H.[Hamilton] threatens to leave me on Tuesday, but I will try to keep her one week more, for we are now deeply engaged in some shell carving that is to be placed at the ends of my bookshelves in my work-room. We have been so much taken up, that we have not either gone out or engaged company at home, that we should have *no inters* [interruptions], only on Wednesday night we went to the Philharmonic concert, which was agreeable enough, and we design to go to the first good comedy that is acted, and then I think I shall have done with public places for the winter season, till February is over. Yesterday morning, just as we were setting out for Dublin to fetch Mrs L.B.[Letty Bushe] and Mrs Montgomery (a very agreeable woman, and friend of Mrs F. Hamilton) Mr and Mrs Vesey came to breakfast, which delayed us an hour. In our way back from Dublin, we called at Mr Smith's (*our Chevenix*) to see a pair of vases, which I think the finest, and prettiest toys I ever saw; indeed they are more than toys, and will serve for decanters or ewers very well. They hold above a quart each, are of a very elegant shape, after the antique, made of the Egyptian pebble, lined with gold, set in the prettiest manner, and ornamented with chased gold perfectly well wrought; he got them unfinished, and finished them here; the price three hundred guineas, they weigh an hundred and fifty. So, *madam*, you see, though we are here a poor, despised, and trampled upon nation, we *have our fine things*, and *costly things*, as well! though not quite as common as in the *superbe Angleterre!* They really are so very pretty that I would rather have them than £500 worth of jewels.   ii pp611–12

Soon her attention turned to the decoration of the chapel ceiling at Delville.

Delville, 10 December 1750

I sat down to my painting, and Bushe to her drawing. In the evening, when tea is over, we settle to our different engagements; she reads aloud Mr Carte's Life of the Duke of Ormonde, and I go on with making shell flowers for the ceiling of the chapel. I have made 86 large flowers, and about 30 small ones; I believe I told you this before, and that I tire you with repetition. Wednesday, Thursday and Friday spent alike.
ii p626

Delville, 12 January 1750/51

I am going on making shell flowers, six of the festoons are finished and fastened on; I have ten more to do, and a wreath to go round the window over the communion-table.   iii p5

Delville 16 March 1750/51

Mr Warde, a clergyman, our landlord at Mount Panther, brought me a present this morning of a *tiled cockle*, that weighs above a hundred weight; it is as fine a shell as ever I saw – it is vulgarly called "the Lion's Claw" and comes from the West Indies; and at this instant looks most magnificent under my cabinet   iii p27

The following no doubt refers to the shell decorations on the Delville grotto. In summer she rose early to start her work.

Mary to her brother Bernard Granville
Delville, 11 June 1751

I am filling a niche with a mosaic of shells and the compliment paid it two days ago was, that "*it was very like Irish stitch.*" These are my occupations till nine (I rise soon after six) and *then painting takes place.*   iii p39

The source for unusual shells was sailors who collected them on their voyages overseas.

Delville, 14 March 1752

Last Tuesday we went to Kingsend [Ringsend], a town by the sea-side, about half a mile from Dublin. A tyde-waiter there sent me word of some fine shells he had to dispose of; unluckily he was not at home, but doing duty on board a ship.   iii p95

She continued her shellwork when she was on her visits to England.

Delville, 6 July 1754

I have not yet got shells large enough for the festoons, and fear it will be in vain to make them here, but I will send a barrel of shells to Sir Charles Mordaunt's, and hope to give myself the pleasure of making it there. Should I do it here there would not be time enough for the putty to dry, and the shells would be all jumbled together before they reached Walton.   iii p284

Delville, 20 July 1754

On examining my shells I find I have none that will by themselves make considerable figure enough for festoons for Sir Charles Mordaunt's cold bath, but will do very well to mix with others, so that it would be in vain to make a festoon here; but I will send (as I am desired) a cask of shells, in which I shall put a basket or box of some for you. iii pp287–88

Delville, 24 March 1759

I have not yet begun painting, as I have had two or three colds in succession. I am going about a little shell ornament for my bow closet, festoons of shell flowers in their *natural colours*, that are to go over the bow window. The coach is at the door, and we are going to Burdoyl [Baldoyle], a strand about six miles off, in search of shells.   iii pp542,543

Delville, 31 March 1759

Mrs Hamilton's work will do for a screen. My box window has provoked me to a good deal of work; I am making festoons with shell-flowers, *chained up* with silver shells, which will look very well on the crimson ground: and next week I hope I shall be able to take up my pencils again.   iii p544

Delville, 12 May 1759

Monday and Tuesday mornings were engaged in shell-work; I shall make my bow-window closet at last an *errant fop*, but *flattery* raises *vanity*, and *vanity* delights *in decorations!*   iii p553

Delville, 18 July 1759

I have one of the kind of oysters mentioned by your Bristol man, commonly called the lion's claw, but mine is a pigmy, only weighs *two hundred weight*.   iii p560

She seems to have devoted less time to shellwork as she grew older, perhaps her needlework and botanical studies took up all her time.

THEATRE

The theatre in 18th century Dublin was a lively place where many of the great names of the stage entertained the metropolitan audience. Mary Delany and her husband attended performances in Dublin frequently, though their first love was music. Also, as entertainment in their own homes, particularly in house parties, amateur acting provided a good source of fun and amusement for the upper level of Irish society.

Here John Dryden's The Spanish Fryar or the Double Discovery is the play they watched.

Dublin, 4 October 1731

I wrote you word on Thursday last, that we designed going to the play that evening. To the play we went, "The Spanish Fryar", tolerably well acted. The house is small, but neat and very well lighted, the gentlemen all sit in the pit.   i p294

Ambrose Philip's play The Distressed Mother was performed by Mary and her friends.

Dublin, 4 January 1732/3

To-morrow is to be acted The Distressed Mother, the part of Hermione by Miss Molesworth, daughter to my Lord Molesworth, Andromache by one Miss Parker, a good and pretty girl, Pyrrhus by Lord Montjoy, Orestes by Mr Burnwell, brother to my Lord Kingsland. Every performer has twelve tickets to dispose of. The scene of action is to be the council-chamber, all the Bishops, Judges, and Privy Counsellors are to be there; Lord Montjoy brought us all tickets last night, so *we are happy*, whilst half the girls in town are trembling for fear they should not be admitted.   i p392

After their marriage the Delanys patronised the theatre, and enjoyed the performances of great celebrities in that most exciting time of Dublin theatre rivalry. The letter below describes a visit to Nicholas Rowe's Fair Penitent, a sentimental drama. Performing in it was David Garrick (1716–79), one of the most famous actors of the age, who later became a friend and entertained Mary and her friend the duchess of Portland at his Thameside home. Also in this performance was Swift's friend, Thomas Sheridan (1721–88), the Irish actor manager who took over the management of the old Smock Alley Theatre in Dublin and then left for Drury Lane, London, returning in 1745 to dominate Dublin theatrical affairs until 1758 when competition from new theatres, including Barry's, drove him back to England. He attracted the great Garrick and a host of brilliant actors of the age to play in Dublin. Thomas was the father of the great actor and playwright, Richard Brinsley Sheridan. As if this was not enough, the Delanys were also to see in this performance, Spranger Barry (1719–77) another famous Irish actor manager, who built and managed the Crow Street Theatre with Henry Woodward in 1758. The rivalry between the Dublin theatres was notorious.

Mr and Mrs Spranger Barry in the characters of Jaffier and Belvidera in Venice preserved, *1776.*

Delville, 13 February 1745/6

To-morrow I go to the Fair Penitent to see our three famous actors together. Garrick performs the part of Lothario, Sheridan Horatio, and Barry Altamont. Sheridan I have not seen, my brother has: he is here in great reputation. Barry is the handsomest man and figure altogether that ever I saw upon the stage, and a promising actor. The ingenious Letty and Mrs Green [the Dean's niece] go with me. Next week Esther is to be performed [one of Handel's works]; the rehearsal will be on Tuesday.
 ii pp423–24

Delville, 10 November 1750

Last night I went with my guest, Mrs Hamilton, to see Macbeth, and was very well entertained with it. Sheridan acted Macbeth very well, the other parts very tolerably done, Lady Macbeth by Mrs Bland – a very handsome clever woman, acts with spirit, but wants judgment.   ii p615

Peg Woffington, referred to below, was an Irish actress who was launched by Madam Violante, the famous rope-dancer, at her amusement booth in Dublin. Peg played in the Smock Alley Theatre and then in Covent Garden where she took London by storm in 1740. Though blessed with an enchanting face and magnetic personality, her voice was harsh. She became David Garrick's mistress and at the time of her return to Dublin in 1751, she was made president, and only female member, of the Beefsteak Club.

Delville, 18 January 1752

Mrs [Peg] Woffington is much improved, and did the part of Lady Townley last Saturday better than I have seen it done since Mrs Oldfield's time. Her person is fine, her arms a little *ungainly*, and her voice disagreeable, but she pronounces her words perfectly well, and she speaks sensibly. Mr Sheridan is a *just* actor, but rather a *dull one*; he is going to give a play gratis to raise a sum of money to erect a monument to Swift; he has many of the Dean of St Patrick's letters that show he was a most friendly and generous man.   iii pp79–80

Colley Cibber's play is on the programme here: he was the famous actor manager of Drury Lane Theatre in London.

Delville, 14 March 1752

Mrs Hamilton and her daughter to dine here, who is to be of our party and lie here, Finglass being too far to go after the play. It is "The Nonjuror". I have never seen it, and they say Mrs Woffington does her part extremely well; she is a fine figure, but she *spoils* her appearance by the immoderate size of her hoops.   iii p98

Here Mary Delany comments unfavourably on the actor Barry, who at that time enjoyed a reputation equal to Garrick, in a performance of William Congreve's Mourning Bride, his only tragedy.

The actress Peg Woffington (1718-60) by Lucius Barber (fl. 1749-67).

Delville, 3 February 1759

Mrs Delany [referring to herself in the third person] with company went to the Mourning Bride to see the new play house, and Mrs Fitzhenry performed the part of Zara which I think she does incomparably!

I have digressed from my account of the play, which on the whole was tolerably acted, though I don't like *their celebrated* Mr Barry : he is tall and ungainly, and does not speak sensibly, nor look his part well: he was Osmyn; Almeyra was acted by a very pretty woman, who I *think* might be made a *very good actress*, her name is Dancer [afterwards Mrs Barry].   iii pp538,539

There was controversy over what should be seen on the stage then, as now.

Delville, 17 March 1759

Mrs Hamilton, and Mrs Forth, and Miss Hamilton, who spent the day with us: we read *Law against the Stage*: have you read it? He is warm and vehement, and *runs away* with his argument, often begging the question. This manner of treating the subject will never convince, and prevents the good and just things he says from having the efficacy they ought to have! I cannot but think that plays well chosen, which expose and punish vice and distinguish and reward virtue, are very allowable entertainments, and might be calculated to do a great deal of good. I own as the stage is *now* managed, when many immoral, bad plays are encouraged, they are dangerous, but *that* is the fault of *the manager* and those who go to them that they do not *choose better.*   iii p541

Delville, 7 December 1764

Plays and burlettas [farces] are much in vogue, and are liked and disliked according to the various humours of their audience. I have, as it is time, given up all public hurley-burleys, but enjoy the recital of them very well.   iv p40

As the dean became more frail, their visits to public performances ceased. When she was widowed and back in London, she resumed her theatre-going.

Thomas Sheridan, from portrait by R. Stewart.

MUSIC

In Mary Delany's circle of friends, music making was a pastime which many enjoyed. She was an accomplished performer on the harpsichord. As a child she heard George Frederick Handel play in her Aunt Stanley's house. Her brother Bernard Granville became Handel's friend and his collection of Handel manuscripts went eventually to the British Museum. Mary, together with her family, helped to forward Handel's reputation in England and Ireland. Like the dean, Mrs Delany was an enthusiast for opera. At the time they were attending public performances, Italian music was all the rage.

Many public performances of music were given in support of charitable institutions and other concerts were organised by musicians in a subscription series. Dublin audiences eagerly awaited the visits of professional musicians. They were particularly sympathetic to Handel, whose oratorio the Messiah was first performed in Dublin's Fishamble Street "Musick Hall" in 1742. Michael Arne, brother of Thomas, in collaboration with Matthew Dubourg, the leader of the viceroy's musicians, arranged a series of subscription concerts in Dublin of Handel's oratorios in 1743.

There were also the talented amateurs who contributed to the musical life of the capital, particularly the Academy of Music formed in 1757 by Mary's godson, Garrett Wesley, 2nd lord Mornington, who is said to have earned his eventual earldom from George III to his musical talent. Their performances were very often arranged for charities.

In her domestic surroundings there was much music, traditional as well as classical: wherever she lived she employed musicians for entertainment and dancing. In County Down, they had a harper named Fitz Simons, and in Delville they had both fiddlers and harpers on occasion.

Killalla, 7 August 1732

Our fiddler has left us, so there's an end of dancing for some time, but we expect a famous piper and haut-boy, and then we shall foot it again most furiously.   i p370

Hollymount, 28 June 1745

We have got an Irish harper in the house, who plays a great variety of tunes very well; he plays to us at our meals, and to me whilst I am drawing.   ii p368

Turlogh Carolan (1678–1738), one of the greatest of the traditional Irish harpers, also composed airs which enjoyed great popularity at all levels of society.

Mount Panther, ?August 1750

You have never mentioned Carolan's tunes since you said you had received them,

Arthur O'Neill (eighteenth century harper).

have you tried them? I think some are very pretty: *Sir Toby Buck* and *Michll [Michael] O'Connor* are great favourites.   ii p580

In the letter below, Mary mentions Matthew Dubourg (1703–67) whom she met when she first visited Ireland. He was a pupil of Francesco Geminiani, the great violinist and friend of Handel, and was the leader of the viceroy's musicians in Dublin, a post he continued to hold besides other appointments and engagements until 1765.

Dublin, 4 October 1731

I wrote you word on Thursday last, that we designed going to the play that evening. Company dined here, among whom were Mr Hamilton and Mr Usher. I am always made to play on the harpsichord after dinner, and great honours I have received on that account, more than I am sure I merit.

   On Friday we went to a concert of music, but our sport there was very near being spoiled, for most of the performers were at the Castle, playing to their Graces [the lord lieutenant and his wife, the duke and duchess of Dorset], and did not think fit to come among us till past eight at night: we then had two or three pieces of music very well performed, Dubourg being the violino primo. On Saturday we dined and supped at Mrs Usher's, where we always are very handsomely entertained and in a friendly manner.   i p294

Mary and her sister had had a good musical education which included thorough base, the English term for basso continuo which was also used to refer to theory of harmony in general.

Delville, 4 December 1731

I am to go to a concert of musick for Mrs Barber's [poetess protegee of Swift and family friend of the Delanys] benefit; it is half-an-hour after three, and I fear I shall be called before I have filled my sheet of paper. I hope you do not neglect your harpsichord, especially thorough-base. There's an end of our hopes of operas; but last Monday we had a ridotto [an entertainment of music and dancing], which everybody liked very well. I was not there, my eyes being out of order. The gentlemen subscribed two moiders a piece, and have two tickets each night to dispose of to ladies. There are in this town two subscription concerts on that footing, so that the women are at no expense for their entertainments.   i p325

Handel's Messiah was performed for the very first time in Dublin on the 12th April, 1742 with Dubourg playing lead violin. Dr Delany, a widower at that time, is said to have been so moved by Mrs Cibber's performance that he shouted out "woman, for this, be all thy sins forgiven". Susanna Cibber was sister to the English song writers and impresarios Thomas and Michael Arne, who spent long periods in Dublin.

Delville, 21 December 1745

Last Monday the Dean and I went to the rehearsal of the Messiah for the relief of poor debtors; it was very well performed, and I much delighted. You know how much I delight in music, and that piece is very charming; but I had not courage to go to the performance at night, the weather was so excessively bad, and I thought it would be hazardous to come out of so great crowd so far, that is my kind guardian thought so for me.   ii p408

Handel was much admired and performed although John Gay's satrical opera the Beggars' Opera, first performed in 1728, was a perennial favourite.

Delville, 26 April 1746

This has been a week of hurry with me indeed. On Thursday I went to the music for the benefit of the hospital of Incurables, which was crowded – the piece performed was [Handel's] Alexander's Feast; and yesterday went to see the Beggars' Opera. We have had glorious news from Scotland. I hope, in God, the affair of the rebellion is now at an end, and that we shall meet in peace. All these gay doings have interrupted my painting, and I much fear I shall hardly have time to finish what I meant *to bring with me*, for it must have some time to dry before it is packed up.   ii pp436–37

Delville, 17 June 1750

I am glad the Foundling Hospital was so full, and carried on with such decency; I am sure it pleased our friend Handel [a performance of his Messiah], and I love to have him pleased.   ii p556

Delville, 27 October 1750

Yesterday evening we went to a concert to hear a new French fiddler, Morella by name, he has a particularly fine execution, plays with great ease and prettiness, but as it was all *nonsense music* I am not sure I shall like his taste, till I hear him play music *of consequence*; and I believe, on the whole, he has *too many tricks to please me* often.   ii p610

Handel's Utrecht Te Deum which she hears here was probably the first sacred music of his performed in Dublin in April 1736 at a benefit concert for the Mercer's hospital.

Delville, 30 November 1750

Yesterday we were at a charitable music, performed in the round church of Dublin [St Andrew's Round Church near Suffolk Street]; we had Corelli's 8th concerto, Mr Handel's Te Deum Jubilate, and two anthems; I cannot say there was so great a crowd as I wished to see on the occasion. We had promised to breakfast and dine at Lucan this day, and to come home by moonshine, but wind and rain prevented our design. I never heard a fiercer storm than it has been all night, and is but little abated. ii p620

Her brother's friendship with Handel enabled her to pass on admiring messages to the great composer, which must have assuaged his feelings over the disappointing reception of some of his works, like the oratorio, Theodora, written in summer 1750, which he regarded highly.

Mary to her brother Bernard Granville
Welsborne [her sister's home], 3 December 1750

I hope you find Mr Handel well. I beg my compliments to him: he has not a more real admirer of his great work than myself; his wonderful Messiah will never be out of my head: and I may say my heart was raised almost to heaven by it. It is only those people who have not felt the pleasure of devotion that can make any objection to that performance, which is calculated to raise our devotion, and make us truly sensible of the power of the divine words he has chose beyond any human work that ever yet appeared, and I am sure I may venture to say ever will.

   If anything can give us an idea of the last day it must be that part "The trumpet shall sound, the dead shall be raised". It is few people I can say so much to as this, for they would call me an enthusiast; but when I wish to raise my thoughts above this world and all its trifling concerns, I look over what oratorios I have, and even my poor way of fumbling gives me pleasing recollections, but I have nothing of the Messiah, but "*He was despised*". Does Mr Handel do anything new against next Lent? surely Theodora will have justice at last, if it was to be again performed, but the generality of the world have ears and *hear not*. Mr Dewes is vastly afraid I shall make the boys love music, which he thinks would interfere with their necessary studies, but I doubt they have all good ears, and the little girl really can sing a tune, and he allows me to make her a musician if I can.   ii pp623–24

Delville, 10 December 1750

On Tuesday morning next, the rehearsal of the Messiah is to be for the benefit of debtors on Thursday evening it will be performed. I hope to go to both; our new, and *therefore* favourite performer Morella is to play the first fiddle, and conduct the whole. I am afraid *his French taste* will prevail; I shall *not be able to endure* his introducing *froth and nonsense* in that sublime and awful piece of music. What makes me fear this will be the case, is, that in the closing of the eighth concerto of Corelli, instead of playing it *clear and distinct*, he filled it up with *frippery and graces which quite destroyed the effect* of the sweet notes, and solemn pauses that conclude it.   ii p626

Mary to her brother Bernard Granville
Delville, 18 December 1750

I was at the rehearsal and performance of the Messiah, and though *voices* and *hands* were wanting to do it justice, it was very tolerably performed, and gave me great pleasure 'tis heavenly. Morella conducted it, and I expected would have *spoiled it*, but was agreeably surprized to find the contrary: he came off with great applause. I thought it would be impossible for his wild fancy and fingers to have kept within bounds: but Handel's music inspired and *awed him*. He says *(but I don't believe him)* that he *never* saw any music of Handel's or Corelli's till he came to Ireland. I heard him play at the Bishop of Derry's a solo of Geminiani's which he had never seen; he played it cleverly, as his execution is extraordinary, but his taste in the adagio part was *ill suited* to the music. He is young, modest, and well-behaved, as I am told, and were he to play *under* Mr Handel's direction two or three years, would make a surprizing player. We are so fond of him here, that were it known I gave this hint, I should be *expelled* all musical society, as they so much fear he should be tempted to leave us. Pray make my compliments to Handel. Is *Theodora* to appear next Lent? Compliments to Hanover Square [Handel lived in Hanover Square].
ii pp629–30,631

Judas Maccabeus and Joshua were part of a series of Handel's "militaristic" oratorios composed after the Highland Rebellion in 1745 and 1746. They were a financial success for the composer, and a fittingly loyal celebration of the Hanoverian dynasty.

Delville, 12 January 1750/51

Next Tuesday we propose going to the rehearsal of Judas Maccabeus, for the Infirmary of Incurables.   iii pp5–6

Delville, 2 February 1750/51

We went to the rehearsal of Joshua last Tuesday; were charmed with it, never heard it before, but it was so cold on Thursday I had not courage to go to the night perform-ance of it.   iii pp12–13

Handel's oratorio Deborah, a very dramatic piece written in 1733, had enjoyed some success.

Delville, February 1750/51

Last Monday we went to the rehearsal of Deborah. Dr Moss, you must known, is the chief manager and operator of the Lying-in Hospital, and has gardens laid out for the entertainment of company in the manner of Vauxhall and Ranalagh; and in order to gather together subscribers for the next season he gave a *gratis breakfast* and a fine concert of music in a large room which was not opened before, and is in the gardens. The music allured us, and we went, D.D. with us, at about half an hour after eleven, the concert to begin at 12. When we came, with some difficulty we squeezed into the room, which they say is 60 feet long, and got up to the breakfast table, which had been well pillaged; but the fragments of cakes, bread and butter, silver coffee-pots, and tea-kettles without number, and all sorts of spring flowers were strewed on the table, shewed it had been set most plentifully and elegantly. The company, indeed, looked as if their principal design of coming was for a breakfast. When they had satisfied their hunger the remains were taken away, and such a torrent of rude mob (for they deserved no better name) *crowded in* that I and my company *crowded out* as fast as we could, glad we escaped in whole skins, and resolving never more to go to the throng of a *gratis* entertainment. We got away with all speed, without hearing a note of the music and went to pay a visit to Mrs Dillon and Lady Austin, and have engaged them to spend next Monday here. The Dean fled from his colours: he followed us into the room, and retired as fast as possible. The bustle and odd mixture of (for there was from the highest to the lowest) was matter of mirth to us in the evening, when we had a little recovered our fatigue.   iii p19

Besides attending public performances, the Delanys enjoyed music played by young amateurs at home and encouraged them.

Delville, February 1751

On Saturday at my neighbour's, Mrs Eccles, where Miss Bushe and I went to drink tea. We met a Miss Veraselle, a French merchant's daughter, a sickly young woman, who lodges at Glasnevin for her health. I soon found she was musical and a performer on the *six-stringed base*, and exprest a desire of hearing her; upon which, with a great deal of good humour, she suffered Mrs Eccles to send for her base, and played an hour to us most agreeably. She has a neat execution and pretty taste; and seems quite a mistress of the instrument, but I made no advances there to an acquaintance, not knowing how she might be entangled with a family; and as my visitors in Dublin are numerous, I keep myself here as clear from company as I can, or I should have no time to myself. They say she also sings prettily.   iii pp17–18

Delville, 16 March 1751

I have been provoked, and yet entertained and pleased in spite of all my anger, at being interrupted just as I came to page the 5th [of her letter]. Rap, rap at the door; and in walked a lady and gentleman, Hamilton by name, that Mrs Bushe introduced to me; *she* is a surprising ready player on the harpsichord – she played Mr Purcell's overture, and one of Handel's, as readily as if she had played them seven years, she has a neat pretty finger, and if she would undergo the slavery of practice, could do what she pleased; but as she plays so agreeably without, and is so much mistress of music, it is not worth her while.   iii p27

Apart from Handel, the music was very influenced by the Italian masters.

Delville, 26 January 1752

Our music was chiefly Italian – the *Stabat Mater* sung by Guadagni (whom you heard sing in Mr Handel's oratorios) and Mrs Oldmixon; Dubourg the principal violin: it was well performed, and some of the duet parts are very pretty. They had more music after we left them, but we staid till *nearly* ten, which was a late hour for us.   iii p81

There were earlier musical ensembles than the Musical Academy formed by her godson Garrett Wesley.

Delville, 14 March 1752/3

Wednesday morning there was a concert, given by gentlemen performers for the benefit of poor debtors; it began with a breakfast, of which we did not choose to

Two sisters of the Leslie family at the harpsichord, by James Latham (1696–1747).

partake but went just before the music began; Mr Brownlow played a voluntary on the organ, but I cannot say it had a good effect, his playing on the harpsichord is much better, and what I believe he has been more used to. This society of gentlemen have a concert among themselves every Wednesday, and admit the ladies of their acquaintance with tickets; but this charity-concert was at half guinea tickets, and I believe they raised a great sum. There is a Capt. Read, who plays on the German flute to great perfection; we could not stay it out as we were to have company to dine with us, all Mr Forde's family.   iii p96

Handel became blind in 1751, the following is a reference to his oratorio Samson; the subject of this oratorio and the author were, of course, in the same poignant predicament.

Delville, 25 November 1752

Poor Handel! how feelingly must he recollect the "*total eclipse*": I hear he has now been couched, and found some benefit from it.   iii p177

Thomas Roseingrave (1688–1766), the performer mentioned below, was the son of Daniel, organist of St Patrick's Cathedral, and educated in Italy where he met Domenico Scarlatti. In 1725 he was made organist at Handel's local church, St George's, Hanover Square. He had been an outstanding performer and improviser, and also composed and taught music, but most important, he introduced the works of Scarlatti to the English. He retired to Dublin where he lived with his brother Ralph, organist of St Patrick's.

Delville, 12 January 1753

So we went; nothing extraordinary happened; they sent for a Miss Barry, a famed physician's daughter, to sing and entertain us, which she did; she has a sweet voice. Tuesday we spent at the Bishop of Derry's; D.D. was engaged to the Sheriffs' feast, but came to us there as soon as we had dined. Mr Rosingrave, (who I believe you must have remembered at dear Lady Sunderland's, and who was sent away from St George's church on account of mad fits,) is now in Ireland, and at times can play very well on the harpsichord. He came to the Bishop of Derry's – he remembered me and my playing; I own *his playing* gave me *some pangs* – it brought so fresh to my mind the happy hours of friendship I have passed with Lady Sunderland. I was not very well all day, and came home with strong symptoms of a violent cold.   iii p194

Mary met Handel at the home of her friend Anne Donnellan in London.

Spring Gardens, 12 December 1756

I promised Don. to call on her and meet Mr Handel, which I did; he was not in spirits any more than myself, but his playing is *always* delightful!   iii p454

Neal's music hall in Dublin where the 'Messiah' was first performed.

The 2nd lord Mornington, the founder of the Musical Academy was made earl of Mornington in 1760, some said, on account of his musical gifts. He was Garrett Wesley, Mary Delany's godson.

Delville, 30 December 1758

I believe I never told you of a musical academy what was opened last year in Dublin. The performers all gentlemen and ladies. Lord Mornington president; Mr Cane O'Hara vice-president; Lady Tyrone lady patroness: *her employment* is to go with the young ladies that sing in the orchestra; it is kept in one of the rooms built for the charity musics. The *gentlemen only* subscribe, and are admitted by ballot, and the profits arising are for loans to poor tradesmen. I was once there; it was a public night (which they have once a month), there was a gallant appearance of ladies in rows one above another, not less than 300!

The Italian taste prevails too much, and takes off the pleasure I should otherwise have in their performance, which is better than I could have imagined. The chief and most applauded singer is a Miss Stuart, a perfect Mingotti (with all her *trills and squalls*), but a great command and cleverness of voice. Mr Brownlow plays charmingly on the harpsichord: he gave us two whip-syllabub lessons *"perfectly neat!"*.

Lord Mornington's performance [on the violin] you know: they have a private meeting once a week, every lady performer has the liberty of introducing two ladies. The design is good, and I am glad there are spirits to execute it; but I think *you and I* should not want a fire in December if our Mary was to mount the stage and perform before such an audience!   iii pp531–32

Delville, 17 March 1759

Tuesday the rehearsal of Endymion; very well for lady singing, but I did not think it well enough to venture going in a storm to the performance of it; and was better regaled with Mrs Hamilton and Mrs Forth who spent the day with us.   iii p541

The Granville family were very well acquainted with Handel, and Mary's brother Bernard was especially friendly. Mr Smyth who writes here with news of the composer's death was Handel's amanuensis and biographer; he had been a pupil to Thomas Roseingrave.

Mr Smyth to her brother Bernard Granville
London, 17 April 1759

According to your request to me when you left London, that I would let you know when our good friend departed this life, *on Saturday last at 8 o'clock in the morn died the great and good Mr Handel.* He was sensible to the last moment; made a codicil to his will on Tuesday, ordered to be buried privately in Westminster Abbey, and a monument not to exceed £600 for him. I had the pleasure to reconcile him to his old friends; he saw them and forgave them, and let all their legacies stand!

In the codicil he left many legacies to his friends, and among the rest he left me £500, and has left to you the two pictures *you formerly gave him.*

He has left the Messiah to the Foundling Hospital, and one thousand pounds to the decayed musicians and their children, and the residue of his fortune to his niece and relations in Germany. He has died worth £20,000 and left legacies with his charities to nearly £6000. He has got by his oratorios this year £1952 12s 8d.   iii pp549,550

Delville, 5 May 1759

I was very much pleased with Court's [her sister's eldest son] lines on Mr Handel; they are very pretty and very just. D.D. likes them extremely. I could not help feeling a damp on my spirits, when I heard that great master of music was no more, and I shall now be *less able* to bear any other music than I used to be. I hear he *has* shewed his *gratitude* and his *regard* to my brother by leaving him some of his pictures; he had *very good ones.* I believe when my brother wrote last to me, which was from Calwich, he had not had an account of his legacy; it was from Mrs Donnellan I had it, to whom Handel has left 50 pounds. I want to know what the pictures are? I am sure you were pleased with the honours done him by the Chapter at Westminster. iii pp550–51

The improvments at Delville included an organ for the chapel.

Delville, 6 October 1759

Yesterday morning D.D. and I went to see an organ made by a very ingenious man and musician, Mr Smith; it is just of a size to fit the nitch in the chapel. It has nine stops; two or three of them harsh and disagreeable, but the flute and stop diapason, and half an open diapason are very agreeable, and I believe are all I shall ever use. Its being ready to put up immediately will tempt us I believe to purchase it, though it is not very perfect in its kind: if you have any pretty hymns or psalms set for organ or harpsichord, pray send them to me under franks, for I *suppose* I shall be the chief organist.   iii p568

In 1760 George II died and was succeeded by his son George III. Eventually Mary became a close friend of his family and enjoyed their help and favour in her old age.

In the letter below she describes one of the great figures of Dublin music in the mid century, Francesco Geminiani (1687–1762). He was an Italian violinist who composed and taught in the fashion of his master, Corelli. He inspired the Irish harper Carolan to compose a concerto in the Italian style.

Delville, 4 March 1760

Is the mourning general with you? Here we are all most dismal. I put on my mourning when I go into the *grande monde*, which I did yesterday to Geminiani's concert; it was pretty full. I went at the head of ten. The Duchess of Bedford and Lady Car[oline] Russell were there. The music began at half an hour after seven; I was extremely pleased with it: there is a spirit of harmony and prettiness of fancy which no other music (besides our dear Handel's) has. He played one of his own solos most wonderfully well for a man of eighty-six years of age, and one of his fingers hurt; but the sweetness and melody of the tone of his fiddle, his fine and elegant taste, and the perfection of *time and tune* make full amends for some failures in his play occasioned by the weakness of his hand; and his clever management of passages too difficult for him to execute with the spirit he used to do was very surprizing. On the whole I was greatly entertained, though it is the fashion to shrug up the shoulders and say: "*Poor old man!* Did you ever hear such a close? *No shake at all!*" with impertinent etceteras, I felt *quite peevish* at their remarks. The great ladies and their attendant peers were so impatient to get to *their cards* and to their dancing, that a message was sent to Geminiani to "*shorten the musical entertainment.*" I was quite provoked the concert was not above one hour; I could have sat three hours more with pleasure to have heard it. I have invited Geminiani to come and see me, and hope to hear this music again some way or other. Oh! how I wished my brother here, and how often have I done that!   iii pp586–87

Mary's love for and interest in music continued to be an important occupation in the years of her widowhood; she also encouraged her niece and great niece to play the harpsichord.

DRAWING AND PAINTING

Mary Delany was competent in drawing and painting although her real talents lay in designing and working her needlework, her shellcraft and her cutpaper work. She was an enthusiastic amateur sketcher and had taken lessons with several London drawing masters, possibly with William Hogarth, and Lewis and Joseph Goupy. In the age predating photography and cheap reproductions of art, she went to great lengths to copy paintings she desired for her home and the Delville chapel. She and her friends kept sketch books to record patterns for their various handcraft projects and also to practise drawing from nature, and still life. They learned from each other. Painting was a challenge, and help had to come from various sources; first a painting had to be borrowed; then colours had to be ground, then came all the different stages of preparation for painting, getting the canvas ready, deadcolouring the background and finally painting and repainting the subjects. Mary entered into the task with great energy.

Dublin, 3 February 1731/32

Miss Bush is abroad again [after smallpox], and comes very often to us:
   I believe I told you she has a fine genius for painting; she is hard at work for me, she paints both in oil and water-colours. I have enclosed you a little scrap of her drawing, which she scratched out by candlelight in a minute. I hope you draw sometimes. I fancy if you copied some landscapes, and did them in Indian ink, you would like it better than faces. I am sure, with very little application, you would do them very well; but copy only from the best prints.   i p336

This is a reference to one of her sketchbooks, an example of which survives in the National Gallery of Ireland collection.

Delville, 4 January 1745/6

I have now finished my three and thirtieth drawing for my book, and am reduced to the fruit of my imagination. I have made one landscape after my own whim, which is a favorite of the Dean's. But his partiality takes place of his judgment. [Lady Llanover notes this addition in the Dean's hand : "*She should say may be suspected to take*"].   ii p410

Delville, 11 January 1745/6

I spoke to Mr Barber [Rupert Barber the enamellist] about copying Lady Stanley's picture [their aunt Stanley]; and as soon as I receive my brother's commands will set about it. Pray let me know if he would have the little Cupid and the whole copied *just as it is.*
   Yesterday arrived our ingenious Letty: she has brought good health and fat sides, and I am very happy to have her; she has spread before me some of her drawings that she has done since I saw her, and they are charming. I lent her some prints of Claude

The Temple at Castleward, Co. Down, by Mary Delany, 7 July 1762.

Lorraine, that she has copied to great perfection; and now we shall paint and draw and chatter together as fast as our hands, eyes, and tongues can go.   ii p412

Delville, 25 January 1745/6

Letty [Bushe] is now drawing some beautiful landscapes in the Indian book Mrs Mead gave me: she drew four in it last year. Her good sense and good humour make her a very desirable companion, without considering the embellishments that enliven the whole. She seems pleased to be here, and is always ready to listen when I want to talk of my English friends, which is no insignificant quality with me.
ii pp415–16

Delville, 8 February 1745/6

The agreeable and ingenious Letty sends her very kind wishes and humble service to you. I shall have a great deal of her handywork to show you; she is so good as to draw almost every day for me, and has inspired me with landscape-drawing out of my own pate; I have invented three which the Dean is very fond of.   ii p422

28 February 1745/6

I gave you or my mother an account of my being engaged in philosophy, besides which I have three oil pictures in hand. I am copying an angel for the Dean after a Guido, finishing a half-length of the famous Duchess of Mazarin for Miss Bushe, and must give my mother's picture (*I have copied for you*) another painting, it does not content me.   ii pp425–26

*Dean Delany's niece was married to Rupert Barber, the enamellist, and they,
with their three children, lived at the bottom of the Delville garden.*

Delville, 15 March 1745/6

Mr Barber has just finished another picture of me in enamel, which Mr Bristowe says,
is better done than any he ever saw of Zincke's, indeed I think it very finely
enamelled; and I hope it will bring him into good business. Lord Massareen sits to
him on Monday, and Mr Bristowe has promised to prevail, if possible, with Lord and
Lady Chesterfield [the lord lieutenant and his lady] to sit to him, and that will bring
him into fashion; he is very industrious, and deserves to be encouraged; his wife is a
very pretty prudent young woman: they have a comical little girl of three years old,
not pretty, but a smart girl, and he proposes to make her a mistress of his art, as soon
as she is capable of learning.   ii p429

Delville, 6 June 1747

The drawing-box and book and everything contained therein are arrived safe, even to
the very nightcaps. I have been so lucky in my journey home, as not to have had
anything the least rubbed, broken, or damaged. I suppose you looked at my Lady
Abbess? [Lady Granville, a cousin] It is really like, though by no means a good
likeness. It was prettily and kindly done; but how without a magical wand it could be
so soon finished I cannot conceive.   ii p461

*Here she mentions one of her drawing masters, probably Lewis Goupy, who
died in 1747.*

*Mary to the duchess of Portland
Delville, 14 February 1748/9*

I wrote your Grace word that I thought [Francis] Hayman the best master I know of,
but am not sure if he will teach. *My poor dear Goupy are you gone?* I am sure you left
nothing like behind you – so modest, quiest, civil, honest and an *incomparable
master!*   ii p505

*Besides copying pictures to decorate their walls, it was fashionable to make
print rooms by pasting prints and borders on walls. Here, the Delanys were
on a visit to the Veseys at Lucan.*

Delville, 30 June 1750

It rained furiously; so we fell to work making frames for prints.   ii p563

Delville, 17 November 1750

I have begun a large Madonna and Child for the chapel, which is a great undertaking;
I have dead coloured the two faces.   ii p616

Delville, 30 November 1750

Miss Forth is better – at Bath, and Mrs Hamilton, I hope, will have her fine little girl preserved to her. Bushe is very well and with me, very busy at this time, drawing in my *Indian book*.

The first part of this week I have spent chiefly in painting the *great Madonna*; I have not yet covered my canvas.   ii pp620,621

Delville, 15 December 1750

I was this morning obliged to work an hour and a half at my picture which by Monday would have been too dry for some softenings that were absolutely necessary, and we dine abroad at Mrs Forde's who is an exact person as to hours.   ii p627

Delville, February 1751

Thursday and Friday Bushe and I worked like dragons; she is finishing a picture in oil colours for Mrs Hamilton, and I finishing some drawings. Harry the Fourth entertained us in the evening. I have enclosed you another description of Lough Lene (commonly called Killarney Lake), by the author of the printed one I sent you before, but more a description and *not so bombastical*; the *view* was drawn by the ingenious Mrs Letitia Bushe, but the *engraver* hath not done justice to the delicacy of her pencil. iii pp16,17

Here Mary determines to copy a portrait of the duchess of Mazarin by Sir Peter Lely which had been engraved several times.

Delville, 16 November 1751

I forget the great news of all, which is that I have quite finished the Raphael and fallen in love with a picture of Lady Mazarin, painted by Sir Peter Lely; though 'tis not the painting of the portrait but *the great resemblance* the person bears to the Duchess of Portland: the face is not to compare to hers, but the figure has all her grace and genteel air. Unluckily *my picture* of her done by Zincke is *turned* the *contrary way*, or I would clap it on the shoulders of this picture, for I could enlarge it in my copy, if the shadows and lights were suited to that of Sir Peter Lely's.   iii p62

Mrs Nuens used to grind Mrs Delany's colours and help with painting; she was a friend of Mary Barber, the poet.

Delville, 23 March 1750/51

Tuesday, Mrs Nuens and I painted: I have now dead-coloured all the figures (which are 4) of the Primate's Raphael: it is a charming picture, but will cost me many a groan before I finish it.   iii p28

Although Mary and her friends made up some frames by themselves, the more valued paintings were set off by expensive gilt frames.

Delville, 6 April 1751

The frame-maker has interrupted me all this morning. I should have dismissed the man for another day, but as time is precious to tradesmen I did not care to disappoint him. He has brought a white and gold frame for the large Madonna, which I think the prettiest I ever saw; and four smaller ones for little flower-pieces, *as ugly.*   iii p32

Mary to her brother Bernard Granville
Delville, 11 April 1751

I have received the six dozen borders all safely, and return you, my dear brother, many thanks for them. They are for framing prints. I think them much prettier than any other sort of frame for that purpose, and where I have *not* pictures, I *must* have prints: otherwise, I think prints best in books. The manner of doing them is to have straining-frames made as much larger than your print as will allow of a border; the straining frame covered with coarse cloth, the print pasted on it, and then the borders, leaving half an inch or rather less of margin round the print. Mr Vesey has a room filled with prints made up in that way and they look very well.   iii pp34–35

Mrs Delany took the opportunity to visit artists working in their studios. John Van Nost, son of a wellknown Dutch artist resident in England, came to Ireland in 1750 and executed several fine portrait busts and tomb memorials.

A dog chasing wild fowl', copied by Mary Delany, 1741.

Delville, 14 March 1752

Nothing can be more beautiful than the environs of Dublin. When we returned, as we were to pass through Dublin, and had some time to spare, we called on a famous statuary, who has been here about two years – Vanhost [Van Nost]. He served his time with Scheemaker, and seems an ingenious man, and a great artist in his way: he takes as strong a likeness as ever I saw taken in marble – his price is forty guineas for the model and bust. If our lawsuits end well, the Dean, I hope, will sit to him. He bought four busts, and bespoke two more for his library – Seneca, Aristotle, Galen, and Horace: they are done in plaster of Paris, and varnished so well that they look like polished marble at a proper distance.   iii pp95–96

Borrowing a coveted picture to copy was quite a delicate business and had to be arranged through friends.

Dangan, 3 June 1752

Mr Stewart, a gentleman of this country who has a fine collection of pictures, has lent me, through Mrs Fortescue's [one of the Wesley daughters] interest, a fine picture of the Transfiguration, an original of Carlo Maratti's – the figures small: Our Saviour, Moses and Elias, St John, St Peter and St James. I shall make a beginning of it before I go to Mount Panther to secure the picture, for the gentleman is whimsical and may change his mind.   iii p130

Perhaps he might well have changed his mind had he known his picture would have remained with the Delanys for a good eight months, despite a reminder.

Delville, 4 November 1752

D.D. had a message from Mr Steward [sic], the gentleman that owns the picture of the Transfiguration I am copying, to desire me to make haste.   iii p168

Delville, 25 November 1752

I have been very busy at my picture; have painted twice over the upper figures in the Transfiguration, and next Tuesday shall go on with the lower figures.
iii pp175–76

She found time to paint her neice some minute playing cards: Lady Llanover tells us they were about an inch long.

Delville, 2 December 1752

Whilst I am writing two young Hamiltons [probably Henry or Edward] are busily employed in the library in copying part of the picture I am copying; they have not applied themselves to drawing above six months, and it would surprise you to see what a progress they have made: they are pretty lads, sons to Mrs H. Hamilton.

I have got a pack of cards for Mary, which I will send her by the first opportunity; the king of the fairies sends them to her: they must be drawn out of their case with a pair of knippers [tweezers], no fingers are small enough.   iii p179

Delville, 9 December 1752

Mrs Nuens, walking from home on Thursday evening, fell down and has sprained her ankle and cut her knee, so that she will be confined some time, but I go on with my picture, have painted five of the figures twice over, and hope in less than a month to finish it quite.   iii p181

Delville, 5 January 1753

I have not painted for three weeks past, but propose beginning next week. The *Transfiguration* I am copying, is only *that part – not* the same as Raphael's, which has added to it the Lunatic that was brought to the disciples at the time of Our Saviour's Transfiguration. This is painted by Carlo Maratti; the figures are Our Saviour, Moses and Elias, Saint John, St. Peter, and St. James; the largest figures are about a foot and half high.   ii pp192–93

In an editorial comment on the following letter Lady Llanover, mother of a large family of girls herself, notes judiciously "the justice of these remarks on the value of innocent recreation and on the superior advantages of drawing as an accomplishment in comparison with music, must be felt in all ages, and is, if possible, more applicable to 1860 than it was to 1753."   iii p207

Delville, 17 February 1753

I agree with Mr Dewes, that an immoderate love to music may draw young people into many inconveniences: I would therefore confine it as much as I could to an amusement, and never allow it to be their business. Painting has *fewer objections*, and generally *leads people into much better company.* I have not many fears for *our* Mary, the good education and the constant good example she is blest with, I hope, will make her another sort of thing than the generality of the young girls.   iii p207

At last she was ready to return Mr Stewart's picture.

Delville, 24 February 1753

I have at last put the finishing stroke to the Transfiguration, and this morning D.D. has carried home the original, and I hope you will see it hung up in its place. It cost me 46 days of 5 hours at a sitting.   iii p209

On the eve of her departure for England, Mary finds the chatty Letty Bushe rather time-consuming.

Delville, 21 April 1753

Mrs Bushe draws and reads and prates when we are together, but I leave her a good deal to herself, having a little finishing in hand in the chapel, which I have a mind to have done before D.D. comes back.   iii p222

Delville, 28 April 1753

I will certainly bring my book of drawings, ashamed of having added so little to it. You know I cannot have a greater pleasure than employing my pen or pencil for you. The book is yours; I only keep it to fill it, which I will do as fast as I can.   iii p226

After her long visit to England, she found that her paintings had suffered in her absence.

Delville, 13 July 1754

I have taken up my pencils again. I found the Madonna with the child asleep quite mildewed, and am copying it *in oil* before I venture to take off the mildew, as that may lose some of the tender touches.   iii p286

Delville, 14 April 1759

Monday, Tuesday, spent at home; Wednesday morning painted and repairing [sic] Guido's Madonna and Sleeping Child, which by the sun's coming on it is much hurt, and shall then finish the copy of the Salvator Rosa I began in London; it belongs to the Bishop of Derry – it is for the chapel.   iii p545

The Delanys had leased a house in London in Spring Gardens and Mary took pictures from Delville to decorate it.

Delville, 5 May 1759

I am very busy in filling up the vacancies in my dressing-room by the pictures Spring Gardens has robbed it of. My present is a picture to go over the chimney – I have borrowed it of Lord Rawdon – a charming Carlo Maratti: the "Riposo" in Egypt, as the Italians call it. The Virgin Mary sitting on the ground with our Saviour standing and looking up in her face; her figure is very sweet and graceful; the background, a landscape with Joseph at a distance. Wednesday, I stuck close to my palette and pencils, and refreshed myself in the evening in my garden.   iii pp552–53

Delville, 12 May 1759

I am now deep in paint; the picture I have undertaken is a large task – if I finish it in three months it must be with industry.   iii p553

Delville, 3 November 1759

Last Wednesday Mrs H. Hamilton and her daughter breakfasted here. After breakfast I went to my painting and settled Mrs Hamilton with water-colours and pencils: she is assisting me in colouring Sheldrake's Herbal. When we were all comfortably settled, the young ladies with their work and Mr Hamilton preparing to read to us, rap, rap at the door; and in came Mrs Clayton, but she was in one of her *best humours*, walked in the garden, and excused my going, so I painted on. In the evening she called on Mrs Hamilton in Anne Street, and told her of her visit. *"There,"* says she, *"I found one painting and another dabbing*, so I thought they wanted not my company, and I walked into the garden," and there she found D.D. as busy with his *pickaxe* and *spade*, and *his labourers round him*, as we were in the house.   iii pp572–73

Mary painted more pictures for the Delville chapel

Delville, 14 December 1751

Tuesday, Wednesday, and Thursday I painted; am copying a head of our Saviour with rays of glory for the ground – a fine head, painted I believe by *Carlo Dolci*; 'tis for the door of the chapel.   iii p67

Delville, 16 February 1760

Lazarus hath made some progress; a fortnight or three weeks hence I hope it will be in a condition to hang up in the chapel; the description of which shall attend you as soon as Mr Barber has leisure to draw the plan.   iii p585

Delville, 24 April 1760

Monday a rage of painting seized me. I took up my pencils and sat down to a picture (at 7 in the morning) I have begun one of David with Goliath's head, as big as the life, from one of the prints in Crozat's collection. I believe I shall be able to finish that and the little Correggio before we go northward; but I was obliged to leave off work before one to dress, and go to Dublin.   iii p590

Delville, 8 May 1760

Saturday painted hard at David, and finished the dead-colouring of it on Monday. He is a comely lad, well clothed in his lion's skin, resting on Goliath's sword, whose head lies on a marble table grim enough; a rich crimsonish and purpleish curtain fills up one side of the picture, and shades part of the giant's head, supposed to be in a room in Saul's palace. I think I shall hardly have time to finish it before we go northward, but as it is chiefly my own composition it will keep till I return to Ireland, if I can't go on with it now. I have *also* a small picture in hand, which I design for the Duchess of Portland *(don't tell her)*, which must be finished; and my pencil has not been quite idle in regard to my dearest sister, though the offering is but a small one.
iii p592

In the final years at Delville Mary was kept busy looking after the ailing dean and consequently had less time for such long drawn out projects as painting, although she kept up her needlework and other crafts.

LITERARY AND SCIENTIFIC INTERESTS

Mary Delany and the dean read to each other in the evening. This allowed Mary to employ her hands and ears simultaneously. She and her friends also read to each other at work, and thus improved their minds at the same time as producing something useful. She continually refers to books they are reading and these extracts below are an indication of their taste, not a bibliography.

One of her contacts in the literary world was Samuel Richardson, (1689–1761) printer and author of *Pamela*, an early novel written in the form of "familiar" letters. He was a great friend of her sister, Anne Dewes and is often mentioned between them. She also took an interest in the collections of scientists like Sir Hans Sloane. This was part of her continuing interest in botany which developed further after she left Ireland.

Mary was intelligent but not earnestly intellectual. She was friendly with many of the ladies in what was nicknamed the "Blue Stocking set" by Admiral Boscawen, particularly Mrs Elizabeth Vesey, her neighbour at Lucan. Mrs Vesey was one of the most popular of that group of literary and intellectual women who held receptions for "rational conversation" in London in the 1750s. Mary's literary tastes seem to be strongly influenced by D.D., indeed she goes so far as to argue against independent judgement in a quarrel with Mrs Clayton. The dean, though a considerable intellectual himself was conservative when it came to the new novels of the day, favouring historical and religious works.

Delville, 4 January 1745/6

We have almost finished Sir Thomas Hanmer's Shakespear; our next study is to the Life of the Admirals [by J.Campbell, LL.D.] which they say is very entertaining. ii p410

Delville, 11 January 1745/6

We have just finish'd Sir T.H's Shakespear. It is a very complete edition. I have been tormented all this morning in looking for two guineas' worth of tickets for a lottery of books, and cannot find them; and with Bushe's chattering and showing me her drawings has run away with my morning.　　ii p413

Delville, 13 February 1745/6

The Dean has subscribed to some philosophical lectures, and they are to be three times a week for six weeks, which with my other employments will fill up my time pretty well; but no occupation shall interfere with my devoirs to my absent friends. ii p422

Delville, 15 March 1745/6

Notwithstanding the bad weather, we have gone every other morning to the philo-sophical lectures, which have entertained me extremely.　　ii pp428–29

Bust of Dean Delany c.1755, by John Van Nost, in the Long Room, Trinity College, Dublin.

Delville, 6 October 1747

Have you ever met with Monsr Saurin's History of the Bible, with cuts done by Picart, Houbrakcn, and others; it is esteemed a very learned and curious book. I never saw it till last week that I found it in the library, but the cuts are not so fine nor so laborious as those in Physique Sacre.

The Fairy Tales (of which we have borrowed eight volumes) have their share of entertaining us. Don't you think we are well occupied?　　ii pp474–45

Samuel Richardson's novel Pamela *appeared in 1741. A few years before this he had acquired a cottage in Fulham, North End, which was familiar country to Mary from her early life there with her Aunt Stanley.*

Delville, 22 September 1750

I am afraid my worthy and much esteemed Mr Richardson will have reason to retract some of the kind things he says of me. I have not yet answered his letter, for my last illness has put me so behind hand in my correspondence, that I don't know when I shall pay my debts.　　ii p592

Delville, 13 April 1751

Bushe being gone, our evenings are spent tête-à-tête. My every-day reading is Dryden's Virgil, but I don't read till candle-light. Do you remember Dryden's dedication to Lord Clifford before his Pastorals; I like it extremely – it is *very witty*. I am glad to find some of the most ingenious books I ever read are now as new to me as if I had never read them: it is, you will say, an extraordinary happiness to find an advantage from a weakness, as this must be owing to my want of memory.

D.D. is busy looking over papers, and I finishing some little useful works, and looking over accounts, necessary work, and so far pleasing as it makes domestic affairs go on with less confusion. I have had a letter from Mr Clerke; he has been confined almost to his chamber for above two months, which is the reason he has not paid the money I directed him to pay. I could not help encouraging Sally [Chapone] going to Mr Richardson, as I thought it might be both an advantage [may be referring to the defence of Swift which Sally intended writing].　　iii p37

Samuel Richardson held reading parties at his Fulham cottage to try out some of his new works; often to audiences of admiring young ladies or his "songbirds", among whom was Hester Mulso, who married Jack, son of Mary's great friend Sally Chapone, in 1761.

Delville, 16 November 1751

We are now reading Cart's History of England which they say is the best which has yet been published: we are still fighting with the Romans – Agricola is the present hero. At eight, prayers – and from that music till supper; and after, a pool at commerce, (to which we invite Gran [Anne Donnellan's maid]) and the young Barbers; they are comical and good-humoured and make us graver folks laugh. Don.

commends Miss Mulso's letters, but she does not so well like the young woman, that is, she admires her sense and ingenuity, but thinks her only *second rate* as to *politeness of manners*; and that Richardson's *high admiration for her* has made him take her *as a model* for his genteel characters, and that is the reason they *are not* so really polished as he thinks them to be.   iii pp59–60

Mrs Delany discusses philosophical persuasions including Robert Clayton's unorthodoxy.

Delville, 22 February 1752/3

If I remember rightly, Sally [Chapone] is a Hutchinsonian. Mrs A. Donnellan is deep that way, Miss Sutton too, and as far as she has made me comprehend, I am struck with their scheme, but don't know enough to talk on the subject. It is perfectly orthodox, and seems to promise perfect satisfaction in regard to the Holy Trinity, and to place it in a much clearer light than I have yet met with, for though I am firm in my belief of it, everything that strengthens that belief is a vast satisfaction. The *Cardinal* [Robert Clayton] will not be archbishop of Tuam; he may thank *his Arian book of Spirit* for that, and he and his lady are most truly mortified.   iii pp94–95

Here she discusses a famous novel published in 1751. This work by Tobias Smollet contained many caricatures of figures in the literary world, for instance, the actor David Garrick, and includes the fictional but scandalous and erotic memoirs of a Lady Vane. It was not a great success and the second edition (1758) was modified.

Mount Panther, 7 October 1752

Yesterday, peacably at home. At candlelight D.D. and I read by turns, and *what do you think* has been part of our study? why truely, Peregrine Pickle! We never undertook it before, but *it is wretched stuff*; only Lady V's history is a curiosity. What a wretch! "For sure at heart was never yet so great a wretch as Helen."   iii p162

She comments on the collection of Sir Hans Sloane (1660–1753). He was born in County Down, and studied medicine in France, afterwards travelling to Jamaica where he collected botanical specimens. He was instrumental in founding the Chelsea Physick garden and left his valuable collection and library to the British Museum on condition that his family was paid £20,000.
    She also mentions the antiquarian George Ballard who published a collection of literary portraits of women in 1752 and included Mrs Delany, much to her annoyance.

Delville, 3 February 1753

I should not have been sorry by way of amusement, when I went to England, to have seen an auction of Sir Hans Sloane's collection; though I think it a great pity so fine a collection should be divided. I hope the King will buy them and build a museum such as a king should have. I have written a few lines to Mr Ballard, which I trouble you with, as I suppose you have franks [for postage].   iii p201

The Granvilles too were collectors, particularly Mary's brother, Bernard, who had no heirs except Anne Dewes' children.

Delville, 3 February 1753

D.D., I thank God, is very well again, busy in settling and cleaning his library and in sprucing his garden: he keeps up his spirits *nobly*. I had last packet a letter from my brother: I have had but one before since the death of Sir Anthony [Westcombe, her mother's brother]. He says he is building a room for his library, 24f by 18; and a drawing-room over it of the same size; that Sir A. W. did not explain sufficiently his meaning about the books, and then transcribes the paragraph: then says, "*that as the collection, together, is very valuable, and as dividing it will much lessen their value, will not the reversion of the whole collection be better for my nephew than the money now? besides, the money I lay out on the house will be of more advantage than what the books can sell for, they being at present a commodity that sells for little or nothing.*" I suppose you and Mr Dewes will be *very well pleased* with this determination; as I think it must be an advantage to the child in the end, and it is pity so fine a library should not be kept up in the family.   iii pp202–203

Delville, 13 July 1754

She [Sally Chapone, her goddaughter] read to me Ben Jonson's *Every Man in his Humour*, a very comical play, full of particular humour.   iii p285

Delville, 7 July 1759

We have got a new book to entertain us in the North [when at Mount Panther] which is greatly commended – Robertson's History of Scotland. Have you read Dr Young's letter to Mr Richardson on original authors, written with the spirit of twenty five rather than fourscore years of age.   iii pp557–58

While they were hard at work painting, they were entertained with history by Edward Hyde, Lord Clarendon (1609–74)). He wrote his History of the rebellion *in the late seventeenth century but it was printed in 1702–4 under his son's supervision. His autobiography appeared in 1759, and must have been hot off the press when Mr Sandford read it to the work party. His works were an important contribution to the art of biography and autobiography, and his* History *was early recognised as a classic historical work.*

Delville, 15 September 1759

Wednesday, a home day, painting. Yesterday, at home; in the evening Mr Sandford read Lord Clarendon to us. He reads well, and I think the Memoires entertaining; Lord Clarendon seems a very honest candid man, and it is very agreeable to know the private thoughts and transactions of a man, who has been of so much consequence in the world, with many little anecdotes which an historian who meant his works should be published in a regular manner would not insert.   iii p565

James Thomson (1700–48) poet and friend of Pope wrote a series of trag-edies referred to but is most famous for his poem 'The Seasons' written in 1726–30. He was influential in launching a cult for the picturesque and developed a distinctive model of topographical poetry which must have increased his appeal to the Delanys with their interest in landscaping.

Delville, 13 October 1759

Whilst I paint in the morning the gentlemen take their turns of reading to me. We are in a course of Thomson's plays. I like Agamemnon extremely, and Edward and Eleonora. I read them when they first came out, but had almost forgotten them; Lord Clarendon (our evening lecture) is almost finished. Gustavus Adophus will be our next book.   iii p571

The Delanys did not admire the novel mentioned below. Laurence Sterne (1713–68) published the first two volumes of Tristram Shandy *in 1759 and made a great stir in the London literary scene. His highly original style, perhaps the earliest example of the "stream of consciousness" school of writers, was also notable for its wit and in his works he parodies the literary form of the early novel.*

Their disapproval countered George Faulkner's (1699–1775) praise. He was Dublin's "prince of printers" and friend of Swift.

Delville, 24 April 1760

The Dean is indeed very angry with the author of Tristram etc. and those who do not condemn the work as it deserves; it *has not* and *will not* enter this house, especially now your account is added to a very bad one we had heard before. We were upon the brink of having it read among us; Mr Sandford heard Faulkner, the printer, cry it up so much, and say it had had a great run in England, and he would have brought it had we not been engaged in other book, and no one would have been more distressed at reading it than himself.

The Delanys were fond of excellence in books, and this example shows how they patronised craftsmen printers. John Baskerville (1706–75), master printer, produced a Milton in 1758; his books were renowned for their presswork and he gave his name to a typeface.

I have truly enjoyed the comfort you have had of my brother's company: as soon as I know he is gone to his works, I shall attack him in his retirement. I would not have Baskerville's Milton sent to Ireland, unless there are two sets, and I have a notion I subscribed as well as the Dean, but am not sure; I know I subscribed for Spenser's works to Mr Amiens.   iii pp588,589

Here is a curious account of a literary squabble which shows Mary in a very conservative light.

Delville, 14 May 1760

D.D. is not a little offended with Mr Sterne; his book [Tristram Shandy] is read here as in London, and seems to divert more than it offends, but as neither I nor any of my particular set have read it, or shall read it, I know nothing of it more than what you have said about it. Mrs Clayton and I had a furious argument about reading books of a bad tendency; I stood up for preserving a purity of mind, and discouraging works of *that kind – she* for trusting to her own *strength* and *reason*, and bidding defiance to any injury such books could do her; but as *I cannot presume* to depend on my own strength of mind, I think it safest and best to avoid whatever may prejudice it. iii p593

The art of letterwriting was practised in the 18th century. Handwriting was a significant indication of education and civilisation; it was of great consequence in Mary's eyes.

Delville, 3 November 1759

I shall be vastly obliged to you for the psalms, and shall value them doubly if written out by Mary, though I would rather employ her pen in letter-writing and get them copied by the organist or any music-writer: nothing but use can make letter-writing pleasant, as that alone can make it easy. I am sure her lively imagination will never be at a loss, and as to her hand, it may settle into an easy *legible one* (though not a fine one), and that with *spelling very correctly* and *writing good English* is as much as need be desired.   iii pp571–72

Mary to her niece Mary Dewes
Delville, 1 September 1760

Your letters, my dear Mary, always are most welcome to me, I think your last was tolerably written considering you have not practised much without lines; *your f's do not stick out their elbows quite so much,* and in time will have a *free and easy air!*

I wish you good success with your spinning; you have undertaken a large work. I shall be very glad to receive your French performances; and if you write or translate but six lines every day it will improve you very much, and at least keep what you have learnt.   iii p600

Mary had always taken a close interest in her neice Mary's upbringing, and although she was not on hand to chaperone her after her mother's death, as godmother, along with Lady Cowper, she advised her on matters of decorum, including the delicate situation which arose with Mr Jean Jacques Rousseau, the philosopher and advocate of nature who was admired by her niece and her brother, Bernard Granville. Lady Kildare, later duchess of Leinster, sister to Lady Louisa Conolly, was interested in engaging him as tutor to her young family.

Mary to Viscountess Andover
Delville, 4 September,1766

I am glad you have seen *the Rousseau*; he is a genius and a curiousity, and his works extremely ingenious, as I am told, but to young and unstable minds *I believe dangerous*, as under the *guise and pomp of virtue* he does advance very erroneous and unorthodox sentiments; it is *not* the "*bon tons*" who say this, but I am too near the *day of trial* to disturb my mind with fashionable whims.

Lady Kildare said she would "offer R. an elegant retreat *if he would educate her children!*" I own I widely differ with her ladyship, and would rather commit that charge to a downright honest parson, I mean as far as to religious principles, but perhaps that was a part that did not fall into her scheme at all. You see, my dear Lady Andover, what rust I am gathering by lying by, I wish it may have the merit of an old coin, and be a testimony of some real value, though I feel too much my own insignificance to think that can be the case. How I have run on!   iv pp76–77

Mary to her niece Mary Dewes
1766

Now for a word about Monsieur Rousseau, who has gained so much of your admiration. His writings are ingenious, no doubt, and were they weeded from the false and erroneous sentiments that are blended throughout his works (as I have been told), they would be as valuable as they are entertaining. I own I am not a fair disputant on this subject from my own knowledge of his works, as I avoid engaging in books from whose *subtlety* I might perhaps receive some prejudice, and I always take alarm when virtue in general terms is the idol, without the support of *religion*, the only foundation that can be our security to build upon; that *great plausiblity and pomp of expression* is deluding, and requires great accuracy of judgment not to be imposed upon by it. I therefore think it the wisest and safest way to avoid those snares that I may not have strength enough to break when once entangled in them. I remember a wise maxim of my Aunt Stanley's when I first came into the great world: – "*avoid putting yourself in danger, fly from temptation, for it is always odds on the tempter's side.*"   iv p80

When she left Ireland, and set up house in England, she befriended two young women who were to become eminent writers: Hannah More (1745–1833), a member of the Blue Stocking circle and author of the poem 'Bas Bleu' (1786), as well as Fanny Burney, later Madame d'Arblay (1753–1840), another of that celebrated company and well known novelist. Through Mary's influence, Fanny Burney became second keeper of the robes to Queen Charlotte. In turn, Fanny had an influence on Mary Delany, going through her letters in later years and writing reminiscences of her.

CHAPTER 8

LAST YEARS: POST SCRIPT

After the dean's death, Mary showed her usual resiliance and fortitude. Theirs had been an extraordinarily aimiable marriage, and her grief at the loss of her companion must have been profound. Nevertheless, with the society of her family, particularly her niece and nephews, she resumed her busy existence. The old Irish life was left behind; the Sandfords disposed of her affairs in Ireland, but she saw them whenever she could and she maintained correspondence with Mrs Francis Hamilton, who remained in Ireland and kept her in touch with that circle.

Her friend Margaret Cavendish, duchess of Portland was also instrumental in the reordering of her life. Much time was spent at Bulstrode in Buckinghamshire with the duchess, especially in the summer, and Mary set up her own little establishment in 1768 at the Thatched House, or "Little Thatch" St James Place. She enjoyed a lively social life, going to the theatre, to concerts of music, and seeing many of her old acquaintances as well as meeting new friends. Among these were several young women whom she helped along their various paths, in some cases, their careers. These included Hannah More, the writer, and Fanny Burney, later Madame D'Arblay, for whom Mary exerted influence in royal circles; as well as Miss Hamilton, daughter of the duke of Hamilton.

It was her interest in botany, enthusiastically shared by the duchess of Portland, which gave rise to a remarkable series of flower portraits executed in cutpaper, started in 1773. She described them as "Plants copied after Nature in paper Mosaick" and *"Hortus Siccus"*. These remain in the British Museum Prints and Drawings collection as a remarkable memorial to her artistic eye and craft skills. This is how the idea came to her as recounted by Lady Llanover.

"Having a piece of Chinese paper on the table of bright scarlet, a geranium caught her eye of a similar colour, and taking her scissors she amused herself with cutting out each flower, by her eye, in the paper which resembled its hue; she laid the paper petals on a black ground, and was so pleased with the effect that she proceeded to cut out the calyx, stalks and leaves in shades of green, and pasted them down; and after she had completed a sprig of geranium in this way the Duchess of Portland came in and exclaimed " What are you doing with the geranium?" having taken the paper imitation for the real flower."   v p215

Dr Erasmus Darwin described the "paper imitations" of plants thus in his *Loves of the Plants*:

> Delany forms her mimic bowers
> Her paper foliage, and her silken flowers;

> Her virgin train the tender scissors ply
> Vein the green leaf, the purple petal dye:
> Round wiry stems the waxen fruit impends.
> Cold Winter views amid his realms of snow
> Delany's vegetable statues blow;

She completed 970 of these exquisite paper collages. The ground work for these creations was probably laid in her love of nature, her genius for handwork, and her accurate eye which had been practised through domestic decorating skills like her shellwork and indeed some cutpaper work (helping her friends like Mrs Vesey of Lucan).

Through her friend the duchess, Mary met Queen Charlotte and King George III who much admired "her works" and encouraged her series of paper Flora by sending specimens from Kew. After the duchess of Portland's death, Mary moved to Windsor in 1785 where, through the generosity of the King and Queen, she was housed and given a pension. Her great niece Georgina Mary Port came to live with her. Her love of children was fulfilled by (a respectful) appreciation of the many Hanoverian babies at Windsor, especially Princess Amelia the last-born.

A good example of her tenderness towards the young is the charming letter to one year old Georgina Mary Port, written with a mixture of affection and admonition, from her great aunt Delany staying at Bulstrode on 16 September, 1772.

This is your birthday, and I wish you joy of its return; perhaps if you knew what a world you are entered into, *so abounding* with evil you would not say "*Ta*" to me for

Margaret, duchess of Portland,
Mary Delany's friend.

Georgina Mary Ann Port, Mary
Delany's grand niece.

my congratulation, but the precepts and example of your excellent parents will teach you how to make so good use of the tryals you will necessarily meet with, that they will not only be supportable but lead to a state of happiness that will have no alloy. This is above your understanding at present, and a rattle or a little squeaking cuckoo will suit you much better; so for the present I leave you to your infantine amusements, which I shall be as ready to contribute to when I can, as I am to testifye how dearly you are beloved by, your great A.D.   iv p457

The last mention of her friends in Ireland is in a letter to Mrs Francis Hamilton dated September, 1786, when she asks to be remembered to them.

She died in 1788, peacefully, in the dignity and achievement of her years and in the company of her great niece, Georgina Mary Port.

Edmund Burke described her thus:

"She was not only the woman of fashion of the present age, but she was the highest bred woman in the world, and the woman of fashion of all ages."

She was indeed a most delightful gentlewoman of her time: she was not connected with scandal or crime; nor was she a cynic or revolutionary. On the whole, Mary accepted the privileges and disadvantages of her position in eighteenth century society although she sniped a little at the restrictions on women's lot. She improved life for her family and neighbours by her activities, she exercised her talents and employed herself constantly at work of one kind or another, in a very expressive, creative way. In this she is very symbolic of feminine achievement in her time and for many women of later generations.

Mary Delany is exceptional in having such a wealth of letters to describe her life, preserved by her family and published by her great grand niece, Lady Llanover. These letters appeal directly to us across the generations: they depict not only the settings of her life, the landscapes and gardens she loved, but also her own contributions to the scene and they convey her strong intelligence, vivacious personality and charm. Her interest in the arts, particularly music and the decorative arts, her enthusiasm for new ideas in landscape gardening and her knowledge of botany, all mark her out above the usual class of interested gentlewoman. The energetic and continuing development of her interests and skills into great old age, particularly her masterpiece of floral depictions, the paper *Flora*, or collages, set her above the ordinary. The record of her eventful busy life in the form of her own letters, that most immediate and personal of literary arts, deserves a wider audience.

ACKNOWLEDGMENTS

This book could not have been written without the help of Margaret McNulty whose idea it was in the first place, and Brian Walker, who had the confidence to publish it.

Otherwise thanks are due to Mrs Ruth Hayden for her great help in locating material and illustrations and to Dudley Snelgrove for his hospitality and help with illustrative material. I would also like to thank the librarians and staff at Newport Borough Library, Gwent; the staff of the British Museum Prints and Drawings room; and the Institute of Irish Studies, Queen's University of Belfast for facilitating my work.

I would like to acknowledge my gratitude to the following individuals. Jack McRobert shared his great knowledge about the Downpatrick area most generously and gave valuable information about Mount Panther and Belville. Maurice Cassidy was a most informative guide round present day Hollymount. Belinda Jupp was most helpful over garden history. Hero Granger Taylor stimulated all sorts of lines of research and was a source of special help and much appreciated hospitality in London. Colonel Michael Percival Price identified some of the Price family. Mr Richard Hanbury Tenison provided interesting information about the Tenison family, and his daughter, Sarah Tolley, was delightfully hospitable. Mr Patrick and Lady Anthea Forde made very helpful suggestions. No-one working in any subject relating to the history of the arts in Ireland can fail to recognise Professor Anne Crookshank's contributions in that field : her sympathetic and helpful encouragment throughout was much appreciated. Professor and Mrs Buchanan also gave generous support and hospitality. My colleague, Patrick McWilliams, was enormously helpful with computer queries. Maureen Carr typed the first drafts. I am grateful to Tony Sheehan for his proof reading.

My family gave me great help and support throughout the work and preparation for this book. In particular, my mother, Mrs Jacqueline Day, was a source of ideas, sympathy and practical help. My aunt, Mrs Georgina Stone, lent books and articles. My sister, Georgina Sampson, gave me valuable reference works and practical help; and my sisters, Catharina Dessain and Susannah Mortensen, helped me to persevere the course. Finally, most important of all, my husband, Fergus Hanna Bell, helped and supported me throughout my work; without his company, I could not have managed to look after Sam Og and write this book.

BIBLIOGRAPHY

An archaeological survey of County Down, H.M.S.O., 1966.

Andrews, J.H.(ed.) Taylor, George and Skinner, Andrew *Maps of the roads of Ireland surveyed in 1777 and corrected down to 1783* (2nd ed.).

Bence-Jones, Mark *A guide to Irish country houses*, revised, Constable, 1988.

Boylan, Henry *Dictionary of Irish biography*, Gill and McMillan, 1979.

Drabble, Margaret (ed.) *Oxford companion to literature*, O.U.P., 1987.

Elrington Ball, J. *The judges of Ireland*, Murray, London, 1926.

Hadfield, Miles *A history of British gardening*, Penguin Books, 1960.

Hayden, Ruth *Mrs Delany: her life and flowers*, B.M. Publications, 1980.

Hogwood, Christopher *Handel*, Thames and Hudson, 1984.

Johnson, R. Brimley *Mrs Delany*, London, 1925.

Kavanagh, Peter *The Irish theatre*, The Kerryman Ltd., Tralee, 1946.

Killanin, Lord and Duignan, Michael V. *The Shell guide to Ireland*, 2nd ed., Ebury Press, 1967.

Leslie, J.B. *Clogher clergy and parishes, an account of the clergy of the Church of Ireland*, Enniskillen, 1929.

Leslie, J.B. and Swanzy, H.B. *Biographical succession lists of the diocese of Down*, Enniskillen, 1936.

Llanover, The Rt Hon. Lady (ed.) *Autobiography and correspondence of Mary Granville*, Mrs Delany, vols i–vi, London, 1861–62.

Malins, Edward *Mrs Delany and landscaping in Ireland*, in Irish Georgian Society Quarterly Bulletin, Vol XI nos 2 & 3, 1968.

Malins, Edward and Glin, The Knight of *Lost demesnes, 1660–1845*, Barrie and Jenkins, 1976.

Maxwell, Constantia *History of Trinity College (1591–1892)*, Dublin University Press, 1946.

Maxwell, Constantia *Country and town in Ireland under the Georges*, Dundalgan Press, 1949.

Maxwell, Constantia *The stranger in Ireland*, Cape, London, 1954.

Nokes, David *Jonathan Swift: A hypocrite reversed*, O.U.P., 1985.

O'Mahony, Charles *The vice roys of Ireland*, London, 1912.

Phillips, W.A.(ed.) *A History of the Church of Ireland from the earliest times to the present day*, O.U.P., 1933.

Sadie, Stanley (ed.) *Grove's dictionary of music and musicians*, Macmillan, 1980.

Stevenson, J. *Two centuries of life in Down 1600–1800*, Belfast, 1920.

Stone, G.W.(ed.) *The London stage 1660–1800 Part 4*, Southern Illinois University Press, 1960.

Vaughan, W.E. (ed.) *A new history of Ireland vol IV (Eighteenth century)* O.U.P. 1986.

INDEX

Where possible nobility are indexed under their family name, not titles. The following abbreviations are used: Bp for Bishop, Abp for Archbishop. Spellings of names and places have been standardised although where Mrs Delany's original spelling is different this is included in brackets. Some explanatory information is also given in brackets. There are no entries for Mary Delany, and entries for her sister Anne Dewes, her principal correspondent, relate to her family.

SOURCES FOR THE ILLUSTRATIONS

The illustrations in this book are reproduced by kind permission of the following institutions and individuals.

The National Gallery of Ireland; Mary Delany's book of pencil, ink and wash sketches, 4, 23, 45, 143, 148, 152, 156, 163, 178, 186, 204, 214, 219, 226, 230, 271, 274; other illustrations, 18, 31, 49, 55, 64, 70, 75, 114, 132, 257.
The Trustees of the British Museum; flower collages from Mary Delany's *Flora*, 91, 106, 110, 180, 217, 225, 241, 245.
The Trustees of the Ulster Museum; the cover painting, 85, 90, 115, 127, 152, 236, 244.
The National Library of Ireland; 42, 88, 140.
The Archaeological Survey for Northern Ireland, crown copyright/Rev. W.E. Milligan, 211.
E.T. Archive/private collection, 98.
The Irish Architectural Archive/Mr J.A. O'Doherty (print by D. Davidson), 169.
The Irish Georgian Society, 103.
The National Museum of Ireland, 237.
The National Portrait Gallery, 248.
The Royal Irish Academy, 224.
The Board of Trinity College Dublin, 280.
The Trustees of the Ulster Folk and Transport Museum/the Governors of the Linen Hall Library, 242.
Mr J.A. O'Doherty (print by D. Davidson), 304.
Private collection; vi, 99, 265.

Other illustration were taken from the following publications.

Bunting's general collection of the ancient music of Ireland (London 1809), 260.
Flower, Newman, *George Frideric Handel, his personality and his times* (London 1923), 267.
Harris, Walter, *The history and antiquities of the city of Dublin* (Dublin 1766), 27, 41, 61, 69.
Le nouveau cuisinier royal et bourgeois, (Amsterdam 1734), 175.
Llanover, the Rt Hon. Lady, ed. *Autobiography and correspondence of Mary Granville, Mrs Delany*, (London 1861–2) vols i–vi, 4, 10, 12, 23, 36, 81, 95, 159, 194, 204, 288.
Maxwell, Constantia, *Dublin under the Georges, 1714–1830* (London 1936), 255, 258.
Miller, Philip, *Gardeners' dictionary* (Dublin 1764), 191.

Neale, J.P., *Views of the seats of noblemen and gentlemen in England, Wales, Scotland and Ireland (1818–1829)*, 103. (Print from Irish Georgian Society.)

Sowerby Jr, G.B.A., *A conchological manual* (London 1852), 247.

Taylor, G. and Skinner, A., *Maps of the roads of Ireland* (Dublin 1783), 108, 123, 201.

The book of Trinity College Dublin (Belfast 1892), 112.

The publishers are grateful to many individuals, and the staff of the above institutions for their enthusiastic support and assistance. It is hoped that this list of sources and acknowledgements is complete.

The Temple at Delville, c.1946.